fourth edition

W9-AWQ-009

# Classrooms That Work

## They Can All Read and Write

**Patricia M. Cunningham**

*Wake Forest University*

**Richard L. Allington**

*University of Tennessee at Knoxville*

PEARSON

Boston • New York • San Francisco
Mexico City • Montreal • Toronto • London • Madrid • Munich • Paris
Hong Kong • Singapore • Tokyo • Cape Town • Sydney

*Senior Series Editor:*   Aurora Martínez Ramos
*Editorial Assistant:*   Mekea Harvey
*Executive Marketing Manager:*   Krista Clark
*Editorial Production Service:*   Omegatype Typography, Inc.
*Composition Buyer:*   Linda Cox
*Manufacturing Buyer:*   Linda Morris
*Electronic Composition:*   Omegatype Typography, Inc.
*Interior Design:*   Denise Hoffman
*Cover Administrator:*   Linda Knowles

For related titles and support materials, visit our online catalog at www.ablongman.com.

Between the time website information is gathered and then published, it is not unusual for some sites to have closed. Also, the transcription of URLs can result in typographical errors. The publisher would appreciate notification where these errors occur so that they may be corrected in subsequent editions.

**Library of Congress Cataloging-in-Publication Data**

Cunningham, Patricia Marr.
  Classrooms that work : they can all read and write / Patricia M. Cunningham, Richard L. Allington.—4th ed.
    p.   cm.
  ISBN 0-205-49394-7  (pbk.)
1. Language arts (Elementary)—United States.  2. Reading (Elementary)—United States.  I. Allington, Richard L.
II. Title.
  LB1576.C855  2006
  372.6'044—dc22

                                                                                    2005058601

Printed in the United States of America
10  9  8  7  6  5  4  3  2  1   RRD-VA   11   10   09   08   07   06

Credits appear on page 308, which constitutes an extension of the copyright page.

*This book is dedicated to all the teachers
who work tirelessly and enthusiastically every day
to provide good balanced literacy instruction
for ALL the children they teach.
In spite of constant criticism and little appreciation,
these teachers create classrooms that
really do work (most of the time!),
in which all children learn to read and write.*

# brief contents

# contents

chapter **8**  *Multilevel Instruction*    **174**

chapter **9**  *Assessment*    **201**

chapter **10**  *Extra Support for Students Who Need It Most*    **215**

# acknowledgments

We want to thank the following reviewers of this edition: Keith Connor; and Allan A. De Fina, New Jersey City University.

We are also indebted to the many others—our colleagues, including especially our spouses, Jim Cunningham and Anne McGill-Franzen, and our students—who have helped us shape the ideas offered in our book.

Patricia M. Cunningham
Richard L. Allington

# chapter 1

# Creating Classrooms
# *That Work*

In 1994, when the first edition of this book was published, it had a bold and optimistic title: *Classrooms That Work: They Can* All *Read and Write*. The claim that *all* children could learn to read and write was, at the time, not widely accepted. Since 1994, the goal of teaching all children has achieved wide acceptance and is most clearly captured in the phrase "No Child Left Behind" (NCLB). While we have many concerns about the way NCLB is being implemented, we were on record long before NCLB existed as believing that the goal of teaching all children to read and write was reasonable and responsible.

In the years since 1994, there has been a great deal of research focused on schools and classrooms that "beat the odds." All over the country—in rural, suburban, and urban areas—there are classrooms where, year after year, *all* the children succeed in learning to read and write. We know what happens in these overachieving classrooms. We know what kind of environment, instruction, and activities the teachers provide that results in all children becoming readers and writers. In this chapter, we will invite you into the classrooms of unusually effective teachers by sharing the observations of some very clever and hardworking researchers. We will then summarize some of the characteristics you would see if you could be a "fly on the wall" in one of these "odds-beating" classrooms.

## *Observing in the Classrooms of Unusually Effective Teachers*

One of the first research studies that actually observed what was happening in classrooms to try to determine effective classroom practice was conducted by Michael Knapp in 140 classrooms in moderate- to high-poverty areas of California, Ohio, and Maryland (Knapp, 1995). After two years of observations, Knapp concluded that classrooms with the highest achievement gains were classrooms in which teachers:

- Emphasized higher-order meaning construction more than lower-order skills
- Maximized opportunities to read
- Integrated reading and writing with other subject areas
- Provided opportunities to discuss what was read

A team of researchers headed by Ruth Wharton-McDonald (Wharton-McDonald, Pressley, & Hampston, 1998) carried out the first extensive observational study to determine what actually happens in the classrooms of outstanding first-grade teachers. Administrators in school districts in upstate New York nominated "exemplary" first-grade teachers as well as "more typical—solid but not outstanding" first-grade teachers. In choosing the exemplary teachers, administrators were asked to consider their own observations of the teacher; teacher, parent, and student enthusiasm; the reading and writing achievement of children in that classroom; and the ability of the teacher to teach children with a wide range of abilities.

Five outstanding teachers and five more typical teachers were identified, and the researchers made multiple visits to their classrooms across one school year. In addition to being observed, the teachers were interviewed across the year about their teaching and how they made decisions. Throughout the year, the observers also looked for indicators of how well the children in these 10 classrooms were reading and writing.

At the end of the year, the researchers reclassified the teachers according to the achievement of the children. Three classes had unusually high achievement. Most of the students in these three classrooms were reading books at or above first-grade level. They wrote pieces longer than a page in length, and their writing showed reasonably good coherence, punctuation, capitalization, and spelling. These three classes with the highest reading and writing achievement also had the highest levels of engagement. Most of the students were working productively on reading and writing most of the time.

The researchers then looked at the observation and interview data from these three classrooms with the highest levels of reading, writing, and engagement and compared them with the data from other classrooms. While there were many similarities across all classrooms, the three outstanding first-grades differed from the others in significant ways:

- All of the teachers provided both skills instruction and reading and writing, but the teachers in the highest-achieving classrooms integrated skills teaching with reading and writing.
- Every minute of time in the highest-achieving classrooms was used well. Teachers in these classrooms turned even mundane routines into instructional events.
- Teachers in the highest-achieving classrooms used lots of scaffolding and coaching—providing support but always trying to get the most out of every child.
- Teachers in the highest-achieving classrooms constantly emphasized self-regulation and self-monitoring.
- In the high-achieving classrooms, there was lots of integration of reading and writing. Reading and writing were also integrated with content areas, and teachers made many cross-curricular connections.
- Teachers in the high-achieving classes had high expectations for their children—both for their learning to read and write and for their behavior. Students knew how they were expected to act and behaved accordingly most of the time.
- Teachers in the high-achieving classrooms were excellent classroom managers.

Encouraged by the results of the Wharton-McDonald study and supported by a large grant, faculty at the University of Albany and other researchers planned and carried out an observational study of first-grade classrooms in five states (Pressley, Allington, Wharton-McDonald, Block, & Morrow, 2001). Thirty exemplary or typical teachers were identified in New York, New Jersey, Texas, Wisconsin, and California, and year-long observations and interviews were conducted in their classrooms. At the end of the year, each teacher identified six students—two low achieving, two middle achieving, and two high achieving—and these children were administered a standardized reading test. Based on the results of this test, a most effective and a least effective teacher were identified for each of the five locations. Comparing observations in the classrooms of the most and least effective teachers revealed the following characteristics of the most effective classrooms:

- Skills were explicitly taught and related to reading and writing.
- Books were everywhere and used in a variety of ways—read aloud by the teacher and read and listened to on tape by the children.
- Children did a lot of reading and writing throughout the day and for homework.
- Teachers had high but realistic expectations of children and monitored progress regularly.
- Self-regulation was modeled and expected. Children were taught to check and reflect on their work and to make wise choices.
- Cross-curricular connections were made as children read and wrote while studying science and social studies themes.
- Classrooms were caring, positive, cooperative environments, in which discipline issues were handled quickly and quietly.
- Classroom management was excellent and teachers used a variety of grouping structures, including whole class, one-to-one teaching, and a variety of small groups.
- Classrooms showed high student engagement. Some 90 percent of the students were engaged in their reading and writing work 90 percent of the time.

The researchers followed up their first-grade observational study by looking at exemplary teachers in fourth grade (Allington & Johnson, 2002). Thirty fourth-grade teachers from five states were identified. Classroom observations took place for 10 days in each classroom. Teachers and children were interviewed. Samples of student writing, reading logs, and end-of-year achievement tests provided information about the reading and writing abilities of the children. From their observations, interviews, and data, the researchers concluded that the following variables distinguished the most-effective classrooms from the less effective classrooms:

- All kinds of real conversations took place regularly in the most effective classrooms. Children had conversations with each other, and teachers had conversations with children.
- Through their conversations and in their instruction, teachers constantly modeled thinking strategies. More emphasis was put on How could we find out? than on right and wrong answers.
- All kinds of materials were used for reading and writing. Teachers "dipped" into reading, science, and social studies textbooks but rarely followed the lesson plans for these materials. Students read historical novels, biographies, and informational books. Magazines and the Internet were used to gather information.

- Word study focused on building interest in words and on looking for patterns in words.
- Learner interest and engagement were important variables in the teachers' planning. Teachers taught the standard curriculum but tailored it to their students' interests, needs, strengths, and weaknesses.
- *Managed choice* was a common feature in these classrooms. Students were often presented with a topic or problem and allowed to choose which part of it they would pursue and what resources they would use.
- Instruction took place in a variety of formats. Whole class, various types of small groups, and side-by-side teaching were seen throughout the day.
- Students were expected to work collaboratively and take responsibility for their learning. Working together was valued. When problems occurred, teachers helped students figure out how to solve these problems so the group could successfully complete its task.
- Reading and writing were integrated with science and social studies. Many of the books chosen for the class to read tied into science and social studies topics.
- Teachers evaluated student work with consideration for improvement, progress, and effort. Self-evaluation was also encouraged and modeled.

In the late 1990s, Barbara Taylor, David Pearson, and other researchers at the Center for the Improvement of Early Reading Achievement (CIERA) began investigating school and classroom practices in schools with unexpectedly high achievement and compared them to what was happening in similar schools in which the children were not "beating the odds" (Taylor, Pearson, Clark, & Walpole, 2000). They identified 70 first-, second-, and third-grade teachers from 14 schools in Virginia, Minnesota, Colorado, and California. Teachers were observed monthly and kept weekly logs of instructional activities. They also completed a questionnaire on their reading/language arts instructional practices. Some of the teachers and principals also participated in interviews. In each classroom, data were gathered for two low and two average readers in the fall and in the spring. When comparing the classroom practices of the most effective teachers with those of the less effective teachers, researchers concluded that the most effective teachers shared these qualities:

- Had higher pupil engagement
- Provided more small-group instruction
- Provided more coaching to help children improve in word recognition
- Asked more higher-level comprehension questions
- Communicated more with parents
- Had children engage in more independent reading

Finally, we want to invite you into classrooms observed by Connie Juel and associates (Juel, Biancarosa, Coker, & Deffes, 2003), who followed 200 low-income urban children from preschool to first grade. Juel and her associates tracked the development of these young children in two important areas—decoding and oral vocabulary. While it is generally accepted that young children need to develop phonemic awareness and phonics skills to become successful readers, meaning vocabulary—that is, the number of words students have meanings for in their speaking and listening vocabularies—is often ignored. Meaning vocabulary, however, is essential to comprehension, and deficits in the oral vocabularies of young children are apt to show up as comprehension deficits in future years.

When the 200 children were evaluated on their decoding and meaning vocabulary skills as they entered preschool, most showed deficits in both areas. The children improved in their decoding skills each year. By the middle of first grade, their average decoding scores were slightly above national norms. While the children did make gains in oral vocabulary between preschool and first grade, they never caught up to national norms. In their vocabulary development, these low-income children were as far behind (nearly one standard deviation) in first grade as they had been in preschool.

Juel and her associates then looked at their classroom observations and coded all the instruction observed into five categories: letter–sound, oral language, anchored word, reading, and writing. The only category of activities that had a positive effect on oral vocabulary was anchored word instruction. Anchored word instruction was defined using an example from *Rosie's Walk* (Hutchins, 1986):

> The teacher had printed the words *pond, mill* and *haystack* on large cards which she places on the floor in front of her students. As she rereads the story, she points to the word cards and asks the students to walk around them the way Rosie walks around each of the locations in the book. The class discusses the meaning of the words *pond, mill* and *haystack.* (p. 13)

The article goes on to explain that the teacher then helps children with the sounds in the words *pond, mill,* and *haystack* but only after having the children actively involved in adding these words to their oral vocabularies. Choosing important words from reading, printing them on cards, and focusing specifically on their meanings is what Juel defines as *anchored word instruction.*

First-graders who had experienced more anchored word instruction had higher oral vocabulary scores. This increase occurred for children who entered preschool with low, average, and high levels of oral vocabulary. Conversely, the oral vocabulary scores of children in classrooms that spent the largest amount of time in letter–sound instruction decreased. This decrease in scores occurred for children who entered preschool with low, average, and high levels of oral vocabulary. Juel concluded her research with one of the best arguments for the need for balanced instruction at all grade levels:

> Ultimately, effective early reading instruction must help students learn to identify words and know their meanings. With so much research emphasizing the importance of early development in both word reading and language skills, we must consider how to provide instruction that fosters students' vocabulary development without losing the promising results of effective instruction in decoding. It does little good, after all, to be able to sound out the words *pond, mill* and *haystack* if you have no idea what they mean. (p. 18)

## *What We Know about Classrooms That Work*

Based on the research studies of effective classrooms, we can draw some firm conclusions about what it takes to create classrooms in which all the children learn to read and write.

### The Most Effective Classrooms Provide Balanced Instruction

*Balance* is an overused word these days, but it is still an important concept in classroom instruction. Balance can be thought of as a "multiple vitamin." We know that many vitamins are required for good health, and we try to eat a balanced diet. Many of us take a multiple vitamin each day as extra insurance that we are getting all the most important nutrients. The most effective teachers provide all the important ingredients that go into creating thoughtful, avid readers and writers. Exceptional teachers teach skills and strategies and also provide lots of time each day for children to read and write. The Juel study, in particular, points out the importance of balance (Juel et al., 2003). When teachers spend too much time on one component—teaching decoding—the development of another important component—oral vocabulary—suffers.

### Children in the Most Effective Classrooms Do a Lot of Reading and Writing

We have long known that the amount of reading and writing children do is directly related to how well they read and write. Classrooms in which all the students learned to read and write are classrooms in which the teachers gave more than "lip service" to the importance of actually engaging in reading and writing. They planned their time so that children did a lot of reading and writing throughout the day—not just in the 100 minutes set aside for reading and language arts.

## Science and Social Studies Are Taught and Integrated with Reading and Writing

In a misguided effort to raise test scores, some schools have eliminated science and social studies in the primary grades and asked teachers just to focus on "the basics." Unfortunately, children who have not had regular science and social studies instruction usually enter the intermediate grades with huge vocabulary deficits. Science and social studies are the "knowledge" part of the curriculum. Young children need to be increasing the size and depth of their meaning vocabularies so that they can comprehend the more sophisticated and less familiar text they will be reading as they get older. Exemplary teachers don't choose reading and writing over science and social studies. Rather, they integrate reading and writing with the content areas. As children engage in science and social studies units, they have daily opportunities to increase the size of their meaning and knowledge stores and real reasons for reading and writing.

## Meaning Is Central and Teachers Emphasize Higher-Level Thinking Skills

In today's society, where almost every job requires a high level of literacy, employers demand that the people they hire be able to communicate well and thoughtfully as they read and write. Low levels of literal comprehension and basic writing are no longer acceptable in the workplace. The most effective teachers emphasize higher-level thinking skills from the beginning. They ask questions that do not have just one answer. They engage students in conversations and encourage them to have conversations with one another. They teach students to problem solve, self-regulate, and monitor their own comprehension. Classrooms in which all the children learn to read and write are classrooms in which meaning is central to all instruction and activities.

## Skills Are Explicitly Taught, and Children Are Coached to Use Them while Reading and Writing

Excellent teachers know what skills children need to be taught, and they teach these skills explicitly—often through modeling and demonstration. More importantly, these excellent teacher never lose sight of the goals of skills instruction. When working with children in a small group or in a one-on-one reading or writing setting, these teachers remind children to use what they have been taught. Because the children are doing lots of reading and writing, they have numerous opportunities to apply whatever skills they are learning.

## Teachers Use a Variety of Formats to Provide Instruction

The argument about whether instruction is best presented in a whole-class, small-group, or individual setting is settled when you observe excellent teachers. Teachers who get the best results from their children use a variety of formats, depending on what they want to accomplish. In addition to providing whole-class, small-group, and individual instruction themselves, excellent teachers use a variety of collaborative grouping arrangements to allow children to learn from one another. Excellent teachers group children in a variety of ways and change these groupings from day to day, depending on what format they determine will best achieve their goals.

## A Wide Variety of Materials Are Used

In some schools today, there is a constant search for the "magic bullet" to increase reading achievement. "What program should we buy?" is the question these schools ask. Not a single one of the exemplary teachers found in the various observational studies was using only one program or set of materials. All the teachers gathered and used the widest range of materials available to them. Administrators who want to restrict teachers to any one set of materials will find no support for this in the research on outstanding teachers.

## Classrooms Are Well Managed and Have High Levels of Engagement

In order to learn, children must be in a safe and orderly environment. If there are lots of disruptions and behavior management issues in a classroom, they will take the teacher's time away from teaching and the children's focus away from learning. All the teachers in the most effective classrooms had excellent classroom management. They expected children to behave in a kind and courteous manner and made these expectations known. These classrooms all had high levels of engagement. Almost all the children were doing what they were supposed to be doing almost all the time. If this seems a bit unreal to you, think about all the factors underlying these well-managed, highly engaging classrooms. Instead of doing a lot of worksheets and repetitive drills, the children were doing a lot of reading and writing. Because the teachers took into account the interests and needs of the children, the children were interested in what they were reading and writing about. The fourth-grade classrooms, in particular, featured a lot of managed choice and collaborative learning. Children spent time investigating topics they cared about with friends with whom they were encouraged to have conversations. Teachers focused their evaluations on improvement and progress and emphasized children becoming self-reliant and responsible for their own learning. Classrooms in which the activities seem real and important to the children are classrooms in which children are more engaged with learning and less apt to find reasons to be disruptive.

## Creating Your Own Classroom That Works—Even Better

From the first edition to the current edition, we have been writing this book for you—the classroom teacher. It has been clear to everyone for decades that the teacher is the most important variable in how well children learn to read and write. While there are many restrictions on what elementary classroom teachers can do, most teachers are still given a great deal of freedom in deciding exactly how their classrooms will be run, how the various materials will be used, what the daily schedule will be like, what kinds of instructional formats they will use, how they will monitor and assess the progress of their students, and how they will create a well-managed, engaging environment. By learning from the most exemplary teachers—teachers who "beat the odds" in helping all their children achieve thoughtful literacy—we can create classrooms that work even better than they have in the past. We hope the practical information contained in the rest of this book will help you make your teaching even more exemplary and more effective.

# chapter 2

# *Creating Enthusiastic, Independent Readers*

I n Chapter One, we described the characteristics of classrooms that work, classrooms in which all the children become the very best readers and writers they can. These classrooms share many important features. Teachers in these classrooms provide a comprehensive curriculum and devote time and energy to all the important components of literacy. They model, demonstrate, and encourage. They emphasize meaning and integrate reading and writing with the content areas. They use a variety of groupings and side-by-side teaching. They use lots of different materials and are not tied to any one published program. They have excellent classroom management, based primarily on engaging their students in meaningful and worthwhile endeavors. Children spend a lot of their time actually engaged in reading and writing.

In this chapter, we will focus on the essential component that must be in place in any classroom where all the children learn to read and write. In order to become literate, children must become readers. Readers are not just children who *can* read—they are children who *do* read. The amount of reading children do is highly correlated with how well they read. The number of words in your meaning vocabulary store is directly related to how much you read, and your reading comprehension is heavily dependent on having meanings for the words you read. *Fluency*—the ability to read quickly and with expression—is also related to how much you read.

Reading is complex, and teaching children to read is equally complex. The fact that children must do a lot of reading to become good readers, however, is simple and straightforward. Because creating enthusiastic and independent readers is the essential foundation upon which all good instruction can be built, we begin this book by describing how to create classrooms in which all children become readers. We hope that as you think about how to make your classroom one in which all children become readers, you will begin by considering how much and how willingly they read and what steps you can take to increase both those levels.

## *Assess and Document Your Students' Independent Reading*

One of the characteristics of the most effective teachers is that they regularly assess how children are progressing toward meeting important goals and then adjust their instruction based on these assessments. Suppose that having all your children read more enthusiastically is one of your most important goals. You will be more apt to achieve this goal if you have some way of knowing where your children are early in the year and how they are progressing toward that goal.

Many teachers do a status assessment early in the year to determine how the children feel about themselves as readers. They file these assessments away and then have the children respond to the same questions halfway through the year and at the end of the year. After the children assess themselves halfway through the year, the teachers give them the reports they completed early in the year and have them compare how they are "growing up" as readers. Both the early-in-the-year reports and the midyear reports are then filed away. At the end of the year, the teachers have children self-report their reading habits one last time. After the students complete the final report, the teachers give them the first and second reports and have them write paragraphs summarizing their change and growth as readers. Many children are amazed (and proud!) to see how much more they like to read. The "Reading and Me" form is one example of the type of report you might use to help you and your students assess their growth as readers.

---
— • Reading and Me • —

My name is _____ .

Here is how I feel about reading as of _____ (today's date).

The best book I ever read was _____ .

I like it because_____ .

The best book I read in the last 4 months was _____ .

I like it because_____ .

My favorite author is _____ .

My favorite kind of book is _____ .

When I am home, I read: (Circle one)

    Almost Never    Sometimes    Almost Every Day    Every Day

This is how I feel about reading right now: (Circle one)

    I love reading.    I like reading.    I don't like reading.    I hate reading.

---

## Make Teacher Read-Aloud an Everyday Event

Do you read aloud to your students at least once every day? Teacher read-aloud has been shown to be one of the major motivators for children's desire to read. In 1975, Sterl Artley asked successful college students what they remembered their teachers doing that motivated them to read. The majority of students responded that teachers reading aloud to the class was what got them interested in reading. More recently, elementary students were asked what motivated them to read particular books. The most frequent response was "My teacher read it to the class" (Palmer, Codling, & Gambrell, 1994). Ivey and Broaddus (2001) surveyed 1,765 sixth-graders to determine what motivates them to read. The responses of this large group of diverse preteens indicated that their major motivation for reading came from having time for independent reading of books of their own choosing and teachers reading aloud to them.

Reading aloud to children is a simple and research-proven way to motivate children of all ages to become readers. When thinking about our struggling readers, however, we also need to consider *what* we are reading aloud. Did you know that most of the fictional books sold in bookstores are sold to women and most of the informational books are sold to men?

## Including Both Fact and Fiction

I (Pat) first heard this report on female/male preferences for fiction versus informational texts on *All Things Considered* while driving home from a workshop I had just done on motivation to read.

I was instantly transported back to a fourth-grade class I taught many years ago. I had five "resistant" readers—all boys—who I tried all kinds of things with to motivate them to read. I can clearly hear their voices telling me that they didn't want to read because "Reading is dumb and silly." At the time, I thought this was just their way of rationalizing the fact that they weren't good readers.

I read to my fourth-graders every day, but I am embarrassed to admit I can't think of a single nonfiction title I read aloud. I read *Charlotte's Web* but never a book about real spiders. What if their "reading is dumb and silly" attitude was engendered by the fanciful text I so enjoyed reading to them?

Reading to children motivates many of them to want to read—and particularly to want to read the book the teacher read aloud. I wonder if my struggling boys' attitude toward reading was an unintended consequence of years of being read to by female teachers who were reading their favorite books—which just happened to be mostly fiction! If I could go back in time, I would resolve to read equal amounts of fiction and informational text. Yes, I would still read *Charlotte's Web,* but I would also read Gail Gibbon's wonderful book *Spiders.*

Now, this doesn't mean that women never read informational texts or that men never read fiction; it just means that males seem to have a preference for information and females for fiction.

Reading aloud matters to motivation, and what we read aloud may really matter to struggling readers. In *True Stories from Four Blocks Classrooms* (Cunningham & Hall, 2001), Deb Smith describes her daily teacher read-aloud session. Each day, Deb reads one chapter from a fiction book, a part of an information book, and an "everyone" book. She chooses the everyone book by looking for a short, simple book that "everyone in her class will enjoy and can read." (She *never* calls these books "easy" books!) By reading from these three types of books daily, Deb demonstrates to her students that all kinds of books are cherished and acceptable in her classroom. Deb follows her teacher read-aloud with independent reading time. The informational books and everyone books are popular choices—especially with her boys who struggle with reading.

Reading aloud to students is more common in primary grades than in upper grades, even though it might be even more important for teachers of older children to read aloud. Most children develop the reading habit between the ages of 8 and 11. Reading aloud to older children provides the motivation for them to read at the critical point when they have the literacy skills to take advantage of that motivation. Intermediate teachers need to make a special effort to read books from all the different sections of the bookstore. Most of us who are readers established our reading preferences in these preteen years. If we read *Cam Jensen* mysteries then, we probably still enjoy reading mysteries today. If we read *Star Wars* and *Star Trek* books then, we probably still enjoy science fiction today. If we packed biographies of famous people and informational books about sports to take to camp, the books we pack in our vacation travel bags today are probably still more information than fiction.

One way you can motivate more of your students to become readers is to read some books in a series and some books by authors who have written many other books.

### Male Reading Models

Most elementary teachers are women, and most struggling readers are boys. A lot of boys believe that "Real men don't read books!" Many schools have reported an increase in students' motivation to read after some "real men" came in to read books to their classes.

Finding these real men and getting them to come to school regularly is not easy, but if you are on the lookout for them, they can often be found. Service organizations such as the Jaycees and the Big Brothers are a place to begin your search. City workers, including policemen and firemen, may also be willing to help. Would the person who delivers something to your school each week be flattered to be asked to come and read to your class? If some construction is being done in your neighborhood, the construction company may feel that it is good public relations to allow its workers to volunteer to come into your classroom for a half hour each week and read to your class.

Cindy Visser (1991), a reading specialist in Washington, reported how her school formed a partnership with the local high school football team. Football players came once a month and read to elementary classes. Appropriate read-aloud books were chosen by the elementary teachers and sent to the high school ahead of time. Interested athletes chose books and took them home to "polish their delivery." On the last Friday of the month, the athletes donned their football jerseys and rode the team bus to the elementary school. The arrival of the bus was greeted by cheering elementary students, who escorted the players to their classes. There, they read to the children and answered questions about reading, life, and, of course, football. This partnership, which was initiated by an elementary school in search of male reading models, turned out to be as profitable for the athletes as it was for the elementary students. The coach reported a waiting list of athletes who wanted to participate and a boost in the self-esteem of the ones who did.

Remember that your students often want to read the book you read aloud. Read aloud one of David Adler's *Cam Jensen* mysteries, and then show students several more of these mysteries that you wish you had time to read aloud to them. Read aloud one of Gail Gibbon's informational books on animals—perhaps *Sharks* or *Whales* or *Dogs*—and then show students the other 40 Gibbon animal books you wish you had time to read to them. Your students who like mysteries may have "choice anxiety" trying to decide which *Cam Jensen* mystery they want to read first, and your animal lover informational readers will not know where to begin with all of Gail Gibbon's wonderful animal books. Unlike most anxiety, this kind of choice anxiety is a good thing!

Many intermediate teachers make a list of different genres, titles, and authors, on which they record the books they have read aloud. In doing so, they can be sure they are opening the doors to all the different kinds of wonderful books there are.

# • Teacher Record Sheet: •
## Books Read Aloud during the School Year

| Type of Book | Title | Author |
|---|---|---|
| Mystery | _____ | _____ |
| Science Fiction | _____ | _____ |
| Fantasy | _____ | _____ |
| Contemporary Fiction | _____ | _____ |
| Historical Fiction | _____ | _____ |
| Multicultural Fiction | _____ | _____ |
| Sports Fiction | _____ | _____ |
| Other Fiction | _____ | _____ |
| Sports Informational | _____ | _____ |
| Animals Informational | _____ | _____ |
| Multicultural Informational | _____ | _____ |
| Science Informational | _____ | _____ |
| Other Informational | _____ | _____ |
| Biography | _____ | _____ |
| Easy Chapter–Series | _____ | _____ |
| Authors with Other Books | _____ | _____ |
| Other | _____ | _____ |

Teachers of older children can show them the whole range of things that adults read by making an extra effort to bring real-world reading materials, such as newspapers and magazines, into the classroom and to read tidbits from these with an "I was reading this last night and just couldn't wait to get here and share it with you" attitude. Teachers who read aloud to older children often keep a book of poetry handy and read one or two poems whenever appropriate. No intermediate-aged student can resist the appeal of Jack Prelutsky's or Judith Viorst's poems. In addition to poetry, your students will look forward to your reading to them if you often read snippets from *The Guinness Book of World Records* and from your favorite joke and riddle books. Be sure to include some of the wonderful new multicultural books in your read-aloud, so that all your students will feel affirmed by what you read aloud to them.

**RECOMMENDED resources**

A treasure trove of good multicultural children's literature is available, and many sources of multicultural books can be found on the Web. Here are two of our favorites:

NEA's list of 50 Multicultural Books Every Child Should Know: **http://nea.org/ readacross/resources/50multibooks**
*Celebrating Cultural Diversity through Children's Literature,* by Robert F. Smith: **http://multiculturalchildrenslit.com**

## Schedule Time Every Day for Self-Selected Reading

The goal of every elementary teacher should be to have all children read for at least 20 minutes each day from materials they have chosen to read. Use an analogy to help your children understand that becoming good at reading is just like becoming good at anything else. Compare learning to read with learning to play the piano or tennis or baseball. Explain that in order to become good at anything, you need three things: (1) instruction, (2) practice on the skills, and (3) practice on the whole thing. To become a good tennis player, you need to (1) take tennis lessons, (2) practice the skills (backhand, serve, etc.), and (3) play tennis. To become a good reader, you also need instruction, practice on the important skills, and practice reading! Point out that sometimes we get so busy that we forget to take the important time each day to read. Therefore, we must schedule it, just like anything else we do.

While at least 20 minutes daily for self-selected reading is the goal, most teachers start with a shorter period of time and increase it gradually as children establish the reading habit and learn to look forward to this daily "read what you want to" time. Some teachers use a timer to signal the beginning and end of the self-selected reading time. When we engage in activities regularly, we establish some natural time rhythms. Using a timer to monitor self-selected reading will help children establish these rhythms. When the timer sounds at the end of the session, the teacher should probably say something like "Take another minute if you need to get to a stopping point."

Once the time for self-selected reading has begun, do not allow children to move around the room looking for books. Some teachers have children choose several pieces of reading material before the time begins and do not allow them to get up and change material until the time ends. In other classrooms, the teacher places a crate of books on each table, and the children choose from that crate. The book crates rotate from table to table so that

**RECOMMENDED resources**

You can find a lot more practical suggestions for self-selected reading at all grade levels in *Self-Selected Reading the Four Blocks Way,* by Cunningham, Hall, and Gambrell (2002).

### Big Buddy Readers

Having easy-to-read books available for older struggling readers will not get you anywhere if those readers refuse to be seen reading "baby books!" One way to get older children to read easy books is to give them a real-life reason to do so. In some schools, older children (big buddies) go to the kindergarten and read aloud to their little buddies books that they have practiced ahead of time. Arranging such partnerships allows older poor readers to become reading models. The buddy system also serves another critical function in that it legitimizes the reading and rereading of very easy books.

Once you have a buddy system set up, you can have the kindergarten teacher send up a basket of books from which each of your big buddies can choose. Tell them that professional readers always practice reading a book aloud several times before reading it to an audience. Then, let them practice reading the book—first to themselves, then to a partner in the classroom, and finally to a tape recorder.

all the children have access to many different books "within arm's reach."

Establishing and enforcing the "No wandering" rule is particularly important for struggling readers. If children have not been successful with reading in the past and they are allowed to move around the room to look for books during the self-selected reading time, then they will be apt to spend more time wandering than reading. Remember that one of your major reasons for committing yourself to this daily self-selected reading time is that you know that how much children read plays a critical role in how well they read. If your good readers read for almost all the allotted time and your struggling readers read for only half the time, the gap between your good and poor readers will further widen as the year goes on. Having a good variety of materials within arm's reach is crucial if struggling readers are going to profit from this precious time you are setting aside each day for self-selected reading.

If you begin with just five or six minutes, kindergartners and early first-graders can engage in self-selected reading even before they can read. Think about your own children or other young children you have known. Those who have been regularly read to often look at their books and pretend they are reading. We should encourage our kindergartners and early first-graders to get in the habit of reading even before they can do it. Many teachers of young children encourage them to "Pretend that you are the teacher and you are reading the book." Kindergarten children are also very motivated to read when they are allowed to pick a stuffed animal or a doll to read to!

## *Accumulate the Widest Possible Variety of Reading Materials*

To have successful self-selected reading, it is crucial that students choose their own reading materials and have lots of materials to choose from. It is also crucial that no students are wandering around the room looking for things to read. Many teachers have a book/

### The Rotating Book Crates Solution

The goal of every teacher of struggling readers should be to have a variety of appealing reading materials constantly and readily available to the children. In one school, four intermediate teachers became convinced of the futility of trying to teach re-sistant children to read with almost no appealing mate-rials in the classroom. The teachers appealed to the ad-ministration and the parent group for money and were told that it would be put in the budget "for next year." Not willing to "write off" the children they were teach-ing this year, each teacher cleaned out her or his closets (school and home), rummaged through the bookroom, and used other means to round up all the easy and appealing books they could find. Then they put these materials into four big crates, making sure that each crate had as much variety as possible. Mysteries, sports, biographies, science fiction, informational books, car-toon books, and the like were divided up equally.

Since the teachers did this over the Christmas holi-day, they decided that each classroom would keep a crate for five weeks. At the end of each five-week period, a couple of students carried the crate of books that had been in their room to another room. In this way, the four teachers provided many more appealing books than they could have if each had kept the books in his or her own classroom.

The four-crate solution was one of those "Necessity is the mother of invention" solutions, which the teachers came up with to get through the year without many books; fortunately, it had serendipitous results. When the first crate left each classroom at the end of the initial five-week period, several children complained that they had not been able to read certain books or that they wanted to read some again. The teacher sym-pathized but explained that there were not enough great books to go around and that their crate had to go to the next room. The teacher then made a "count-down" calendar and attached it to the second crate. Each day, someone tore off a number so the children would realize that they had only 10, 9, 8, 7, and so on days to read or reread anything they wanted to from this second crate. Reading enthusiasm picked up when the students knew that they had limited time with these books.

When the third crate arrived, students dug in imme-diately. A racelike atmosphere developed as children tried to read as many books as possible before the crate moved on. When the fourth (and final) crate arrived, children already knew about some of the books that were in it. Comments such as "My friend read a great mystery in that crate, and I am going to read it, too" let the teachers know that the children were talking to their friends in other classes about the books in the crates!

While the enthusiasm generated by the moving crates of books had not been anticipated by the teach-ers, they realized in retrospect that it could have been. We all like something new and different, and "limited time only" offers are a common selling device. The fol-lowing year, even with many more books available, the teachers divided their books up into seven crates and moved them every five weeks so that the children would always have new, fresh material.

magazine selection time before the beginning of the self-selected reading and require that students have several things they want to read within arm's reach so that no one has any excuse to be going from place to place. (To make doubly sure of this, the teacher often places a crate of good reading material at each student grouping, just in case anyone needs something additional to read.) Students need to understand that reading requires quiet and concentration and that people wandering around are distracting to everyone.

Collecting lots of appealing books requires determination, cleverness, and an eye for bargains. In addition to obvious sources—such as getting free books from book clubs when your students order books, asking parents to donate, begging for books from your friends and relatives whose children have outgrown them, and haunting yard sales and thrift shops—there are some less obvious sources as well. Libraries often sell or donate used books and magazines on a regular basis. Some bookstores will give you a good deal on closeouts and may even set up a "donation basket," where they will collect used books for you. (Take some pictures of your eager readers and have them write letters telling what kind of books they like to read for the store to display above the donation basket.)

Many classrooms subscribe to some of the popular children's magazines. You will have far fewer resistant readers if the latest issue of and back copies of *Jack and Jill, Children's Digest, Cricket, Soccer Junior, Ranger Rick, 3-2-1 Contact, Sports Illustrated for Kids, National Geographic for Kids,* and *Zoobooks* are available for children to read during self-selected reading.

Another inexpensive source of motivating reading materials is the variety of news magazines for children, including *Scholastic News, Weekly Reader,* and *Time for Kids.* They generally cost about $4.00 per copy, and you get a "desk copy" with an order of 10 to 12. Teachers across a grade level often share the magazines, with each classroom receiving two or three copies. These news magazines deal with topics of real interest to kids, and reading interest is always heightened on the day that a new issue arrives.

## *Schedule Conferences So You Can Talk with Children about Their Reading*

Early in the year, when they are getting their students in the habit of reading every day and gradually increasing the time for self-selected reading, most teachers circulate around and have whispered conversations with individual children about their books. Once the self-selected reading time has been well established, teachers often schedule conferences with one-fifth of their students each day. They use this time to monitor individual children's reading, to encourage them in their individual reading interests, and to help them with book selection if they need that help.

If your reading conferences are going to be something your students look forward to (instead of dreading!), you need to think of them as conversations, rather than interrogations. Here are some "conference starters" teachers use to set a positive and encouraging tone for their conferences:

> "Let's see. What have you got for me today?"
>
> "Oh good, another book about ocean animals. I had no idea there were so many books about ocean animals!"
>
> "I see you have bookmarked two pages to share with me. Read these pages to me, and tell me why you chose them."
>
> "I never knew there was so much to learn about animals in the ocean. I am so glad you bring such interesting books to share with me each week. You are turning me into an ocean animals expert!"
>
> "I can't wait to see what you bring to share with me next week!"

One way to make sure your conferences are kid-centered conversations, rather than interrogations, is to put the job of preparing for the conference on the child. Before you begin conferences, use modeling and role-playing to help children learn what their job is in the conference. The children are to choose the book (or magazine) they want to share and bookmark the part they want to share. Make sure your students know they must prepare and be ready for the conference, since you will only have three or four minutes with each student. After role-playing and modeling, many teachers post a chart to remind children what they are to do on the day of their conference.

## • Getting Ready for •
## Your Reading Conference

1. Pick the book or magazine you want to share.

2. Pick a part to read to me and practice this part.

3. Write the title and page # on a bookmark and put the bookmark in the right place.

4. Think about what you want to talk to me about. Some possibilities are:
   • What you like about this book.
   • Why you chose this part to read to me.
   • Other good parts of the book.
   • What you think will happen if you haven't finished the book.
   • What you are thinking about sharing with me next week.
   • Who you think would also like this book.

Rather than arbitrarily assign one-fifth of the class to each different conference day, many teachers divide up their struggling and most advanced readers across the days. In the sample conference schedule that follows, the first child listed on each day is one of the most struggling readers and the second child is one of the most advanced readers.

The teacher often spends an extra minute with the struggling reader scheduled for the day, as struggling readers often need help selecting books they can read. After the child shares the book chosen for that day, the teacher may help him or her select some books to read across the next week. Advanced readers also often need an extra minute to help with book selection, as they often read books that are very easy for them. While reading easy books is good for all of us, it is nice to have a minute to nudge these students forward in their book selection. Clever teachers do this in a seductive rather than a heavy-handed way:

> "Carla, I know you love mysteries, and the other day when I was in the library, I found two mysteries that made me think of you. Listen to this." (Teacher reads "blurb" on the back of each mystery to Carla.)
>
> "Now, I have to warn you: These mysteries are a little longer and harder than the ones you usually read. But you are such a good reader, I know you could handle them if you wanted to read them."

Carla will probably be delighted that the teacher thought of her and believed she could read harder mysteries and will very likely "take the bait" and go off with some mysteries closer to her advanced reading level.

Reading books you want to read motivates you to read more. Sharing those books once a week with someone who "oohs and aahs" about your reading choices is also a sure-fire motivator.

## • Conference Schedule •

| Day 1 | Day 2 | Day 3 | Day 4 | Day 5 |
|---|---|---|---|---|
| Todd | Marisol | Julio | Shandra | Ian |
| Carla | Belinda | Tyrone | Tracy | Maria |
| Patrice | Carlos | Vincent | Tiffany | Mike |
| Tony | Antoine | Elizabeth | Richard | Sandy |
| Alex | Michael | Trisha | Matt | Juan |

# *Make Time for Sharing and Responding*

Children who read also enjoy talking to their classmates about what they have read. In fact, Manning and Manning (1984) found that providing time for children to interact with one another about reading material enhanced the effects of sustained silent reading on both reading achievement and attitudes.

One device sure to spark conversation about books is to create a classroom bookboard. Cover a bulletin board with white paper, and use yarn to divide it into 40 or 50 spaces. Select 40 to 50 titles from the classroom library, and write each title in one of the spaces. Next, make some small construction paper rectangles in three colors or use three colors of small sticky notes. Designate a color to stand for various reactions to the books. One class used these color codes:

- Red stood for "Super—one of the all-time best books I've ever read."
- Blue indicated that a book was "OK—not the best I've ever read but still enjoyable."
- Yellow stood for "Yucky, boring—a waste of time!"

In this class, children were encouraged to read as many of the bookboard books as possible and to put their "autographs" on red, blue, and yellow rectangles and attach them to the appropriate titles. Once a week, the teacher led the class in a lively discussion of the reasons for their book evaluations. Some books were universally declared "reds," "blues," or "yellows," but other books collected evaluations in all three colors. As the weeks went on, everyone wanted to read the red books and some would choose the yellow books to see if they were "really that bad." When most children had read these books, a new bookboard was begun. This time, each child selected a book title or two to put on the bookboard and labeled/decorated the spot for that book.

In some classrooms, the self-selected block ends with a *Reader's Chair,* in which one or two children get to do a book talk each day. Each child shows a favorite book and reads or tells a little about it and then tries to "sell" this book to the rest of the class. The students' selling techniques are quite effective, since these books are usually quickly seen in the hands of many of their classmates.

Other teachers have "reading parties" one afternoon every two or three weeks. Children's names are pulled from a jar and they form groups of three or four, in which everyone gets to share his or her favorite book. Reading parties, like other parties, often include refreshments such as popcorn or cookies. Children develop all kinds of tasty associations with books and sharing books!

Finding time for children to talk about books is not easy in today's crowded curriculum. There is, however, a part of each day that is not well used in most elementary classrooms—the last 15 minutes of the day. Many teachers have found that they can successfully schedule weekly reading sharing time if they utilize the last 15 minutes. Here is how this sharing time works in one classroom.

Every Thursday afternoon, the teacher gets the children completely ready to be dismissed 15 minutes before the final bell rings. Notes to go home are distributed. Bookbags are packed. Chairs are placed on top of the desks. The teacher has previously written down each child's name on an index card. The index cards are now shuffled and the first five names—which will form the first group—are called. These children go to a corner of the room that will always be the meeting place for the first group. The next five names that are called will form the second group and will go to whichever place has been designated for the second group. The process continues until all five or six groups have been formed and all the children are in their places. Now, each child has two minutes to read, tell, show, act out, or otherwise share something from what he or she has been reading this week. The children share in the order that their names were called. The first person called for each group is the leader. Each person has exactly two minutes and is timed by a timer. When the timer sounds, the next person gets two minutes. If a few minutes remain after all the children have had their allotted two minutes, the leader of each group selects something to share with the whole class.

Teachers who use such a procedure to ensure that children have a chance to talk with others about what they read on a regular basis find that children are more enthusiastic about

## Do Incentive Programs and Book Reports Demotivate Reading?

Many schools set up reading incentive programs in an attempt to get children to read real books. These programs can take many different forms. In some, children are given T-shirts that proclaim "I have read 100 books!" and in others, whole classes are rewarded with pizza parties if they have read "the most" books.

These reward systems are set up with the best intentions and may even motivate some children to begin reading. Unfortunately, another message can get communicated to children who are exposed to such incentive programs. The message goes something like "Reading is one of those things I must do in order to get something that I want." Reading thus becomes a means to an end, rather than an end in itself. Many teachers (and parents) report that children only read "short, dumb books" so that they can achieve the "longest list."

Doing book reports is another device used to motivate reading that can often have the opposite effect of

what it was intended to have. When adults are asked what they remember about elementary school that made them like reading, they mention having their teachers read books aloud to the class, being allowed to select their own books, and having time to read them. When asked what things teachers did that made them dislike reading, doing book reports is most commonly mentioned. Likewise, few children enjoy doing book reports, and their dislike is often transferred to the act of reading. Some children report on the same books year after year, and others even admit lying about reading books.

Children who are going to become readers must begin to view reading as its own reward. This intrinsic motivation can only be nurtured as children find books that they "just can't put down" and subsequently seek out other books. Incentive programs and book reports must be evaluated on the basis of how well they develop this intrinsic motivation.

reading. Comments such as "I'm going to stump them with these riddles when I get my two minutes" and "Wait 'til I read the scary part to everyone" are proof that sharing helps motivate reading. The popularity of the books shared with other children is further proof. Having discussions on a specified afternoon each week puts this procedure on the schedule and ensures that it will get done. Using index cards to form the groups is quick and easy and helps ensure that children will interact with many classmates over the course of the year.

## Summary

Most educators and many research studies support the importance of the amount of reading students do. Nagy and Anderson (1984) showed that good readers often read 10 times as many words as poor readers during the school day. Data collected from the 1996 National Assessment of Educational Progress (NAEP) testing indicated the 13-year-olds who reported more independent reading demonstrated better reading comprehension of both narrative and expository text than 17-year-olds who reported less independent reading (Campbell, Voelkl, & Donahue, 1997)! Stanovich (1986) labeled the tendency of poor readers to remain poor readers as "the Matthew effect" and attributed the increasing gap between good readers and poor readers in part to the difference in time spent reading.

Wide reading is highly correlated with meaning vocabulary, which, in turn, is highly correlated with reading comprehension. Students who read more encounter the same words more frequently, and repeated exposure to the same words has been shown to lead to improvements in fluency (Topping & Paul, 1999). A. E. Cunningham and Stanovich (1998) found that struggling readers with limited reading and comprehension skills increased vocabulary and comprehension skills when time spent reading was increased.

Wide reading is also associated with the development of automatic word recognition (Stanovich & West, 1989). Share (1999) reviewed the research and concluded that self-teaching of word recognition occurs while readers are decoding words during independent reading. Good decoders teach themselves to recognize many words as they read for enjoyment.

This chapter has described classroom-tested ways to create classrooms in which children read enthusiastically and independently. Teacher read-aloud is one of the major motivators for independent reading—particularly when the teacher reads aloud from great books in all the different genres. Scheduling time every day for self-selected reading demonstrates the importance of reading and ensures that all children spend some time each day developing the reading habit. Having a wide variety of books and magazines available is critical to the success of self-selected reading—particularly with struggling readers, who may yet to have discovered the perfect books for them. Sharing what they are reading in a weekly conference with the teacher and with peers further motivates students to read and is consistent with a sociocultural view of literacy.

# Building the
# *Literacy Foundation*

Ask most adults when they learned to read, and most will tell you about their experiences in kindergarten or first grade. In reality, learning to read begins much earlier for many children. Think back to your own preschool years. You probably couldn't read in the way we usually think of it. You probably couldn't pick up a brand-new book and read it by yourself. But you probably did have some literacy skills in place before you were ever given any reading instruction in school.

Did you have a favorite book that someone read to you over and over? Did you ever sit down with a younger child or a stuffed animal and pretend you could read that book?

Perhaps it was a predictable book, such as *Are You My Mother?* or *Pat the Bunny* or *Brown Bear, Brown Bear, What Do you See?* While you probably didn't know all the individual words in the book, you could sound like you were reading by telling in book language what was happening on the different pages.

*Pretend reading* is a stage that many 3- and 4-year-olds go through and is probably crucial to the ease with which they learn to read once they start school. Children who pretend to read a book know what reading is—that it has to "sound right" and "make sense." They also know that reading is enjoyable and something all the "big people" can do and thus something they are very eager to be able to do, too. Pretend reading is a way of experiencing what reading feels like even before you can do it and is an indicator of future success in reading.

Did you write before you came to school? Could you write your name and the names of your siblings, cousins, pets, or favorite restaurants?

DAVID
IUN
SARA
PISSA
HUT

Did you ever write a note like this?

I LUVMOME

Did you ever make a sign for your room that looked like this?

KEPOUT

Many 4-year-olds love to write. Sometimes they write in scribbles.

Young children want to do everything that grown-ups can do. For the things they can't do yet, they just pretend they can! They pretend to drive, to take care of babies, to cook—and if they grow up in homes where the grown-ups read and write, they pretend they can read and write. As they engage in these early literacy behaviors, they learn important concepts.

## *Concepts That Form the Foundation for Literacy*

### Why We Read and Write

Ask 5-year-olds from strong literacy backgrounds why people read and write, and they reel off a string of answers:

> "Well, you have to able to read. You read books and signs and cereal boxes and birthday cards that come in the mail and recipes and . . . You write notes and stories and signs and lists and you write on the computer and you send postcards when you are on a trip and you write to your aunt and . . ."

You can tell from these answers that children who come to school with clear ideas about the functions of reading and writing have had lots of real-world experiences with reading and writing. Reading and writing are things all the bigger people they know do, and they intend to do them, too!

### Background Knowledge and Vocabulary

A lot of what we know about the world, we have learned from reading. This is also true of young children. When parents or other people read to young children, they don't just read; they also talk with the children about what they are reading:

> "Do you know what that animal is called?"
>
> "Yes, it's a bear. The bears in this story are not real bears. We can tell because we know that real bears don't wear clothes or live in houses. Where could we go to see a real bear?"
>
> "Maybe we can find a book about real bears the next time we go to the library."

Comprehension is very highly correlated with prior knowledge and vocabulary. The more you know about any topic, the greater will be your understanding of what you read related to that topic. Your store of background knowledge and vocabulary directly affects how well you read. Young children who have had many books read to them simply know more than children who haven't.

## Print Concepts

Print is what you read and write. Print includes all the funny little marks—letters, punctuation, spaces between words and paragraphs—that translate into familiar spoken language. In English, we read across the page in a left-to-right fashion. Because our eyes can see only a few words during each stop (called a *fixation*), we must actually move our eyes several times to read one line of print. When we finish that line, we make a return sweep and start all over again, left to right. If there are sentences at the top of a page, a picture in the middle, and more sentences at the bottom, we read the top first and then the bottom. We start at the front of a book and go toward the back. These arbitrary rules about how we proceed through print are called *conventions*.

*Jargon* refers to all the words we use to talk about reading and writing. Jargon includes such terms as *word, letter, sentence,* and *sound.* We use this jargon constantly as we try to teach children how to read:

"Look at the **first word** in the **second sentence.**"
"How does that **word begin**?"
"What **letter** has that **sound**?"

Children who have been read to and whose early attempts at writing have been encouraged often walk in the door of kindergarten with these critical print conventions and jargon. From being read to in the "lap position," they have noticed how the eyes "jump" across the lines of print as someone is reading. They have watched people write grocery lists and thank-you letters to Grandma, and they have observed the top-to-bottom, left-to-right movement. Often, they have typed on the computer and observed these print conventions. Because they have had people to talk with them about reading and writing, they have learned much of the jargon. While writing down a dictated thank-you note to Grandma, Dad may say,

"Say your **sentence** one **word** at a time if you want me to write it.
I can't write as fast as you can talk."

When the child asks how to spell *birthday,* he may be told,

"It **starts with** the **letter** *b*, just like your dog, Buddy's, name. *Birthday*
and *Buddy* **start with the same sound and the same letter.**"

Concepts That Form the Foundation for Literacy

Knowing these print concepts is an essential part of the foundation for becoming literate. Young children who have had lots of informal early experiences with reading and writing have already begun to develop understandings about print conventions and jargon.

## Phonemic Awareness

The ability to recognize that words are made up of a discrete set of sounds and to manipulate those sounds is called *phonemic awareness,* and children's level of phonemic awareness is very highly correlated with their success in beginning reading. Phonemic awareness develops through a series of stages, during which children first become aware that language is made up of individual words, that words are made up of syllables, and that syllables are made up of phonemes. It is important to note here that it is not the jargon children learn. Five-year-olds cannot tell you there are three syllables in *dinosaur* and one syllable in *Rex.* What they can do is clap out the three beats in *dinosaur* and the one beat in *Rex.* Likewise, they cannot tell you that the first phoneme in *mice* is *m,* but they can tell you what you would have if you took the "mmm" off *mice—ice.* Children develop this phonemic awareness as a result of the oral and written language they are exposed to. Nursery rhymes, chants, and Dr. Seuss books usually play a large role in this development.

Phonemic awareness is an oral ability. You hear the words that rhyme. You hear that *baby* and *book* begin the same. You hear the three sounds in *bat* and can say these sounds separately. Only when children realize that words can be changed and how changing a sound changes the word are they able to profit from instruction in letter–sound relationships.

Children also develop a sense of sounds and words as they try to write. In the beginning, many children let a single letter stand for an entire word. Later, they put in more letters and often say the word they want to write, dragging out its sounds to hear what letters they might use. Children who are allowed and encouraged to "invent-spell" develop an early and strong sense of phonemic awareness.

## Some Concrete Words

Another area that demonstrates that early and easy readers know things about how words work is the use of *concrete words.* If you were to sit down with children in their first week of school and try to determine if they can read by giving them a simple book to read or testing them on some common words, such as *the, and, of,* and *with,* you would probably conclude that most of them can't read yet. But many young children do know some words. The words they know are usually "important-to-them" concrete words—*David, tiger, Pizza Hut, Cheerios.* Knowing a few words is important, not because you can read much with a few words but because in learning these first words, you have accomplished a critical task. You have learned how to learn words, and the few words you can read gives you confidence that you can learn words.

## Some Letter Names and Sounds

Many children know some letter names and sounds when they come to school. They can't always recognize all 26 letters in both upper- and lowercase, and they often don't know the sound of *w* or *c,* but they have learned the names and sounds for the most common letters. Usually, the letter names and sounds children know have come from those concrete words they can read and write. Many children have also learned some letter names and sounds through repeated readings of alphabet books and through making words with magnetic letters on the refrigerator. In addition, children have learned some letter names and sounds as adults have spelled out words they were trying to write. This immersion in print has allowed children to make connections among the letters they have seen in many places.

## Desire to Learn to Read and Write

Children who have had lots of early literacy encounters can't wait to learn to read! All the big people can do it, and they can't but want to! We all know of children who have come home disappointed after the first day of school because "We were there all day and didn't learn to read!" This "can't wait" attitude motivates and sustains them through the work and effort required to learn to read.

## The Foundation

From early reading and writing experiences, children learn these critical concepts:

- Why we read and write
- Background knowledge and vocabulary
- Print concepts
- Phonemic awareness
- Some concrete words
- Some letter names and sounds
- Desire to learn to read

These concepts are not, however, all or nothing. Some children come to school with all of the concepts quite well developed. Some children come with some developed but not all. Some children come with few of these concepts. Successful classrooms for young children are filled with lots of activities to help all children move along in their development of these crucial concepts.

## *Activities for Building the Foundation*

### Reading to Children and Self-Selected Reading Time

The previous chapter outlined the importance of doing activities to promote enthusiastic and independent readers. If you have committed yourself to reading aloud to children and including a time for self-selected reading each day, you are well on your way to helping children build a firm foundation for learning to read. Many children are read to at home and are encouraged as they "pretend read" favorite books and attempt to read signs, labels, and other environmental print. For these children, your teacher read-aloud and independent reading encouragement will just move them further along in their literacy development. For children who have not had these experiences before coming to school, daily teacher read-aloud and self-selected reading time will give them a successful start in building the foundation for literacy.

Reading to children and providing time for children to read by themselves will also help children build their oral vocabularies. You may want to capitalize on an anchored vocabulary activity found to be effective in helping low-income young children build their oral vocabularies by picking important words from the books you read aloud to them and focusing their attention on those words. Find or copy a picture to go with each word. Put these words together in a book, with each page having one picture and the word that goes with it. Label the book according to the category the word belongs in. Make these books available for self-selected reading, and you will have lots of simple books that even your most struggling readers can find success with and enjoy.

### Supporting and Encouraging Writing

Some people believe that if children are allowed to write before they can spell and make the letters correctly, they will get into bad habits that will be hard to break later. There is a certain logic in this argument, but the logic does not hold up to scrutiny when you actually look at what children do before they come to school. Just as many children "read" before they can read by pretend reading a memorized book, they "write" before they can write. Their writing is not initially decipherable by anyone besides themselves, and sometimes they read the same scribbling different ways! They write with pens, markers, crayons, paint, chalk, and normal-sized pencils with erasers on the ends. They write on chalkboards, magic slates, paper, and, alas, walls! You can encourage and support fledgling attempts at writing in numerous ways.

*Model Writing for the Children*   As children watch you write, they observe that you always start in a certain place, go in certain directions, and leave spaces between words. In addition to these print conventions, they observe that writing is "talk written down." There are numerous opportunities in every classroom for the teacher to write as the children watch—and sometimes help—with what to write.

In many classrooms, the teacher begins the day by writing a morning message on the board. The teacher writes this short message as the children watch. The teacher then reads the message, pointing to each word and inviting the children to join in on any words they know. Sometimes, the teacher takes a few minutes to point out some things students might notice from the morning message:

"How many sentences did I write today?"

"How can we tell how many there are?"

"What do we call this mark I put at the end of this sentence?"

"Which words begin with the same letters?"

"Which is the shortest word?"

These and similar questions help children learn conventions and jargon of print and focus their attention on words and letters.

***Provide a Variety of Things to Write With and On***  Young children view writing as a creation and are often motivated to write by various media. Many teachers grab free postcards, scratch pads, counter checks, pens, and pencils and haunt yard sales—always on the lookout for an extra chalkboard or an old but still working typewriter. A letter home to parents at the beginning of the year, asking them to clean out desks and drawers and donate writing utensils and various kinds of paper, often brings unexpected treasures. In addition to the usual writing media, young children like to write with sticks in sand, with paintbrushes or sponges on chalkboards, and with chocolate pudding and shaving cream on tables.

***Help Children Find Writing Purposes through Center Activities***  Children need to develop the basic understanding that writing is a message across time and space. Once they have that understanding, they are able to identify a purpose for a piece of writing. For most young children, the purpose of writing is to get something told or done. Children will find some real purposes for writing if you incorporate writing in all your classroom centers. Encourage children to make grocery lists while they are playing in the housekeeping center. Menus, ordering pads, and receipts are a natural part of a restaurant center. An office center would include various writing implements, a typewriter or computer, along with index cards, phone books, and appointment books.

Children can make birthday cards for friends or relatives or write notes to you or their classmates and then mail them in the post office center. They can make signs (Keep Out! Girls Only!) and post them as part of their dramatic play. When children put a lot of time into building a particularly wonderful creation from the blocks, they often do not want to have it taken apart so that something else can be built. Many teachers keep a large pad of tablet paper in the construction center. Children can draw and label records of their constructions before disassembling them.

Once you start looking for them, there are numerous opportunities for children to write for real purposes as they carry out their creative and dramatic play in various centers.

***Provide a Print-Rich Classroom***    Classrooms in which children are encouraged to write have lots of print in them. In addition to books, there are magazines and newspapers. There are also charts of recipes made and directions for building things. Children's names are on their desks and on many different objects. There are class books, bulletin boards with labeled pictures of animals under study, and labels on almost everything. Children's drawings and all kinds of writing are displayed. In these classrooms, children see that all kinds of writing are valued. Equally important, children who want to write "the grown-up way" can find lots of words to make their own.

***Accept the Writing They Do***    Accepting a variety of writing—from scribbling to one-letter representations to invented spellings to copied words—is the key to having young children "write" before they can write. Talk to your students on the very first day of school about the forms they can use for writing. Show them examples of other children's scribbles, pictures, single letters, vowel-less words, and other kinds of writing. Tell them they all started out at the scribble stage, and they will all get to conventional writing. For now, they should use the stage of writing that is most comfortable to share the message they have, and you will help them move along to the next stage.

## Teach Concrete Words

All children need to be successful in their first attempts at word learning. If the words you focus on with your beginners are the most common words—*the, have, with, to*—then those children who have not had many literacy experiences are going to have a hard time learning and remembering these words. The problem with the most common words is that they do not mean anything. *The, have, with,* and *to* are abstract connecting words. Children do need to learn these words (lots more about that in the next chapter), but doing so will be much easier if they have already learned some concrete important-to-them words. Most kindergarten and first-grade teachers begin their year with some get-acquainted activities. As part of these activities, they often have a "special child" each day. In addition to learning about each child, you can focus attention on the special child's name and use that name to develop some important understandings about words and letters.

To prepare for this activity, write all the children's first names (with initials for last names, if two first names are the same) in permanent marker on sentence strips. Cut the strips so that long names have long strips and short names have short strips. Each day, reach into the box and draw out a name. This child becomes the "King or Queen for a Day," and his or her name becomes the focus of many activities. Reserve a bulletin board and add each child's name to the board. (Some teachers like to have children bring in snapshots of themselves or take pictures of the children to add to the board as the names are added.) The following sections describe some day-by-day examples of what you might do with the names.

*Day 1*    Close your eyes. Reach into the box, shuffle the names around, and draw one out. Crown that child "King (or Queen) for the day!" Lead the other children in interviewing this child to find out what he or she likes to eat, play, or do after school. Does she or he have brothers? Sisters? Cats? Dogs? Mice? Many teachers record this information on a chart or compile a class book, with one page of information about each child.

Now focus the children's attention on the child's name—*David.* Point to the word *David* on the sentence strip and develop children's understanding of jargon by pointing out that this *word* is David's name. Tell them that it takes many *letters* to write the word *David,* and let them help you count the letters. Say the letters in *David*—D-a-v-i-d—and have the children chant them with you. Point out that the word *David* begins and ends with the same letter. Explain that the first and the last *d* look different because one is a capital *D* and the other is a small *d* (or uppercase/lowercase—whatever jargon you use).

Take another sentence strip and have the children watch as you write *David.* Have them chant the spelling of the letters with you. Cut the letters apart and mix them up. Let several children come up and arrange the letters in just the right order so that they spell *David,* using the original sentence strip on which *David* is written as a model. Have the other children chant to check that the order is correct.

Give each child a large sheet of drawing paper, and have all of them write *David* in large letters on one side of their papers using crayons. Model at the board how to write each letter as the children write it. Do not worry if what they write is not perfect (or even if it does not bear much resemblance to the letter you wrote). Also resist the temptation to correct what they write. Remember that children who write at home before coming to school often reverse letters or write them in funny ways. The important understanding is that names are words, that words can be written, and that it takes lots of letters to write them.

Finally, have everyone draw a picture of David on the other side of the drawing paper. Let David take all the pictures home!

*Day 2*    Draw another name—*Caroline.* Crown "Queen Caroline" and do the same interviewing and chart making that you did for David. (Decide carefully what you will do for the first child because every child will expect equal treatment!) Focus the children's attention on Caroline's name. Say the letters in *Caroline,* and have the children chant them with you. Help the children count the letters and decide which letter is first, last, and so on. Write *Caroline* on another sentence strip and cut it into letters. Have children arrange the letters to spell *Caroline,* using the first sentence strip name as their model. Put *Caroline* on the bulletin board under *David,* and compare the two. Which has the most letters? How many more letters are in the word *Caroline* than in the word *David?* Does *Caroline* have any of the same letters as *David?* Finish the lesson by having everyone write *Caroline.* Have everyone draw Caroline pictures, and let Caroline take all of them home.

***Day 3*** Draw the third name—*Dorinda.* Do the crowning, interviewing, and chart making. Chant the letters in Dorinda's name. Write it, cut it up, and do the letter arranging. Be sure to note the two *d*'s and to talk about first and last letters. As you put *Dorinda* on the bulletin board, compare it to both *David* and *Caroline.* This is a perfect time to notice that both *David* and *Dorinda* begin with the same letter and the same sound. Finish the lesson by having the children write *Dorinda* and draw pictures for Dorinda to take home.

***Day 4*** *Mike* comes out. Do all the usual activities. When you put *Mike* on the bulletin board, help the children realize that *David* has lost the dubious distinction of having the shortest name. (Bo may now look down at the name card on his desk and call out that his name is even shorter. You will point out that he is right but that Mike's name is the shortest one on the bulletin board right now. What is really fascinating about this activity is how the children compare their own names to the ones on the board, even before their names get there. That is exactly the kind of word/letter awareness you are trying to develop!)

When you have a one-syllable name with which there are many rhymes (*Pat, Jack, Bo, Sue,* etc.), seize the opportunity to help the children listen for words that rhyme with that name. Say pairs of words, some of which rhyme with Mike—*Mike/ball, Mike/bike, Mike/hike, Mike/cook, Mike/like.* If the pairs rhyme, everyone should point at Mike and shout "Mike." If not, they should shake their heads and frown.

***Day 5*** *Cynthia* comes out. Do the various activities, and then take advantage of the fact that the names *Caroline* and *Cynthia* both begin with the letter *c* but with different sounds. Have Caroline and Cynthia stand on opposite sides of you. Write their names above them on the chalkboard. Have the children say *Caroline* and *Cynthia* several times, drawing out the first sound. Help them understand that some letters can have more than one sound and that the names *Caroline* and *Cynthia* demonstrate this fact. Tell the class that you are going to say some words, all of which begin with the letter *c.* Some of these words will sound like *Caroline* at the beginning, and some of them will sound like *Cynthia.* Say some words and have the children say them with you—*cat, celery, candy, cookies, city, cereal, cut.* For each word, have the children point to Caroline or Cynthia to show which sound they hear. Once they have decided, write each word under *Caroline* or *Cynthia.*

***Day 6/Last Day*** Continue to have a special child each day. For each child, do the standard interviewing, charting, chanting, letter arranging, writing, and drawing activities. Then take advantage of the names you have to help children develop an understanding about how letters and sounds work. Here are some extra activities many teachers do with the names:

- Write the letters of the alphabet across the board. Count to see how many names contain each letter. Make tally marks or a bar graph, and then decide which letters are included in the most names and which letters are included in the fewest names. Are there any letters that no one in the whole class has in his or her name?

- Pass out laminated letter cards—one letter to a card, lowercase on one side, uppercase on the other. Call out a name from the bulletin board, and lead the children to chant the letters in the name. Then let the children who have those letters come up and display the letters and lead the class in a chant, cheerleader style: "David—D-a-v-i-d—David—Yeh! David!

***Learning Other Concrete Words***   The activities just described for names can be used to teach lots of concrete words. Many teachers bring in cereal boxes as part of a nutrition unit. In addition to talking about the cereals, children learn the names of the cereals by chanting, writing, and comparing. Places to shop is another engaging topic. Ads for local stores—Wal-Mart, Kmart, Dollar General—are brought in. Children talk about the stores and, of course, learn the names by chanting, writing, and comparing. Food is a topic of universal interest. Menus from popular restaurants—Burger King, McDonald's, Pizza Hut—spark lots of lively discussion from children, and, of course, children love learning to read and spell these very important words. You can teach the color words through chanting, writing, and drawing. When studying animals, add an animal name to an animal board each day. Children love chanting, writing, and drawing the animals.

These activities with the children's names and other concrete words can be done even when many children in the class do not know their letter names yet. Young children enjoy chanting, writing, and comparing words. They learn letter names by associating them with the important-to-them words they are learning.

## Develop Phonemic Awareness

Phonemic awareness includes a variety of understandings and levels. *Phonemic awareness* is the ability to take words apart, put them back together again, and change them. Phonemic awareness activities are done orally, calling attention to the sounds—not the letters or which letters make which sounds. Here are some activities to include in your classroom to ensure that all your children continue to develop in their ability to hear and manipulate sounds in words.

***Use Names to Build Phonemic Awareness***   Capitalize on your children's interest in names by using their names to develop a variety of phonemic awareness skills. The first way that children learn to pull apart words is into syllables. Say each child's name, and have all the children clap the beats in that name as they say it with you. Help children to see that *Dick* and *Pat* are one-beat names, that *Manuel* and *Patrick* are two beats, and so on. Once children begin to understand, clap the beats and have all the children whose names have that number of beats stand up and say their names as they clap the beats with you.

Another phonemic awareness skill is the ability to hear when sounds are the same or different. Say a sound, not a letter name, and have all the children whose names begin with that sound come forward. Stretch out the sound as you make it: "s-s-s." For the "s-s-s" sound, Samantha, Susie, Steve, and Cynthia should all come forward. Have everyone stretch out the "s-s-s" as they say each name. If anyone points out that *Cynthia* starts with a *c* or that *Sharon* starts with an *s,* explain that they are correct about the letters but that now you are listening for sounds.

You can use the names of some of your children to help them understand the concept of *rhyme.* Choose the children whose names have lots of rhyming words to come forward—*Bill, Jack, Brent, Kate, Clark.* Say a word that rhymes with one of the names (*hill, pack, spent, late, park*), and have the children say the word along with the name of the rhyming child. Not all your children's names will have rhymes, but the children who do will feel special and appreciated because they are helping everyone learn about rhyming words.

All your children will feel special if you call them to line up by stretching out their names, emphasizing each letter of each name. As each child lines up, have the class stretch out his or her name with you. The ability to segment words into sounds and blend them back together is an important phonemic awareness ability.

***Encourage Invented Spelling***   Think about what you have to do to "put down the letters you hear" while writing. You have to stretch out the sounds in the word. Children who stretch out words develop the phonemic awareness skill of *segmenting.* It does not really matter when children are just beginning, if they represent all the sounds with the right letters. What matters is the stretching out they are doing to try to hear the sounds. As phonics instruction continues, their invented spelling will more closely match the actual spelling of the word.

***Count Words***   This activity lets you build math skills as you develop the basic phonological awareness concept of separating words. For this activity, each child should have 10 counters in a paper cup. (Anything that is manipulative is fine. Some teachers use edibles, such as raisins, grapes, or small crackers, and let the children eat their counters at the end of the lesson. This makes cleanup quick and easy!) Begin by counting some familiar objects in the room, such as windows, doors, trash cans, and the like, having each child place one of the counters on the desk for each object.

Tell the children that you can also count words by putting down a counter for each word you say. Explain that you will say a sentence in the normal way and then repeat the sentence, pausing after each word. The children should put down counters as you say the words in the sentence slowly and then count the counters and decide how many words you said. As usual, children's attention is better if you make sentences about them:

> Carol has a big smile.
> Paul is back at school today.
> I saw Jawan at the grocery store.

Once the children catch on to the activity, let them say some sentences—first in the normal way, then one word at a time. Listen carefully as they say their sentences because they usually need help saying them one word at a time. Not only do children enjoy this activity and learn to separate words in speech, but they are also practicing critical counting skills!

*Clap Syllables* In addition to using your children's names to develop syllable awareness, you can use any of the environmental print words you are helping children learn. *Cheerios* is a three-beat word. *Kix* takes only one clap and has one beat. Once children can clap syllables and decide how many beats a given word has, help them see that one-beat words are usually shorter than three-beat words—that is, they take fewer letters to write. To do this, write some words that children cannot read on sentence strips and cut the strips into words, so that short words have short strips and long words have long strips. Have some of the words begin with the same letters but be of different lengths, so the children will need to think about word length in order to decide which word is which.

For the category of animals, you might write *horse* and *hippopotamus, dog* and *donkey, kid* and *kangaroo,* and *rat, rabbit,* and *rhinoceros.* Tell the children that you are going to say the names of animals and that they should clap to show how many beats each word has. (Do not show them the words yet!) Say the first pair of words, one at a time—*horse/hippopotamus.* Help children to decide that *horse* is a one-beat word and *hippopotamus* takes a lot more claps and is a five-beat word. Now, show children the two words and say, "One of these words is *horse,* and the other is *hippopotamus.* Who thinks they can figure out which one is which?" Explain that because *hippopotamus* takes so many beats to say, it probably takes more letters to write.

*Play Blending and Segmenting Games* In addition to using the names of your children to help them learn to blend and segment, you can use a variety of other words that help build their meaning vocabularies while simultaneously practicing blending and segmenting. Use pictures related to your unit or from simple concept and alphabet books. Let each child take a turn saying the name of the picture (one sound at a time), and call on another child to identify the picture. In the beginning, limit the pictures to five or six items whose names are very different and short—*truck, frog, cat, pony, tiger.* Once children understand what they are trying to do, they loving playing a variation of I Spy, in which they see something in the room, stretch out its name, and then call on someone to figure out what they have seen and to give the next clue.

***Read Rhyming Books and Nursery Rhymes***   One of the best indicators of how well children will learn to read is their ability to recite nursery rhymes when they walk into kindergarten. Since this is such a reliable indicator and since rhymes are so naturally appealing to children at this age, kindergarten and first-grade classrooms should be filled with rhymes. Children should learn to recite these rhymes, sing the rhymes, clap to the rhymes, act out the rhymes, and pantomime the rhymes. In some primary classrooms, they develop "raps" for the rhymes.

As part of your read-aloud, include lots of rhyming books, including such old favorites as *Hop on Pop; One Fish, Two Fish, Red Fish, Blue Fish;* and *There's a Wocket in My Pocket.* As you read the book for the second time—once is never near enough for a favorite book of young children—pause just before you get to the rhyme and let the children chime in with the rhyming word.

**RECOMMENDED resources**

**Two Wonderful Tongue-Twister Books**

*Alphabet Annie Announces an All-American Album,* by Susan Purviance and Marcia O'Shell (1988)

*The Biggest Tongue Twister Book in the World,* by Gyles Brandeth (1978)

***Read and Invent Tongue Twisters***   Children love tongue twisters, and they are wonderful reminders of the sounds of beginning letters. Use children's names and let them help you create the tongue twisters. Have students say them as fast as they can and as slowly as they can. When students have said them enough times to have them memorized, write them on posters or in a class book.

## Teach Letter Names and Sounds

Through all the activities just described, children will begin to learn some letter names and sounds. You can accelerate this learning with some of the following activities.

***Use Children's Names to Teach Letter Names and Sounds***   When you focus on a special child each day, chanting and writing that child's name and then comparing the names of all the children, many children will begin to learn some letter names and sounds. Once all the names are displayed, however, and most of the children can read most of the names, you can use these names to solidify knowledge of letter names and sounds.

Imagine that these children's names are displayed on the word wall or name board:

| | | | | |
|---|---|---|---|---|
| David | Rasheed | Robert | Catherine | Cindy |
| Mike | Sheila | Sam | Joseph | Julio |
| Amber T. | Matt | Erin | Shawonda | Bianca |
| Erica | Kevin | Adam | Delano | Brittany |
| Bill | Tara | Amber M. | Octavius | Kelsie |

Begin with a letter that many children have in their names and that usually has its expected sound. With this class, you might begin with the letter *r*. Have all children whose names have an *r* in them come to the front of the class, holding cards with their names on them. First count all the *r*'s. There are 11 *r*'s in all. Next have the children whose names contain an *r* divide themselves into those whose names begin with an *r*—*Robert* and *Rasheed;* those whose names end with an *r*—*Amber T.* and *Amber M.*; and those with an *r* that is not the first or the last letter—*Brittany, Erica, Tara, Erin, Catherine, Larry.* Finally, say each name slowly, stretching out the letters, and decide if you can hear the usual sound of that letter. For *r*, you can hear them all.

Now choose another letter, and let all those children come down and display their name cards. Count the number of times that letter occurs, and then have the children divide themselves into groups according to whether the letter is first, last, or in between. Finally, say the names, stretching them out, and decide if you can hear the usual sound that letter makes. The letter *D* would be a good second choice. You would have *David* and *Delano* beginning with *d; David* and *Rasheed* ending with *d; Cindy, Shawonda,* and *Adam* having a *d* that is not first or last. Again, you can hear the usual sound of *d* in all these names.

Continue picking letters and having children come up with their name cards until you have sorted for some of the letters represented by your names. When doing the letters *s, c, t,* and *j,* be sure to point out that they can have two sounds and that the *th* in *Catherine* and the *sh* in *Sheila, Shawonda,* and *Rasheed* have their own special sounds. You probably should not sort out the names with an *h* because although *Shawanda, Sheila, Rasheed, Catherine,* and *Joseph* all have *h*'s, the *h* sound is not represented by any of these. The same would go for *p,* which only occurs in *Joseph.* When you have the children come down for the vowels—*a, e, i, o,* and *u*—count and then sort the children according to first, last, and in between but do not try to listen for the sounds. Explain that vowels have lots of different sounds and that the children will learn more about the vowels and their sounds all year.

***Use Favorite Words with Pure Initial Sounds as Key Words***   Capitalize on the concrete words you have been teaching your children by choosing one or two of these words to represent each of the important sounds. Use your children's names when they have the appropriate sounds and then use other concrete words you have been learning.

When teaching the first letter–sound relationships, begin with two letters that are very different in look and sound and that are made in different places of the mouth—*b* and *l,* for example. Also choose two letters for which your children's names can be the examples. Show the children the two words, *Bill* and *Larry,* which will serve as key words for these letters. Have the children pronounce the two key words and notice the positions of their tongues and teeth as they do. Have Bill stand in the front of the room and hold the word *Bill.* Also have Larry hold a card with his name on it. Say several concrete words that begin like *Bill* or *Larry*—*bike, lemon, box, book, ladder, lady, boy*—and have the children say them after you. Have them notice where their tongues and teeth are as they say the words. Let the children point to the child holding the sign *Bill* or *Larry* to indicate how each word begins.

***The Alphabet Song and Alphabet Books***   "The Alphabet Song" has been sung by generations of children. Not only do children enjoy it, but it seems to give them a sense of all the letters and a framework in which to put new letters as they learn them. Many children come to school already able to sing "The Alphabet Song." Let them sing it and teach it to

everyone else. Once the children can sing the song, you may want to point to alphabet cards (usually found above the chalkboard) as they sing. Children also enjoy "being the alphabet" as they line up to go somewhere. Simply pass out your laminated alphabet cards—one to each child, leftovers to the teacher—and let the children sing the song slowly as they line up. Be sure to hand out the cards randomly, so that no one always gets to be the *A* and lead the line or has to be the *Z* and bring up the rear every day!

Wonderful alphabet books are also available. You can read these books aloud over and over. Your children can select these books to "read" during their self-selected reading. Teacher aides, as well as parent and grandparent volunteers, can "lap read" these in the reading corner and so on. Your class can create their own alphabet book modeled after their own favorite alphabet book. Be sure to focus on the meanings of the words in all alphabet books you use, so that children will add words to their oral vocabularies.

*Letter Actions*    Young children love movement! Teach children actions for the letters, and they will remember those letters. Write a letter on one side of a large index card and an action on the other. The first time you teach each letter, make a big deal of it. Get out the rhythm sticks and the marching music when you *march* for *M*. Go out on the playground and do *jumping jacks* for *J*. Play *hopscotch* and *hop* like bunnies for *H*.

Once the children have learned actions for several letters, you can do many activities in the classroom without any props. Have all the children stand by their desks and wait until you show them a letter. Then, they should do that action until you hide the letter behind your back. When they have all stopped and you have their attention again, show them another letter and have them do that action. Continue this with as many letters as you have time to fill. Be sure to make comments such as "Yes, I see everyone marching because *M* is our marching letter."

In another activity, pass out the letters for which children have learned the actions to individual children. Each child then gets up and does the action required and calls on someone to guess which letter he or she was given. In Follow the Letter Leader, the leader picks a letter card and does that action. Everyone else follows the leader, doing the same action. The leader then picks another card and the game continues.

Teachers have different favorites for letter actions, and you will have your own favorites. Try to pick actions with which everyone is familiar and that are only called by single names. Following is a list of actions we like:

| | | | |
|---|---|---|---|
| bounce | hop | nod | vacuum |
| catch | jump | paint | walk |
| dance | kick | run | yawn |
| fall | laugh | sit | zip |
| gallop | march | talk | |

The action for *s* is our particular favorite. You can use it to end the game. Children say, "It is not an action at all," but remember that "*s* is the sitting letter." You may want to take pictures of various members of your class doing the different actions and make a book of actions they can all read and enjoy.

## *Summary*

Emergent literacy research began with the work of Charles Read (1975) and his mentor, Carol Chomsky (1971). Read's work described for many of us at the time what we were seeing in the writing of young children. Read taught us that young children's spellings are developmental and could be predicted by analyzing the consonant and vowel substitutions students consistently made. Chomsky's article "Write First, Read Later" was seminal in helping to shift instruction toward the field that came to be known as *emergent literacy.*

Much of the emergent literacy research has been done in the homes of young children, tracing their literacy development from birth until the time they read and write in conventional ways (Sulzby & Teale, 1991). From this observational research, it became apparent that children in literate home environments engage in reading and writing long before they begin formal reading instruction. These children use reading and writing in a variety of ways and pass through a series of predictable stages on their voyage from pretending and scribbling to conventional reading and writing. When parents read to children, interact with them about the print they see in the world (signs, cereal boxes, advertisements), and encourage and support their early writing efforts, children establish a firm foundation for learning to read.

This chapter summarizes the crucial understandings essential to successful independent reading and writing. Through early reading and writing experiences, children learn why we read and write. They develop background knowledge and vocabulary, print concepts, and phonemic awareness. They learn some concrete important-to-them words and some letter names and sounds. Most important, they develop the desire to learn to read and gain self-confidence in their own ability to become literate. Classrooms in which all children develop a firm foundation of emergent literacy provide a variety of reading, writing, and word activities to help all children get off to a successful start in literacy.

# Developing Fluent
# Decoders and Spellers

When you are reading or writing, your brain is busy constructing meaning and simultaneously identifying or spelling words. Most of the time, you don't even know that you are identifying or spelling words because you have read or written these words so many times that their identification and spelling has become automatic.

*Automatic* means "without any conscious effort or thought." The concept of automaticity is critical to your understanding of the words/meaning construction relationship

because your brain can carry out many automatic functions simultaneously. Your brain can do only one nonautomatic function, however. Meaning construction is the nonautomatic function. When your brain is stopped by a word you can't immediately and automatically identify or spell, your attention is diverted from the meaning to the word. In order to read and write fluently, readers and writers must be able to immediately recognize and spell the vast majority of words.

Even when you can instantly recognize most words, you will occasionally come to a word you have never before seen. Imagine that while reading, you encounter the word *desufnoc.* When your eyes see the letters of a word you have never seen before, your brain cannot immediately identify that word. You must stop and figure it out. This figuring out may include determining the pronunciation for the word and the meaning for the word. In this case, you can probably pronounce *desufnoc,* but since no meaning is triggered by your pronunciation, this word can't just join the others in your working memory and help them construct some meaning to shift to long-term memory. Your reading is stalled by the intrusion of this unknown word. You have to either figure out what it is and what it means or continue reading, hoping the other words—the *context*—will allow you to continue to construct meaning, even though you don't know the word *desufnoc.* A bit confused (which is *desufnoc* backward), you press forward!

In order to become fluent readers who can concentrate most of their attention on comprehension, beginning readers must learn to recognize immediately the most frequently occurring words. Words such as *have, of, the, on, was,* and many others occur again and again in everything we read and everything we write. We call these words *high-frequency words.* The sooner children learn to instantly and automatically read and spell these words, the faster they will progress in learning to read.

In addition to learning to instantly recognize and spell the most frequent words, children must learn how to figure out the pronunciations and spellings of words they do not know. All proficient readers have the ability to look at regular words they have never seen before and assign probable pronunciations. Witness your ability to pronounce these made-up words:

cate      frow      perdap      midulition

Now of course, you were not reading because having only pronounced these words, you would not construct any meaning. But if you were in the position of most young readers, who have many more words in their listening/meaning vocabularies than in their sight-reading vocabularies, you would often meet words familiar in speech but unfamiliar in print. Your ability to rapidly figure out the pronunciations of "unfamiliar-in-print" words would enable you to make use of your huge store of "familiar-in-speech" words and thus create meaning.

Before we go on, how did you pronounce the made-up word *frow?* Did it rhyme with *cow* or with *snow?* Because English is not a one-sound, one-letter language, there are different ways to pronounce certain letter patterns. Even so, the number of different ways is limited, and with real words, unlike made-up words, your speaking vocabulary lets you know which pronunciation to assign.

Not only do readers use their phonics knowledge to read words they have not seen before, but this same knowledge also enables them to write. If the four made-up words had been dictated to you and you had to write them, you would have spelled them reasonably close to the way we spelled them.

All good readers and writers develop this ability to come up with pronunciations and spellings for words they have never read or written before. Many poor readers do not. When good readers see a word they have never before seen in print, they stop briefly and study the word, looking at every letter in a left-to-right sequence. As they look at all the letters, they are not thinking of a sound for each letter, because good readers know that sounds are determined not by individual letters but by letter patterns. Good readers look for patterns of letters they have seen together before and then search their mental word banks, looking for words with similar letter patterns. If the new word is a big word, they "chunk" it—that is, they put letters together to make familiar chunks.

Based on their careful inspection of the letters and their search through their mental bank for words with the same letter patterns, good readers try out a pronunciation. If the first try does not result in a word they have heard and stored in their mental word bank, they will usually try another pronunciation. Finally, they produce a pronunciation that they recognize as sounding like a real word that they know. They then go back and reread the sentence that contained the unfamiliar-in-print word and see if their pronunciation makes sense, given the meaning they are getting from the context of surrounding words. If the pronunciation they came up with makes sense, they continue reading. If not, they look again at all the letters of the unfamiliar word and see what else would "look like this and make sense."

Imagine a young boy reading this sentence:

The dancer came out and took a bow.

Imagine that he pauses at the last word and then pronounces *bow* so that it rhymes with *low.* Since that is a real word that he remembers hearing, his eyes then glance back and he quickly rereads the sentence. He then realizes, "That doesn't make sense." He studies all the letters of *bow* again and searches for similar letter patterns in his mental word bank. Perhaps he now accesses words such as *how* and *now.* This gives him another possible pronunciation for this letter pattern, one that is also recognized as a previously heard word. He tries this pronunciation, quickly rereads, realizes his sentence now "sounds right," and continues reading.

From this scenario, we can infer the strategies this good reader used to successfully decode an unfamiliar-in-print word:

1. Recognize that this is an unfamiliar word, and look at all the letters in a left-to-right sequence.
2. Search your mental word bank for similar letter patterns and the sounds associated with them.
3. Produce a pronunciation that matches that of a real word that you know.
4. Reread the sentence to cross-check your possible pronunciation with meaning. If meaning confirms pronunciation, continue reading. If not, try again!

Had the unfamiliar word been a big word, the reader would have had to use a fifth strategy:

5. Look for familiar morphemes, and chunk the word by putting letters together that usually go together in the words you know.

To be a good reader, you must be able to automatically recognize most words and you must be able to quickly decode the words you do not immediately recognize. To be a good writer, you must be able to automatically spell most of the words and come up with reasonable spellings for the words you cannot automatically spell. This chapter will provide activities for helping all children become automatic and fluent decoders and spellers.

## Teaching High-Frequency Words

In English, about 120 words make up half of all the words we read and write. In order to read and write, children must learn to quickly and automatically recognize and spell these most common words. The most common words are usually meaningless, abstract, connecting words (*of, and, the, is,* etc.). Children use these words in their speech, but they are not aware of them as separate entities.

Read these sentences in a natural speech pattern, and notice how you pronounce the italicized words:

> What *do* you see?
> I want that piece *of* cake.
> What are *they*?

In natural speech, the *what* and the *do* are slurred together and sound like "wudoo." The *of* is pronounced like "uh." The *they* is tacked on to the end of *are* and sounds like "ah-thay."

All children use high-frequency words such as *what, of,* and *they* in their speech, but they are not as aware of these words as they are of the more concrete, tangible words, such as *want* and *pie.* To make learning to read and write even more difficult, many of these high-frequency words are not spelled in regular, predictable ways. *What* should rhyme with *at, bat,* and *cat. Of* should be spelled *u-v. They,* which clearly rhymes with *day, may,* and *way,* should be spelled the way many children do spell it—*t-h-a-y.*

When you consider that most high-frequency words are meaningless, abstract words that children use but do not realize are separate words and that many of these words are irregular in spelling/pronunciation, it is a wonder that any children learn to recognize and spell them! In order to read and write fluently, however, children must learn to instantly recognize and automatically spell these words.

Since these words occur so often, children who read and write will encounter them in their reading and need to spell them as they write. Many teachers have found it effective to display high-frequency words in a highly visible spot in their classrooms and provide daily practice with these words. Teachers often refer to the place where the words are displayed as their *word wall.*

*Upper Grades Word Wall*

*Primary Grades Word Wall*

Teaching High-Frequency Words

*Doing* a word wall is not the same thing as *having* a word wall. Having a word wall might mean putting all these words up somewhere in the room and telling students to use them. In our experience, struggling readers cannot use these words because they do not know them or know which is which! Doing a word wall means the following:

- Being selective and "stingy" about what words go up there, limiting the words to those really common words that children need a lot in writing
- Adding words gradually—five or six a week
- Making the words very accessible by putting them where everyone can see them, writing them in big black letters, and using a variety of colors so that the constantly confused words (*went, want, what, with, will, that, them, they, this,* etc.) are in different colors
- Practicing the words by chanting and writing them, because struggling readers are not usually good visual learners and can't just look at and remember words
- Doing a variety of review activities to provide enough practice so that children can read and spell the words instantly and automatically
- Making sure that word wall words are spelled correctly in any writing students do

Teachers who *do* word walls (rather than just *have* word walls) report that *all* their children learn these critical words.

## Selecting Words for the Wall

The selection of words varies from classroom to classroom, but the selection principle is the same: Include words students will need often in their reading and writing and that are often confused with other words. First-grade teachers who are using a basal reader usually select some high-frequency words taught in that basal. Other teachers select their words from a high-frequency word list. In addition to using high-frequency words, first-grade teachers often begin their word walls with the names of their children and add an example word for each letter in the alphabet—even if there is no high-frequency word for that letter.

Beyond first grade, teachers should look for words commonly misspelled in the children's writing and add them to the wall. The misspelled words include many homophones, and these should be added with a picture or phrase clue attached to all but one of the words. For example, add a card with the number 2 next to *two* and attach the word *also* and the phrase *too late* next to *too.* Children learn to think whether they are writing the number *two,* the "too late *too,*" or "the other one." Once high-frequency words are on the wall, teachers may add words with a particular pattern—beginning letters, rhyming pattern, vowel pattern, ending—to provide examples of this pattern.

## 120 High-Frequency Words Often Found on Primary Word Walls

|  |  |  |  |  |  |
|---|---|---|---|---|---|
|  | brother | *fun | is | *old | teacher | want |
|  | *but | get | *it | on | *tell | was |
|  | *can | girl | *like | other | *that | we |
| about | can't | give | little | our | the | *went |
| after | *car | go | *look | *out | their | were |
| again | children | good | *made | over | them | what |
| *all | come | *had | *make | people | *then | *when |
| *am | could | has | many | *play | there | where |
| *and | *day | have | me | pretty | they | who |
| are | *did | he | *more | *ride | they're | *why |
| *at | do | her | *my | said | *thing | *will |
| be | don't | here | *new | *saw | this | with |
| because | *down | him | *nice | *school | to | won't |
| before | *eat | his | *night | *see | too | you |
| *best | favorite | house | no | she | two | your |
| *big | for | *how | *not | sister | *up | |
| *black | friend | I | of | some | us | |
| *boy | from | *in | off | *talk | very | |

*Asterisked words help with decoding and spelling lots of rhyming words.

## Displaying the Words

Write the words with a thick, black, permanent marker on pieces of different-colored paper. Place the words on the wall above or below the letters they begin with. When confusable words are added, make sure they are on a different color of paper from the other words they are usually confused with. Most teachers add five new words each week and do at least one daily activity in which the children find, chant, and write the spellings of the words.

## Chanting and Writing the Words

To begin the word wall practice, students write numbers on a sheet of paper, from one to five. The teacher calls out five words, putting each word in a sentence. As the teacher calls out each word, one child finds and points to that word on the wall. Next, the students clap and chant the spelling of each word in a rhythmic fashion. After chanting, they write each

## 90 Words Commonly Found on Intermediate Word Walls

| | | | |
|---|---|---|---|
| | doesn't | *knew | that's | *weather (rain) |
| | don't | *know | *their | *we're (we are) |
| | enough | laugh | then | went |
| about | especially | let's | *there (here) | *were |
| again | everybody | myself | they | what |
| almost | everyone | *new (old) | *they're (they are) | when |
| also | everything | *no (yes) | thought | *where |
| always | except | off | *threw (caught) | *whether |
| another | excited | *one (1) | *through | who |
| anyone | favorite | our | *to | *whole |
| are | first | people | *too (Too late!) | with |
| beautiful | friends | probably | trouble | *won |
| because | getting | really | *two (2) | won't |
| before | have | *right (wrong) | until | wouldn't |
| *buy (sell) | *hole (donut) | said | usually | *write |
| *by | I'm | school | very | *your |
| can't | into | something | want | *you're (you are) |
| could | *it's (it is) | sometimes | was | |
| didn't | *its | terrible | *wear (shirt) | |

*Clues are attached to homophones and may include pictures and opposite words.

word on their papers. Many teachers tie this daily writing of five words into handwriting instruction and model for the children how to make each letter as the children write the words. When all five words have been written, the teacher leads the students to check/fix their own papers.

On the day new words are added, the new words are called out, clapped, chanted, and written. These new words are often reviewed on the second day. During the rest of the week, however, any five words from the wall can be called out. The words with which children need much practice are called out almost every day.

## "On-the-Back" Activities

Most teachers allot 10 minutes each day for the daily word wall practice. Early in the year, it takes the whole 10 minutes to call out, chant, write, and check five words. But as the year goes on, children become much faster at chanting, writing, and checking the words and can do five words in 5 or 6 minutes. At this point, the teacher can add "on-the-back" activities (called this because children turn over their word wall papers and do these activities on the back). On-the-back activities are designed to provide additional practice with word wall words and to help children learn that knowing some of the words on the wall can help them spell lots of other words. Several of the most popular and productive on-the-back activities are described in the sections that follow.

*Learning to Spell Rhyming Words*    Half the high-frequency words do not follow logical patterns—but half do. Many teachers put stars on word wall words that children can use to help them spell lots of rhyming words. This activity helps children learn how to use the starred words to spell lots of other words. To begin this activity, the teacher might say something like this:

> "All of the words we have on our word wall are important words because we see them over and over again in the books we read and they help us write. But some words are important in another way. Some of the words on our wall will help us spell lots of other words that rhyme with them. *Went* is one of those helpful words."

The teacher circles *went*, which was one of the five words called out today.

> "Today, we are going to practice using *went* to spell five other words we use a lot in our writing. Turn your paper over and write *went* on the top line. I am going to say a sentence that someone might be writing, and I want you to listen for the word that *went* will help you spell."
>
> I had a wreck and put a big dent in my car door.
>
> "Which word will *went* help you spell?"

A child volunteers that *went* will help you spell *dent* because *went* and *dent* rhyme. The teacher has the children all say *went* and *dent* to confirm that they rhyme, and everyone writes *dent* under *went*.

Next, the teacher says,

> "I am going to say another sentence. Listen for the word *went* will help you spell."
>
> We have to pay a lot of rent for our apartment every month.

A child volunteers that *rent* and *went* rhyme. All the children say *rent* and *went* to confirm this, and everyone writes *rent* under *went* and *dent*. The teacher continues, saying three more sentences that children might be writing:

> I spent all my money on a gift for my mom.
> We slept in a tent at camp.
> My cousin's name is Brent.

After each sentence, a volunteer tells the word that *went* will help spell, the children say the two words to confirm the rhyme, and everyone writes the rhyming word.

When the teacher does this on-the-back rhyming activity, she or he has the children write five preselected words that rhyme with one of the word wall words. The teacher gives the children a sentence they might be writing, and they decide which word the target word will help them spell. This more closely models what children actually have to do to use this rhyming strategy to spell words they are writing and helps ensure transfer to their writing. It is important to note that the teacher, not the children, is coming up with the sentences. Asking children to create the sentences will turn this into a 30-minute activity, rather than a 3-minute one, and they might suggest rhyming words with a different spelling pattern.

This rhyming on-the-back activity can be used with all the starred words on your word wall and will greatly increase the number of words children can spell. Here are some sentences you might give them if you have the word *eat* on your word wall:

> My favorite team *beat* my Dad's favorite team.
> It was so cold last night that we had to turn on the *heat*.
> We had company and I had to get my room clean and *neat*.
> Having my grandma come for my birthday was a real *treat*.
> Our coach says we have to try hard to win, but we must never *cheat*.

When you do these rhyming activities, be sure to give children the rhyming words, rather than ask them to tell you the rhyming words. Some rhymes have more than one pattern, and by controlling which words you have children spell, you can avoid using words such as *feet* and *Pete,* which have different patterns. They will eventually have to learn to use their visual checking system to determine the correct pattern, but the first step is to get them spelling by pattern, rather than putting down one letter for each sound.

Here are a few more examples for starred words from the word wall:

> *At* will help you spell *cat, bat, hat, brat,* and *flat.*
> *Look* will help you spell *cook, book, hook, brook,* and *crook.*
> *Ride* will help you spell *side, wide, bride, glide,* and *tide.*
> *Black* will help you spell *Jack, pack, snack, stack,* and *track.*
> *Night* will help you spell *fight, light, might, flight,* and *tight.*
> *And* will help you spell *hand, sand, band, stand,* and *brand.*
> *Can* will help you spell *Dan, man, ran, tan,* and *plan.*
> *Will* will help you spell *Bill, fill, pill, still,* and *spill.*
> *Make* will help you spell *bake, cake, rake, lake,* and *brake.*

There is another rhyming on-the back format that is harder but closer to what children actually have to do to use the word wall words to spell words they need while writing. To do this rhyming format, make sure that all the words you call out for children to write on the front of the page have some words that rhyme and share the same spelling pattern. You might call out the words: *make, thing, like, went,* and *will.*

Help the children to notice that all these words are starred words and that they have stars because they can help with spelling lots of other rhyming words. Tell children that you are going to pretend to be writing and need to spell a word that rhymes with one of these five words. Tell them some sentences you might be writing, emphasizing the word you need to spell, and let them decide which of the five helpful words they wrote on the front of the page will help you:

> I had a cavity and the dentist had to *drill* my tooth.
> I was so scared when I saw the huge *snake.*
> My brother *spent* his whole allowance on baseball cards.
> My sister likes it when I push her on the *swing.*
> We took a long *hike* up the mountain.

Once you have begun to use this new rhyming format, alternate it with the easier one, in which your sentences use rhymes for only one of the words. The harder format helps children who are ready to learn how thinking of a rhyming word can help them spell lots of words. The easier format is important for children who are still developing their sense of rhyme and how rhyme helps them spell.

*Learning to Spell Words with Endings*  Another on-the-back activity helps children learn how to spell word wall words that need endings. Imagine that these were the five word wall words you called out for the children to locate, cheer for, and write:

girl    boy    friend    brother    sister

Have the children turn their papers over and write the words *boys, sisters, brothers, friends,* and *girls.*

On another day, call out five words that can have *ed* endings, such as *want, look, jump, kick,* and *play.* Then have the children write these words with the *ed* ending on the back. On another day, do a similar activity with words to which *ing* can be added.

For easy endings activities, work with only one ending and do not include words that need spelling changes. Once students get good at adding *s, ed,* and *ing,* do some more complex on-the-back activities by including different words and endings. Imagine that your students have written these five words on the front:

want    eat    look    talk    play

Have them turn their papers over and tell them something like this:

> "Today, we are going to work on how to spell these word wall words when they need different endings. I will say some sentences for you to write, and you listen for the word wall word that has had an ending added."
>
> My friends and I love *eating* at McDonald's.
>
> We were *looking* for some new shoes.
>
> I was *talking* on the phone to my Grandma.
>
> My mom *wants* the new baby to be a girl
>
> My friend spent the night and we *played* Nintendo 'til 11:00.

After you read each sentence, the children identify the word wall word and the ending, decide how to spell it, and write it on their papers.

As the children get good at adding *s, ed,* and *ing,* include some endings with spelling changes—the *e* dropped, a *y* changed to *i,* or a letter doubled. Since you will decide ahead of time what the children will write, everyone will be writing the words correctly. This additional information about how to spell words with a variety of endings and spelling changes really moves the accelerated learners along in their spelling ability.

When students are good at spelling word wall words with the most common endings, include some words in which *y, ly, er,* and *est* are added. Show them how they can spell *jumpy* and *rainy* by adding *y* to *jump* and *rain* and how *nicely* and *friendly* are formed by adding *ly*. You can add *er* and *est* to *new* and *pretty. Talk, jump, kick, ride,* and *eat* can become the person who does them by adding *er.* Of course, you will help the children decide what spelling changes they need as they write these words.

## Reading, Writing, and Word Walls

Once you have a word wall growing in your room, there will be no doubt that your students are using it as they are reading and writing. You will see their eyes quickly glance to the exact spot where a word that they want to write is displayed. Even when children are reading, they will sometimes glance over to the word wall to help them remember a particularly troublesome word.

Word walls provide children with an immediately accessible dictionary for the most troublesome words. Because the words are added gradually, stay in the same spots forever, are alphabetical by their first letters, are visually distinctive by different colors of paper, and are used in daily practice in finding, writing, and chanting, most children learn to read and spell almost all of the word wall words. Because the words you selected are words they need constantly in their reading and writing, their recognition of these words will become automatic and their attention can be devoted to less frequently occuring words and to constructing meaning as they read and write.

## *Developing Fluency*

*Fluency* is the ability to read quickly, accurately, and automatically and with appropriate expression. Fluency is critical to reading comprehension because of the attention factor. Our brains can attend to a limited number of things at a time. If most of our attention is focused on decoding the words, little attention is left for the comprehension part of reading—putting the words together and thinking about what they mean. The National Reading Panel (2000) explains this relationship between reading comprehension and fluency:

> If text is read in a laborious and inefficient manner, it will be difficult for the child to remember what has been read and to relate the ideas expressed in the text to his or her background knowledge. (p. 11)

In Chapter Two, we described how to create enthusiastic and independent readers. One of the reasons for establishing self-selected reading as a regular component in every elementary classroom is that fluency develops as children do lots of reading—and particularly lots of easy reading. In the previous section of this chapter, we described how to help children automatically recognize high-frequency words. The ability to instantly and automatically recognize high-frequency words contributes much to fluent reading.

One of the major ways that we become fluent readers is to read something over several times. The first time, a lot of our attention is on identifying the words. The second time, we are able to read in phrases, as our brain puts them together into meaningful units. The third time, we read more rapidly, with good expression and in a seemingly effortless way. There are a variety of ways to include repeated readings as part of your classroom routines. In the following sections, we will describe five ways many teachers have found to work well with children across the elementary grades: echo reading, choral reading, taped reading/listening, timed repeated reading, and paired repeated reading.

## Echo Reading

One teacher had been doing echo reading for months when a child suddenly asked, "What's an *echo?*" The teacher tried to explain it and discovered that many children had never heard an echo. After some "field research," the teacher located a spot in the auditorium where sound would echo, and the children all got to hear their voices echoing back to them. Echo reading made a lot more sense to them after that, and they tried to "be the echo." It is easy to forget that our children don't know everything we know. If your children have never heard an echo, you might try to find a place to take them where they can have firsthand experience with this phenomenon.

Once children know what an echo does—that it repeats exactly what was said—it is easy to engage them in echo reading. Echo reading is usually done one sentence at a time, with the teacher's voice reading the sentence first and the children's voices being the echo. Echo reading is often done with short, easy text that has only one sentence on a page. Echo reading is fun to do when the text has different voices. *Brown Bear, Brown Bear, What Do You See?* by Bill Martin, *I Went Walking* by Sue Williams, and *Hattie and the Fox* by Mem Fox are favorites for echo reading. Echo reading is also appropriate for reading plays. First read the whole play in an echo reading format, using different voices for the different characters. As you read, ask children to think about each character and which character they would like to be when you read the play again.

## Choral Reading

Choral reading works best for poetry, stories with refrains, and books with lots of conversation. The whole class can read, or you can assign groups and parts. Many teachers use old favorites, including nursery rhymes and finger plays. *The Itsy Bitsy Spider, Five Little Pumpkins, Rudolph the Red-Nosed Reindeer,* and *Peter Cottontail* are naturals for choral reading. Choral reading is also a wonderful way to reread books such as *The Lion and the Mouse* and *Brown Bear, Brown Bear,* in which characters talk to each other.

To conduct a choral reading, begin by reading the rhyme to the children. You may want to echo read it with them a time or two. If you have the rhyme in a "big book," use that. If not, reproduce it on a chart. After reading it together, children enjoy pantomiming these rhymes while other children read them.

## Taped Reading/Listening

Another way teachers provide opportunities for children to do repeated readings is to have them read along with an audiotape or CD recording of a book or story. There are lots of variations on this activity and lots of different names for it.

Be patient and allow the student to listen to or read the selection during any free time or at home. When the student is able to read the selection fluently without the aid of the recording, he or she should receive praise and ample opportunities to read the selection to parents, other teachers, fellow students, and young children in kindergarten or first grade. Although the student has not really memorized the selection (the student could not read the selection without having the book to follow), a combination of memorization and reading enables the student to have the real experience of successful, effective, and fluent reading.

Several students can receive such instruction simultaneously, each one with a different book. The limit is defined by how many tape recorders or CD players are available. A group of students can also learn the same book simultaneously, if you have multiple copies of an appropriate book or magazine article.

Find a selection that will interest the student and that is not too long or too difficult. Choose a selection that is appealing and dramatically read. Then instruct the student to listen to the recording and follow along in the book until he or she can read the text fluently.

## Timed Repeated Reading

For a timed repeated reading, you need a passage of interest to the student that is at the student's instructional level. The passage should be short, no more than 150 words. Give the student the passage, and tell him or her to read it silently and to get ready to read it orally with few errors and at a comfortable rate. After silent reading, have the student read the passage to you; count the oral reading errors (the three most frequently occurring errors are words left out, words changed, and words added in), and time the reading. If the student makes more than five errors per 100 words, the passage is too difficult and an easier one should be chosen. If the student makes no more than five errors per 100 words, tell the reader the time it took and help her or him correct any errors. Then have the student practice reading the material again.

Repeat this process until the student has read the passage three or four times. While some students are practicing, another can be reading to you, which makes it possible to use repeated readings with a small group of readers.

## Paired Repeated Reading

Paired repeated reading is just like timed repeated reading but without timing. In other words, the student reads and rereads a passage but only to make fewer errors, not to increase rate.

Partner up two children who like each other and who are at about the same reading level, and have them take turns reading and recording errors. Children like listening to each other read and counting errors. Model and role-play for the whole class how you want them to do paired repeated reading, and be sure they understand that they are not allowed to interrupt each other during reading but must wait until the reading is finished before helping the reader make corrections. Children like to do paired repeated reading when they can do it with a friend and when they get to pick the book and pages they will practice reading.

## Teaching Phonics and Spelling Patterns

While children are learning to read and spell high-frequency words and doing lots of easy and repeated reading to develop fluency, they also need to be learning to decode unfamiliar words. Once children know the common sounds for most letters, they need to start paying attention to the patterns in words so that they can use these patterns to decode and spell words. Many activities can help children notice patterns in words. Four versatile lesson formats—*Guess the Covered Word, Using Words You Know, Making Words,* and *Reading/Writing Rhymes*—will be described in the next few sections.

RECOMMENDED
**resources**

The book *Phonics They Use* (Cunningham, 2005) has many more activities for helping children learn decoding and spelling patterns. For grade-level specific ideas of decoding and spelling activities, see *Month by Month Phonics for First Grade* (Cunningham & Hall, 1997), *Month by Month Phonics for Second Grade* (Hall & Cunningham, 1998), *Month by Month Phonics for Third Grade* (Cunningham & Hall, 1998), and *Month by Month Phonics for Upper Grades* (Cunningham & Hall, 1998).

### Guess the Covered Word

Many words can be figured out by thinking about what would make sense in a sentence and seeing if the consonants in the word match what you are thinking of. You must learn to do two things simultaneously—think about what would make sense and think about letters and sounds. Struggling readers often prefer to do one or the other but not both. Thus, they may guess something that is sensible but ignore the letter sounds they know, or they may guess something that is close to the sounds but makes no sense in the sentence! Doing a weekly Guess the Covered Word activity will help students combine these strategies effectively.

Before class begins, write four or five sentences on the board that start with your students' names, follow a similar word pattern, and end with words that vary in their initial sounds and word length.

Rasheed likes to play *soccer.*
Kate likes to play *softball.*
Rob likes to play *basketball.*
Juan likes to play *hockey*

Cover the last word in each sentence with a sticky note, tearing or adjusting it to the length of the word.

Begin the activity by reading the first sentence and asking students to guess the covered word. Write three or four guesses on the board, next to the sentence. Next, uncover the first letter. Erase the guesses that do not begin with that letter. Have students continue offering guesses that make sense and begin with the correct letter. Write their responses on the board. Keep the students focused both on meaning and on beginning letters.

When the first letter is revealed, some students will guess anything that begins with that letter. For example, if the first letter is an *s,* they may guess *sand.* Respond with something like "*Sand* does begin with an *s,* but I can't write *sand* because people don't play *sand.*" Finally, uncover the whole word and see if any guesses were correct. Repeat the procedure on the remaining sentences.

Once students understand how Guess the Covered Word works, include some sentences in which the covered word begins with the digraphs *sh, ch, th,* and *wh.* Explain that the rules of this game require you to show the children all the letters up to the first vowel. Then show them some sentences that contain the digraphs *sh, ch, th,* and *wh* as well as single consonants. Include examples for both sounds of *c.* Vary your sentence pattern and where in the sentence the covered word is.

> Corinda likes to eat *cherries.*
> *Watermelon* is Chad's favorite fruit.
> Jessica likes strawberries on her *cereal.*
> Bo likes strawberry *shortcake.*
> Melinda bakes pies for *Thanksgiving.*
> I don't know *which* pie I like best.

Guess the Covered Word works for teaching and reviewing *blends,* groups of letters in which you can hear the sounds blended together, such as *br, pl,* and *str.* As with digraphs, vary the sentence pattern and where in the sentence the covered word is.

> Justin likes to swim in the *summer.*
> Curtis plays baseball in the *spring.*
> *Skiing* is Jennifer's favorite sport in the winter.
> Jennifer likes to *skate,* too.
> Val likes to play all kinds of *sports.*

Be sure that when you uncover the beginning letters, you uncover everything up to the vowel. If you have uncovered an *s* and someone guesses the word *snow,* tell him or her that that was good thinking for the *s.* Then, have everyone say *snow* slowly and hear the *n.* Say something like "My rule is I have to show you everything up to the vowel, so if the word were *snow,* I would have to show you not just the *s* but the *n,* too."

Sometimes, struggling readers get the idea that the only time you use reading strategies is during reading! It is important to show them how cross-checking can help them figure out words when they are reading all kinds of things. You might write a paragraph such as the following that is related to your science topic—in this case, mammals. Cover the words in the usual way, and have the whole sentence read before going back to guess without any letters and then with all the letters up to the vowel.

Mammals are warm-blooded animals. Their body *temperature* stays the same regardless of the weather. All mammals at some time in their *lives* have hair. For *whales,* they have hair only before they are born. Mammals nurse their babies and give them more *protection* than other animals. Mammals also have larger *brains* than any other group of animals.

One more way to vary Guess the Covered Word is to cover some words in a "big book." Use the same procedure of guessing without any letters and then with all the letters up to the vowel. Help the children to verbalize that one thing you can do to decode words is to read the whole sentence and then think what would make sense, be about the right length, and have *all* the correct letters up to the vowel.

## Using Words You Know

Using Words You Know is an activity designed to help students learn to use the words they already know to decode and spell lots of other words. Here are the steps of a Using Words You Know lesson:

**1** Show students three to five words they know, and have these words pronounced and spelled. For our sample lesson, we will tell students that some of the ways they travel—including bikes, cars, vans, and trains—can help them spell other words.

**2** Divide the board, a chart, or a transparency into four columns, and head each column with one of these words: *bike, car, van,* or *train.* Have students set up the same columns on their own papers and write these four words.

**3** Tell students that words that rhyme usually have the same spelling pattern. The spelling pattern in a short word begins with the vowel and goes to the end of the word. Underline the spelling patterns *i-k-e, a-r, a-n,* and *a-i-n,* and have students underline them on their papers.

**4** Tell students that you are going to show them some new words and that they should write each one under the word with the same spelling pattern. Show them words that you have written on index cards. Let a different student go to the board, chart, or transparency and write each new word there as the other students write the word on their papers. Do not let the students pronounce a word aloud until it has been written on the board.

Then help the students pronounce the words by making them rhyme. Here are some words to use:

| | | | | |
|---|---|---|---|---|
| pain | Spain | pan | jar | sprain |
| hike | Fran | spike | than | star |

(5) Explain to students that thinking of rhyming words can help them spell. This time, do not show them the words but rather say the words. Have students decide which words they rhyme with and use the spelling pattern to spell them. Here are some words you might pronounce and have them spell:

| | | | | |
|---|---|---|---|---|
| strike | stain | clan | hike | far |
| strain | bran | brain | scar | Mike |

(6) End this first part of the lesson by helping students verbalize that in English, words that rhyme often have the same spelling pattern and that good readers and spellers do not sound out every letter but rather try to think of a rhyming word and read or spell the word using the pattern in the rhyming word.

For the second part of the lesson (probably on the next day), use the same procedures and four key words again:

(1) Head four columns on the board, chart, or transparency and have students head four columns on their papers with these words and underline the spelling patterns. Explain to the students that using the rhyme to help read and spell words works with longer words, too.

(2) Show students these words written on index cards, and have them write each word under the appropriate word. Once the word has been written on the board or chart, have students pronounce the word, making the last syllable rhyme:

| | | | | |
|---|---|---|---|---|
| guitar | motorbike | complain | maintain | orangutan |
| suntan | dislike | entertain | hitchhike | Superman |

(3) Now say these words and have students decide which word the last syllable rhymes with and use that spelling pattern to spell it. Give help with the spelling of the first part, if needed:

| | | | | |
|---|---|---|---|---|
| Batman | lifelike | restrain | remain | boxcar |
| unchain | contain | trashcan | hijack | began |

(4) Again, end the lesson by helping students notice how helpful it is to think of a rhyming word you are sure how to spell when trying to read or spell a strange word.

In Using Words You Know lessons, you should always choose the words students will read and spell. Do not ask students for rhyming words because, especially for the long vowels, there is often another pattern. *Crane, Jane,* and *rein* also rhyme with *train,* but you

Teaching Phonics and Spelling Patterns

### Most Common Spelling Patterns

Knowing 37 spelling patterns will allow children to read and spell over 500 words commonly used by young children (Wylie & Durrell, 1970). Many teachers display each pattern with a word and picture to help children learn the pattern that will help them spell many other words.

Here are the 37 high-frequency spelling patterns (with possible key words):

| | | | | | |
|---|---|---|---|---|---|
| ack (black) | ail (pail) | ain (train) | ake (cake) | ale (whale) | ame (game) |
| an (pan) | ank (bank) | ap (cap) | ash (trash) | at (cat) | ate (skate) |
| aw (claw) | ay (tray) | eat (meat) | ell (shell) | est (nest) | ice (rice) |
| ide (bride) | ick (brick) | ight (night) | ill (hill) | in (pin) | ine (nine) |
| ing (king) | ink (pink) | ip (ship) | it (hit) | ock (sock) | oke (Coke) |
| op (mop) | ore (store) | ot (hot) | uck (truck) | ug (bug) | ump (jump) |
| unk (trunk) | | | | | |

should only use words that rhyme and have the same pattern. You can do Using Words You Know lessons with any words children can already read and spell. To plan a lesson, select known words that have lots of rhyming words with the same spelling pattern. A rhyming dictionary, such as *The Scholastic Rhyming Dictionary* (Young, 1994), is a great help in finding suitable rhyming words.

## Making Words

Making Words is a very popular activity with both teachers and children. Children love manipulating letters to make words and figuring out the secret word that can be made with all the letters. While children are having fun making words, they are also learning important information about phonics and spelling. As children manipulate letters to make words, they learn how making small changes, such as changing just one letter or moving two letters around, results in completely new words. Children also learn to stretch out words and listen for the sounds they hear and the order of those sounds. When you change the first letter, you also change the sound you hear at the beginning of the word. Likewise, when you change the last letter, you change the sound you hear at the end of the word. These ideas seem commonplace and obvious to those of us who have been reading and writing for almost as long as we can remember. But they are a revelation to many beginners—one that gives them tremendous independence in and power over the challenge of decoding and spelling words.

The Making Words activity is an example of a type of instruction called *guided discovery.* In order to truly learn and retain strategies, children must discover them. But some children do not seem to make discoveries about words very easily on their own. In a Making Words lesson, the teacher guides them toward those discoveries by carefully sequencing the words they are to make and giving them explicit guidance about how much change is needed.

Making Words lessons have three steps. In the first step, you make words. Begin with short, easy words and move to longer, more complex words. The last word is always the secret word—a word that can be made with all the letters. As the children make each word, a child who has made it successfully goes up to the pocket chart or chalk ledge and makes the word with big letters. Children who have not made the word correctly quickly fix their word to be ready for the next word. The small changes made between most words encourages even those children who have not made a word perfectly to fix it, because they soon realize that spelling the current word correctly increases their chances of spelling the next word correctly. In each lesson, have students make 10 to 15 words, including the secret word that can be made with all the letters. When it is time to make the secret word, give children one minute to try to come up with the word. After one minute, if no one has discovered the secret word, then give the children clues that will allow them to figure it out.

In the second step of a Making Words lesson, sort the words into patterns. Many children discover patterns just through making the words in the carefully sequenced order, but some children need more explicit guidance. This guidance happens when all the words have been made and you guide the children to sort them into patterns. Depending on the sophistication of the children and the words available in the lesson, words might be sorted according to their beginning letters—all the letters up to the vowel. Alternatively, to focus on just one sound–letter combination, you may ask children to sort out all the words that begin with *sp* or *sn*. Once the words with these letters have been sorted, you and the children should pronounce the words and discover that most words that have the same letters also have the same sound. This is an important discovery for all emerging readers and writers.

Another pattern that children need to discover is that many words have the same root word. If they can pronounce and spell the root word and if they can recognize the root word with a prefix or suffix added, they can decode and spell many additional words. To some children, every new word they meet is a new experience! They fail to recognize how new words are related to already known words and thus are in the difficult, if not impossible, position of starting from "scratch" and trying to learn and remember every new word. To be fluent, fast, automatic decoders and spellers, children must learn that *play, playing, played, plays, player,* and *replay* all have *play* as their root and use their knowledge of how to decode and spell *play* to quickly transfer to these related words. Whenever possible from the letters available, Making Words lessons should include related words. Tell the children that people are related by blood and that words are related by meaning. Ask the children to find any related words and sort them out and then create sentences to show how these words are related.

In every lesson, sort the rhyming words. Each lesson should contain several sets of rhyming words. Children need to recognize that words that have the same spelling pattern from the vowel to the end of the word usually rhyme. When you sort the words into rhyming words and point out that the words that rhyme have the same spelling pattern, children learn rhyming patterns and how to use words they know to decode and spell lots of other words.

The final step of a Making Words lesson is the transfer step. All the working and playing with words you do while making words will be worth nothing if children do not use what they know when they need to use it. Many children know letter sounds and patterns and do not apply this knowledge to decode unknown words they encounter during reading or to spell words they need while writing. All teachers know that it is much easier to teach children phonics than it is to actually get them to use it. This is the reason that you need to end every Making Words lesson with a transfer step.

Once you have the words sorted according to rhyme, tell children to pretend they are reading and come to a new word. As you say this, write a word that has the same spelling pattern and rhymes with one set of rhyming words. Show this word to a child and ask that child to come up and put on the board or chart the new word with the words it rhymes with. Do not allow anyone to say the new word until it has been lined up under the other rhyming words. Then you can lead the children to pronounce the rhyming words they made and the new word. Next, show them one more word and ask a child to do the following:

> "Pretend you're reading and come to this new word. Put it with the words that would help you figure it out."

Once you have decoded two new words using the rhyming patterns from the words you made, help the children transfer their letter–sound knowledge to writing. To do this, ask children to pretend they are writing and need to spell a word:

> "Pretend you're writing and you need to spell the word *stray*. You stretch out *stray* and hear the beginning letters *str*. If you can think of the words we made today that rhyme with *stray*, you will have the correct spelling of the word."

The children decide that *stray* rhymes with the *ay* words they made and that *stray* is spelled *s-t-r-a-y*. Finish the lesson by having them spell one more word by deciding which of the words they made it rhymes with.

Here is an example of how you might conduct a Making Words lesson and cue the children to the changes and words you want them to make.

*Beginning the Lesson*    Give all the children the letters *a, e, e, h, k, l, n,* and *t.* Display these same letters—big enough for all to see—in a pocket chart or along the chalk ledge. The vowels should be in a different color from the other letters, and the letter cards should have lowercase letters on one side and capital letters on the other side.

To prepare for this lesson, write the words the children are going to make on index cards. These will be placed in the pocket chart as the words are made and will be used for the sort and transfer steps of the lesson.

Begin the lesson by having each child hold up and name each letter as you hold up the big letter in the pocket chart. Give these instructions:

"Hold up and name each letter as I hold up the big letter. Let's start with your vowels. Show me your *a* and your two *e*'s. Now show me your *h, k, l, n,* and *t.* You all have eight letters. In a few minutes, we will see if anyone can figure out the secret word that uses all eight letters. Make sure all your letters are showing their lowercase side to start with. When we are making a name, I will cue you and look to see who remembers to turn the first letter in that name to the capital side. Let's get started making words."

***Step 1: Making Words*** Give students these instructions:

> "Use three letters to spell the word *ate*. We *ate* lunch at my grandma's on Sunday.

Find someone who spelled *ate* correctly, and send that child to spell *ate* with the big letters.

> "Move the letters around and turn *ate* into *eat*. I like to *eat* at my grandma's."
>
> "Start over and use three letters to spell *Ken*. *Ken* is the boy who delivers my newspaper."

Quickly send someone with the correct spelling to use the big letters. Make sure he or she spelled *Ken* with a capital *K*. Keep the pace brisk. Do not wait until all the children have *Ken* spelled with their little letters. It is fine if some children are making *Ken* as *Ken* is being spelled with the big letters.

> "Change just one letter and turn *Ken* into *ten*. I have *ten* fingers and *ten* toes."
>
> "Make sure you have *ten* spelled correctly. Add just one letter to spell *then*. I had a snack, and *then* I did my homework."

Continue sending the children to make the words with the big letters. Remind the children to use the big letters to check what they have made with their letters, fixing each of their own words as needed before going on to the next word. Move the lesson along at a fast pace.

> "Start over and use four letters to spell *late*. No one came to school *late* this morning."
>
> "Change one letter to spell the name *Kate*. We read a story about a girl named *Kate*."
>
> "Start over and use four letters to spell another name, *Hank*. Perhaps a new boy will move here next week and his name will be *Hank*."
>
> "Change one letter and turn *Hank* into *tank*. It costs a lot of money to fill up my gas *tank*."
>
> "Add one letter to spell *thank*. In this classroom, we always say 'Thank-you.'"
>
> "Start over and use five letters to spell *ankle*. When I was little, I broke my *ankle*."

"Start over and use five letters to spell *eaten*. The lost boy was not hurt, but he was hungry because he hadn't *eaten* for 24 hours."

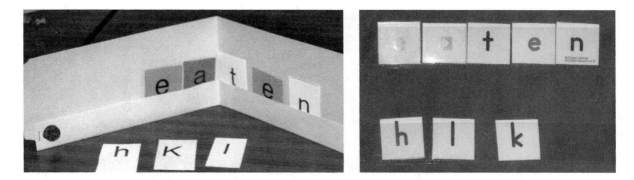

"I have just one word left. It is the secret word you can make with all your letters. See if you can figure it out."

Give students one minute to figure out the secret word, and then give them clues, if needed.

"Our secret word today is a name . . . In fact, it is the name of a girl in our class . . . It starts with *K*."

Let someone who figures it out (hopefully, Kathleen) go to the big letters and spell the secret word—*Kathleen*. Then have all the children make the word *Kathleen* and enjoy the fact that their friend, Kathleen, was the secret word!

***Step 2: Sorting the Words into Patterns***     Have the children read aloud with you all the words made in the lesson. Then have them sort out the related words. Remind the children that related words share a root word and some meaning. After the words *eat* and *eaten* are sorted, say a sentence that contains the two words:

> "The first thing the boy did was to *eat* a sandwich because he hadn't *eaten* in 24 hours."

Next, sort out the rhyming words. Send several children to the pocket chart to find rhyming words with the same pattern and line these up with rhymes, one under the other.

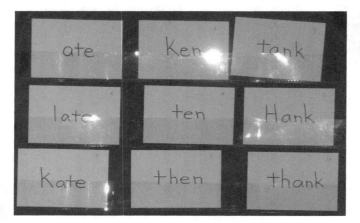

***Step 3: Transfer***     Tell the children to pretend that they are reading and come to a new word. Show one child the word *blank* written on an index card. Let that child put *blank* under *Hank, tank,* and *thank,* and then have all the children pronounce all three words, using the rhyming words they made to decode the new word, *blank.* Do the same thing with *plate.*

Next, tell children to pretend they are writing and need to spell a word:

> "Let's pretend Terry is writing and trying to spell the word *skate.*"

Have the children tell you that *skate* begins with *sk,* and write *sk* on an index card. Then have the children pronounce the sets of rhyming words in the pocket chart and decide that *skate* rhymes with *ate, late,* and *Kate.* Have them use the *a-t-e* pattern to finish spelling *skate.* Do the same thing with *Frank.*

When you have finished the lesson, the rhyming words you have made will be lined up in the pocket chart along with two new words the children helped you read and two new words they helped you spell.

***Other Making Words Lessons***  To do the first several lessons, include only one vowel and make fewer words:

**Letters:**  a  b  l  s  t

**Make:**  as  at  lab  tab  sat  bat  bats  stab  last  blast

**Sort for:**  l  b
-ab  -at  -ast

**Transfer Words:**  cab  fast  past  rat

**Letters:**  o  g  n  r  s  t

**Make:**  so  no  go  got  rot  not  rot  rots  sort  song  snort  strong

**Sort for:**  g  n  r  s
-o  -ot  -ort  -ong

**Transfer Words:**  clot  sport  long  slot

**Letters:**  i  g  n  p  r  s

**Make:**  in  sin  pin  pig  rig  rip  sip  snip  sing  ring  rings  spring

**Sort for:**  s  p  r
-in  -ing  -ig  -ip

**Transfer Words:**  strip  string  twin  twig

## Steps in Planning a Making Words Lesson

1. Choose your secret word, a word that can be made with all the letters. In choosing this word, consider child interest, the curriculum tie-ins you can make, and the letter–sound patterns to which you can draw children's attention through the sorting at the end.

2. Make a list of other words that can be made from these letters. (Go to www.wordplays.com and enter your secret word to see *all* the words that can be made from these letters.)

3. From all the words you could make, pick 12 to 15 words using these criteria:
   • Words that you can sort for the pattern you want to emphasize
   • Little words and big words to create a multilevel lesson. (Making little words helps your lower-achieving students; making big words challenges your highest-achieving students.)
   • Words that can be made with the same letters in different places (*barn/bran*) so children are reminded that ordering letters is crucial when spelling words
   • A proper name or two to remind the children that we use capital letters
   • Words that most students have in their listening vocabularies

4. Write all the words on index cards and order them from smallest to biggest.

5. Once you have the two-letter words together, the three-letter words together, and so on, order them so you can emphasize letter patterns and how changing the position of the letters or changing/adding just one letter results in a different word.

6. Store the cards in an envelope. Write the words in order on the envelope, the patterns you will sort for, and the transfer words.

Try to tie in lessons with what the children are reading or with something they are studying. Here are some December lessons:

| | |
|---|---|
| **Letters:** | e e n p r s t |
| **Make:** | net pet pets pest nest rest rent sent spent enter pester present (and serpent) |
| **Sort for:** | n p r<br>-et -est -ent |
| **Transfer Words:** | wet west chest vent |

| | |
|---|---|
| **Letters:** | a e c d l n s |
| **Make:** | as an can Dan and sand land clan clean dance dances cleans candles |
| **Sort for:** | c cl<br>-an -and |
| **Transfer Words:** | band stand bran hand |

## Steps in Teaching a Making Words Lesson

1. Place the large letter cards needed in a pocket chart or along the chalk tray.

2. Have children pass out letters or pick up the letters needed.

3. Hold up and name the letters on the large letter cards, and have the children hold up their matching small letter cards.

4. Write the numeral 2 (or 3 if no two-letter words are in this lesson) on the board. Tell them to take two letters and make the first word. Have them say the word after you stretch out the word to hear all the sounds.

5. Have a child who makes the first word correctly make the same word with the large letter cards on the chalk tray or pocket chart. Do not wait for everyone to make the word before sending a child to make it with the big letters. Encourage anyone who did not make the word correctly at first to fix the word when he or she sees it made correctly.

6. Continue to make words, giving students clues, such as "Change the first letter only" or "Move the same letters around and you can make a different word" or "Take all your letters out and make another word." Send a child who has made the word correctly to make the word with the large letter cards. Cue students when they are to use more letters by erasing and changing the number on the board to indicate the number of letters needed.

7. Before telling students the last word, say, "Now it's time for the secret word—the word we can make with all our letters. I am coming around to see whether one of you has made the secret word in your holder." If someone has figured it out, send that child to make the big word. If not, tell them the word and let everyone make it.

8. Once all the words have been made, take the index cards on which you wrote the words and place them one at a time (in the same order that children made them) along the chalk ledge or in the pocket chart. Have children say and spell the words with you as you do this. Have the children sort these words for patterns—including beginning sounds and rhymes.

9. To encourage transfer to reading and writing, show students how rhyming words can help them decode and spell other words. Write two words on index cards and have students put these two new words with the rhyming words and use the rhyming words to decode them. Finally, say two words that rhyme and have students spell these words by deciding which words rhyme with them.

Lessons in which the secret words are sports related are always motivating:

| | |
|---|---|
| **Letters:** | a o o b f l l t |
| **Make:** | at bat fat all ball fall tall tool fool boat flat float football |
| **Sort for:** | -at -all -oo -oat |
| **Transfer Words:** | stall stool chat goat |

| Letters: | a a e b b l l s |
|---|---|
| Make: | all lab slab blab ball bell sell seal sale bale able sable baseball |
| Sort for: | -al -ab -ale -ell -able |
| Transfer Words: | cable spell flab whale |

*Making Big Words*   When working with older students and with more than eight letters, print the letters on strips and duplicate them. Have the children cut the strips into letters and use them to make words.

| Letters on strip: | e e e i c d n p s t |
|---|---|
| Make: | nice need deep seep seen dent sent cent scent spend steep dense tense scene nicest insect decent descent deepest neediest inspected centipedes |
| Sort for: | est (ending) ent eep ense seen/scene sent/cent/scent |
| Transfer Words: | spent creep creepiest steepest |

| Letters on strip: | e e o u y l m m n n p t |
|---|---|
| Make: | ump yum plum lump lumpy melon lemon lemony employ moment monument employment unemployment |
| Sort for: | ment um ump |
| Related Words: | employ, employment, unemployment; lump, lumpy; lemon, lemony |
| Transfer Words: | bump bumpy grump grumpy |

## Reading/Writing Rhymes

Reading/Writing Rhymes is another activity that helps students learn to use patterns to decode and spell hundreds of words. In addition, all beginning letters are reviewed every time you do a Reading/Writing Rhymes lesson. Once all the rhyming words are generated on a chart, students write rhymes using these words and then read each other's rhymes. Because writing and reading are connected to every lesson, students learn how to use these patterns as they actually read and write.

To do a Reading/Writing Rhymes lesson, you will need a deck of cards containing all the beginning sounds. The 3 × 5 index cards are laminated and have the single-letter consonants written in blue, the blends in red, and the digraphs and other two-letter combinations in green. On one side of each card, the first letter is a capital letter. The deck contains 50 beginning letter cards that include:

**Single consonants:** b c d f g h j k l m n p r s t v w y z

**Digraphs (two letters, one sound):** sh ch wh th

**Other two-letter, one-sound combinations:** ph wr kn qu

**Blends (beginning letters blended together, sometimes called clusters):** bl br cl cr dr fl fr gl gr pl pr sc scr sk sl sm sn sp spr st str sw tr

At the beginning of the lesson, distribute all the cards to the students. In most classrooms, each child gets two or three cards. Once all the cards are distributed, write the spelling pattern you are working with 10 to 12 times on a piece of chart paper. As you write it each time, have the children help spell it and pronounce it.

Next invite all the children who have a card they think makes a word to come up to place their card next to one of the written spelling patterns and to pronounce the word. If the word is indeed a real word, use the word in a sentence and write that word on the chart. If the word is not a real word, explain why you cannot write it on the chart. Write names with capital letters, and if a word is both a name and not a name, such as *will* and *Will,* write it both ways. When all the children have come up who think they can spell words with their beginning letters and the spelling pattern, call children up to make the words not yet there by saying something like, "I think the person with the *qu* card could come up here and add *qu* to *ill* to make a word we know." Try to include all the words that any of the children will have in their listening vocabularies, but avoid obscure words. If the patterns you wrote to begin the chart get made into complete words, add as many more as needed:

```
ill
bill       skill
Bill       mill
fill       drill
chill      grill
Jill       pill
gill       quill
Kill
will
Will
still
spill
Kill
dill
```

Once the chart of rhyming words has been written, work together in a shared writing format to write a couple of sentences using lots of the rhyming words. Next, have the students write some silly sentences. If children choose to, you should let them write with a friend. Give them a limited time—9 minutes—to write. When the time is up, gather the children together and, if they want to, let them read their silly sentences to the class.

Reading/Writing Rhymes can also be used to teach spelling patterns for words with two common patterns. Head the chart with the two patterns and distribute the beginning letter cards. Children line up who think their beginning letters make a real word. Write the word on the correct side of the chart. If both patterns make a real word (*plain, plane*), write each word in the appropriate column and talk about the different meanings of the words. If a rhyming word is spelled with another pattern (*reign, Maine*), write it at the bottom of the chart with an asterisk. Here is the chart for the *ain/ane* long vowel spelling pattern:

| ain | ane | |
|-----|-----|---|
| rain | cane | |
| brain | crane | |
| train | sane | |
| pain | pane | |
| plain | plane | * reign |
| brain | Jane | Maine |
| vain | Vane | |
| chain | Shane | |
| gain | mane | |
| grain | Zane | |
| stain | | |
| strain | | |
| Spain | | |
| sprain | | |

All the common vowel patterns can be taught through Reading/Writing Rhymes. You should always choose the patterns that generate the most rhymes, and when there is more than one common spelling for a rhyme, include both—or in some cases all three—spelling patterns. Children enjoy writing the silly sentences. Following is an example written by two friends working from the *ain/ane* chart:

> Jane went to Spain with Zane and Shane. They went on a plane then took a train. Shane tripped on a chain and fell in the lane in the rain. He had a sprain in his leg and a lot of pain and needed a cane.

## Strategies for Big Words

Big words present special decoding problems. Most of the words we read are one- and two-syllable words, but polysyllabic words often carry most of the content. Decoding and spelling polysyllabic words is based on patterns, but these patterns are more sophisticated and require students to understand how words change in their spelling, pronunciation, and meaning as suffixes and prefixes are added. The *g* in *sign* seems quite illogical until you realize that *sign* is related to *signal, signature,* and other words. Finding the *compose/ composition* and *compete/competition* relationship helps students understand why the second syllable of *composition* and *competition* sound alike but are spelled differently.

To decode and spell big words, children must (1) have a mental store of big words that contain the spelling patterns common to big words; (2) chunk big words into pronounce-able segments by comparing the parts of new big words to the big words they already know; and (3) recognize and use common prefixes and suffixes. The activities in this section are designed to help children build a store of big words and use these big words to decode and spell other big words.

## Big Word Boards

Reserve one of the bulletin boards in your room for use as a Big Word Board. As you teach science and social studies units or read literature selections, identify 15–25 big words that are key to understanding. Write these on large index cards with a black, thick permanent marker. Do not overwhelm your students by presenting all the words at once. Rather, add three or four each day as you introduce these words. As you put the words on the board, have the students chant the spelling (cheerleader style) with you. Then have them close their eyes and chant the spelling again. Next, have them write a sentence that uses as many of the words as they can and still have a sensible sentence.

Once the words are displayed on the board, draw students' attention to these words as they occur in lectures, films, experiments, or discussions. As students write about what they are learning, encourage them to use the big words and to refer to the board for the correct spellings. Help students develop a positive attitude toward learning these big words by pointing out that every discipline has some critical big words; using these words separates the pros from the amateurs.

The following list of words appeared on a Big Word Board while students were studying Antarctica:

| | | |
|---|---|---|
| Antarctica | geologic | regulation |
| exploration | exploitation | conservation |
| conservationists | minerals | petroleum |
| controversial | development | resources |
| environmentalists | environment | continent |
| vacationers | policies | confrontation |
| geologists | inhospitable | international |

As you can see, the big words students need as they read and write about Antarctica are numerous. Notice also how many of the common polysyllabic patterns are illustrated by just this one set of words. Students who can read and write *exploration, exploitation, regulation, conservation,* and *confrontation* now have several known big words that end in the reliable but totally unexplainable letter pattern *t-i-o-n,* which we pronounce "shun"! The words *geologists, conservationists,* and *environmentalists* contain the suffix *ists,* which usually transforms a word from "the thing" to "the people who work on or worry about the thing." Including two important forms of the same base word—*conservation/ conservationists, environment/environmentalists, geologic/geologists*—allows students to see how the endings of words often change what part of the sentence they can be used in. If your students are not very sophisticated word users, you can greatly extend the control they have over language by pointing out how words change and by pointing out the similarities and differences in pronunciation, use, and spelling.

## Modeling How to Decode Big Words

When you model, you show someone how to do something. In real life, we use modeling constantly to teach skills. We would not think of explaining how to ride a bike. Rather, we would demonstrate and talk about what we were doing as the learner watched and listened to our explanation. Vocabulary introduction is a good place to model how you figure out the pronunciation of a word for students. Modeling is more than just telling them pronunciation; it is modeling the thinking that goes on when you meet up with a big word.

The word should be shown in a sentence context so that students are reminded that words must have the correct letters in the correct places and must make sense. Here is an example of how you might model for students one way to decode the word *international.* Write on the board or overhead:

> The thinning of the ozone layer is an international problem.

> "Today, we are going to look at a big word that is really just a little word with a prefix added to the beginning and a suffix added to the end."

Underline *nation* in the sentence you have just written.

> The thinning of the ozone layer is an inter<u>nation</u>al problem.

> "Who can tell me this word? Yes, that is the word *nation.* Now, let's look at the prefix that comes before *nation.*"

Underline *inter.*

> The thinning of the ozone layer is an <u>inter</u>national problem.

> "This prefix is *inter.* You probably know *inter* from words such as *interrupt* and *internal.* Now, let's look at what follows *inter* and *nation.*"

Underline *al.*

> The thinning of the ozone layer is an internation<u>al</u> problem.
>
> "You know *al* from many words, such as *unusual* and *critical."*

Write *unusual* and *critical* and underline the *al.*

> unusu<u>al</u> critic<u>al</u>
>
> "Listen as I pronounce this part of the word."

Underline and pronounce *national.*

> The thinning of the ozone layer is an inter<u>national</u> problem.

> "Notice how the pronunciation of *nation* changes when we put *a-l* on it. Now let's put all the parts together and pronounce the word—*inter nation al.* Let's read the sentence and make sure *international* makes sense."

Have the sentence read and confirm that ozone thinning is indeed a problem for many nations to solve.

> "You can figure out the pronunciation of many big words if you look for common prefixes, such as *inter;* common root words, such as *nation;* and common suffixes, such as *al.*"

> "In addition to helping you figure out the pronunciation of a word, prefixes and suffixes sometimes help you know what the word means or where in a sentence we can use the word. The word *nation* names a thing. When we describe a nation, we add the suffix *al* and have *national.* The prefix *inter* often means between or among. Something that is *international* is between many nations. The Olympics are the best example of an *international* sporting event."

This sample lesson for introducing the word *international* demonstrates how a teacher can help students see and use morphemes—meaningful parts of words—to decode polysyllabic words. Notice that the teacher points out words that students might know and that have the same parts. In addition, meaning clues provided by the morphemes are provided whenever appropriate.

A similar procedure could be used to model how you would decode a word that did not contain suffixes or prefixes. For the word *resources,* for example, the teacher would draw students' attention to the familiar first syllable *re* and then point out the known word *sources.* For *geologic,* the teacher might write and underline the *geo* in the known word *geography* and then point out the known word *logic. Policies* might be compared to *politics* and *agencies.*

Modeling is simply thinking aloud about how you might go about figuring out an unfamiliar word. It takes just a few extra minutes to point out the morphemes in *international* and to show how *policies* is like *politics* and *agencies.* But taking these extra few minutes is quickly paid back as students begin to develop some independence in figuring out those big words that carry so much of the content.

## The Nifty-Thrifty-Fifty

English is the most morphologically complex language. Linguists estimate that for every word you know, you can figure out how to decode, spell, and build meanings for six or seven other words, if you recognize and use the morphemic patterns in words. Activities in this section teach students how to spell a Nifty-Thrifty-Fifty store of words to decode, spell, and build meaning for thousands of other words. These 50 words include examples for all the common prefixes and suffixes as well as common spelling changes. Because these 50 words help with so many other words, we have named them the Nifty-Thrifty-Fifty.

The Nifty-Thrifty-Fifty words should be introduced gradually, and students should practice chanting and writing them until their spelling and decoding become automatic. The procedures for working with these words and their important parts follow:

**1** Display the words, arranged by first letter, someplace in the room. Add four or five each week. You may want to use a bulletin board or hang a banner above a bulletin board and attach the words to it. The words need to be big and bold so that they are seen easily from wherever the students are writing. Using different colors makes them more visible and attractive. Many teachers use large colored index cards or write them with different colors of thick, bold permanent markers.

**2** Explain to students that in English, many big words are just smaller words with prefixes and suffixes added to the word. Good spellers do not memorize the spelling of every new word they come across. Rather, they notice the patterns in words and these patterns include prefixes, suffixes, and spelling changes that occur when these are added.

**3** Tell students that one way to practice words is to say the letters in them aloud in a rhythmic, chanting fashion. Tell students that although this might seem silly, it really is not because the brain responds to sound and rhythm. (That is one of the reasons you can sing along with the words of a familiar song even though you could not say the words without singing the song and also why jingles and raps are easy to remember.) Point to each word and have students chant it (cheerleader style) with you. After "cheering" for each word, help students analyze the word, talking about its meaning and determining the root, prefix, and suffix, and noting any spelling changes. Here is an example of the kind of word introduction students find most helpful:

> **composer**—A composer is a person who composes something. Many other words, such as *writer, reporter,* and *teacher,* are made up of a root word and the suffix *er,* meaning a person or thing that does something. When *er* is added to a word that already has an *e,* the original *e* is dropped.
>
> **discovery**—A discovery is something you discover. The prefix *dis* often changes a word to an opposite form. To *cover* something can mean to hide it. When you *discover* it, it is no longer hidden. *Discovery* is the root word *cover* with the added prefix *dis* and suffix *y.* There are no spelling changes.
>
> **encouragement**—When you encourage someone, you give them encouragement. Many other words, such as *argue, argument* and *replace, replacement,* follow this same pattern. The root word for *encourage* is *courage.* So *encouragement* is made up of the prefix *en,* the root word *courage,* and the suffix *ment.*
>
> **hopeless**—Students should easily see the root word *hope* and the suffix *less.* Other similar words are *painless* and *homeless.*
>
> **impossible**—The root word *possible* with the suffix *im.* In many words, including *impatient* and *immature,* the suffix *im* changes the word to an opposite.
>
> **musician**—A musician is a person who makes music. A *beautician* helps make you beautiful, and a *magician* makes magic. *Musician* has the root word *music* with the suffix *ian,* which sometimes indicates the person who does something. None of the spelling changes but the pronunciation changes. Have students say the words *music* and *musician, magic* and *magician,* and notice how the pronunciation changes.

**(4)** Once you have noticed the composition for each word, helped students see other words that work in a similar way, and cheered for each word, have students write each word. Writing the word with careful attention to each letter and the sequence of each letter helps students use another mode to practice the word. (Do not, however, assign students to copy words five times each. They just do this "mechanically" and often do not focus on the letters.) Students enjoy writing the words more and focus better on them if you make it a riddle or game. You can do this simply by giving clues for the word you want them to write:

1. Number 1 is the opposite of *discouragement.*
2. Number 2 is the opposite of *hopeful.*
3. For number 3, write the word that tells what you are if you play the *guitar.*
4. For number 4, write what you are if you play the *guitar* but you also make up the songs you play.
5. Number 5 is the opposite of *possible.*
6. For number 6, write the word that has *cover* for the root word.

After writing the words, have students check their own papers, once more chanting the letters aloud and underlining each as they say it.

**(5)** When you have a few minutes of "sponge" time, practice the words by chanting or writing. As you are cheering or writing each word, ask students to identify the root,

## Nifty-Thrifty-Fifty Transferable Chunks

| | | | | | |
|---|---|---|---|---|---|
| | | | impression | im | sion |
| | | | independence | in | ence |
| | | | international | inter | al |
| | | | invasion | in | sion |
| | | | irresponsible | ir | ible |
| antifreeze | anti | | midnight | mid | |
| beautiful | | ful (y-i) | misunderstand | mis | |
| classify | | ify | musician | | ian |
| communities | com | es (y-i) | nonliving | non | ing (drop e) |
| community | com | y | overpower | over | |
| composer | com | er | performance | per | ance |
| continuous | con | ous (drop e) | prehistoric | pre | ic |
| conversation | con | tion | prettier | | er (y-i) |
| deodorize | de | ize | rearrange | re | |
| different | | ent | replacement | re | ment |
| discovery | dis | y | richest | | est |
| dishonest | dis | | semifinal | semi | |
| electricity | e | ity | signature | | ture |
| employee | em | ee | submarine | sub | |
| encouragement | en | ment | supermarkets | super | s |
| expensive | ex | ive | swimming | | ing (double m) |
| forecast | fore | | transportation | trans | tion |
| forgotten | | en (double t) | underweight | under | |
| governor | | or | unfinished | un | ed |
| happiness | | ness (y-i) | unfriendly | un | ly |
| hopeless | | less | unpleasant | un | ant (drop e) |
| illegal | il | | valuable | | able (drop e) |
| impossible | im | ible | | | |

prefix, and suffix and talk about how these affect the meaning of the root word. Also have them point out any spelling changes.

**6** Once students can automatically, quickly, and correctly spell the words and explain to you how they are composed, it is time to help them see how these words can help them decode and spell other words. Remind students that good spellers do not memorize the spelling of each word. Rather, they use words they know and combine roots, suffixes, and prefixes to figure out how to spell lots of other words. Have the students spell words that are contained in the words and words you can make by combining parts of the words.

Have each word used in a sentence and talk about the meaning relationships when appropriate. Note spelling changes as needed. From just the eight words—*composer,*

## Nifty-Thrifty-Fifty Transfer Words

Here are just some of the words students should be able to decode, spell, and discuss meanings for by using parts of all 50 words:

| | | | |
|---|---|---|---|
| | refinish | declassify | powerlessness |
| | relive | decompose | superpower |
| conform | repose | deform | finalize |
| conformity | reclassify | deformity | finalizing |
| inform | revalue | prearrange | finalization |
| informer | recover | resign | weighty |
| informant | rediscover | resignation | weightier |
| information | electrical | designation | weightiest |
| misinform | displease | significant | weightless |
| uninformed | discontinue | significance | undervalue |
| formation | disposal | freezer | friendlier |
| formal | musical | freezing | friendliest |
| transform | continual | freezable | friendliness |
| transformation | employer | subfreezing | unfriendliness |
| performer | employment | underclass | unpleasantness |
| responsibility | unemployment | overexpose | historical |
| responsive | unemployed | underexpose | historically |
| responsiveness | employable | superimpose | expressive |
| honesty | unemployable | undercover | impressive |
| dishonesty | difference | forecaster | repressive |
| honestly | consignment | forecasting | invasive |
| legally | nationality | forecastable | noninvasive |
| illegally | nationalities | miscast | invasiveness |
| responsibly | internationalize | antidepressant | hopefully |
| irresponsibly | interdependence | overture | hopelessly |
| arranging | depress | empower | predispose |
| rearranging | depression | empowerment | predisposition |
| placing | depressive | powerful | deodorant |
| replacing | deport | powerfully | beautician |
| misplacing | deportation | powerfulness | electrician |
| report | deportee | powerless | |
| reporter | devalue | powerlessly | |

*discovery, encouragement, hopeless, impossible, musician, richest,* and *unfriendly*—
students should be able to decode, spell, and discuss meanings for the following words:

| | | | | |
|---|---|---|---|---|
| compose | encourage | music | dispose | enrichment |
| pose | courage | rich | discourage | uncover |
| discover | hope | friend | discouragement | richly |
| cover | possible | friendly | enrich | hopelessly |

(7) Continue adding words gradually, going through the above procedures with all the words. Do not add words too quickly, and provide lots of practice with these words and the other words that can be decoded and spelled by combining parts of these words. Because this store of words provides patterns for so many other words, you want your students to "overlearn" these words so that they can be called up instantly and automatically when students meet similar words in their reading or need to spell similar words while writing.

## The Wheel

The popular game show *Wheel of Fortune* is based on the idea that having meaning and some letters allows you to figure out many words. On *Wheel of Fortune*, meaning is provided by the category to which the word belongs. A variation of this game can be used to introduce big words and to teach students to use meaning and all the letters they know. Here is how to play The Wheel.

Remind students that we can figure out many words (even if we cannot decode all the parts) as long as we think about what makes sense and keep the parts that we do know in the right places. Ask students who have watched *Wheel of Fortune* to explain how it is played. Then explain how your version of The Wheel will be different:

1. Contestants guess all letters without considering if they are consonants or vowels.
2. They must have all letters filled in before they can say the word.
3. The word must fit in a sentence rather than in a category.
4. They will win paper clips instead of great prizes!
5. Vanna will not be there to turn letters!

Write a sentence on the board, and draw a blank for each letter of an important word. Here is an example:

> If you were to travel to Antarctica, you would be struck by its almost unbelievable _ _ _ _ _ _ _ _ _ _ _.

Have a student begin by asking "Is there a . . . ?" If the student guesses a correct letter, fill in that letter. Give that student one paper clip for each time that letter occurs. Let the student continue to guess letters until he or she gets a "No!" When a student asks about a letter that is not there, write the letter above the puzzle and go on to the next student.

Make sure that all letters are filled in before anyone is allowed to guess. (This really shows students the importance of spelling and attending to common spelling patterns!) Give the person who correctly guesses the word five bonus paper clips! As with other games, if someone says the answer out of turn, immediately award the bonus paper clips to the person whose turn it was. The student having the most paper clips at the end is the winner!

For our example, a student might ask whether there is an *r?* ("Sorry, no *r!*") The next student asks for an *s.* One *s* is filled in.

> If you were to travel to Antarctica, you would be struck by its
> almost unbelievable _ _ s _ _ _ _ _ _ _.

The student is given one paper clip and continues to ask questions. "Is there a *t?*" "Yes, one *t!*"

> If you were to travel to Antarctica, you would be struck by its
> almost unbelievable _ _ s _ _ _ t _ _ _.

The student asks for an *o.* Two *o*'s are filled in and the student receives two more paper clips.

> If you were to travel to Antarctica, you would be struck by its
> almost unbelievable _ _ s o _ _ t _ o _.

Next the student asks for an *i* and then for an *n.*

> If you were to travel to Antarctica, you would be struck by its
> almost unbelievable _ _ s o _ _ t i o n.

After much thought, the student asks for an *m.* Unfortunately, there is no *m,* so play passes to the next student, who asks for an *e,* an *a,* a *d,* and an *l* and correctly spells out *d e s o l a t i o n!* (The teacher points out that *desolation* is also the emotion felt by the previous student who came so close to winning!) Play continues with another big word introduced in a sentence context.

Students who are introduced to vocabulary by playing The Wheel pay close attention to the letter patterns in big words. They also get in the habit of making sure that the word they figure out, based on having some of the letters, fits the meaning of the sentence in which it occurs.

## *Summary*

Reading is a complex process in which you have to identify words from which you construct meaning. Writing is equally (if not more!) complex. Both reading and writing require that the most common words be read and spelled automatically—without thought or mediation—so that the brain's attention can focus on meaning. When children are first starting to read and write, their word identification and spelling will not be automatic.

Teaching them how to read and spell high-frequency words and providing lots of varied practice reading will help children develop fluency.

As they are learning high-frequency words and developing fluency, children also need to learn patterns so that they can quickly decode and spell words they have not yet learned. The patterns in short words are the *onsets*—commonly called beginning letters—and the *rimes*—spelling patterns. In big words, *morphemes*—prefixes, suffixes, and roots—are the patterns that allow readers to quickly decode and spell longer words.

Few instructional studies have compared different types of phonics instruction. After reviewing the research on phonics instruction, Stahl, Duffy-Hester, and Stahl (1998), concluded that there are several types of good phonics instruction and that there is no research base to support the superiority of any one particular type. The National Reading Panel (NRP) (2000) reviewed the experimental research on teaching phonics and determined that explicit and systematic phonics is superior to nonsystematic or no phonics but that there is no significant difference in effectiveness among the kinds of systematic phonics instruction. The NRP also found no significant difference in effectiveness among tutoring, small-group, or whole-class phonics instruction.

Newer approaches to teaching phonics often use guided and independent spelling activities to teach letter–sound relationships and their application (Stahl, Duffy-Hester, & Stahl, 1998). A number of studies have supported integrating phonics and spelling instruction with young children (Ehri & Wilce, 1987; Ellis & Cataldo, 1990). Juel and Minden-Cupp (2000) noted that based on their observations, the most effective teachers of children who entered first grade with few literacy skills combined systematic letter–sound instruction with onset–rime, compare–contrast activities instruction and taught these units with applications in both reading and writing.

Phonics and spelling instruction in the upper grades has not been investigated much, but some understanding about the new words encountered in these grades provides some instructional direction. In 1984, Nagy and Anderson published a landmark study in which they analyzed a sample of 7,260 words found in books commonly read in grades 3–9. They found that most of these words were polysyllabic words and that many of these big words were related semantically through their morphology. Some of these relationships are easily noticed. For instance, the words *hunter, redness, foglights,* and *stringy* are clearly related to the words *hunt, red, fog,* and *string.* Other more complex word relationships exist between words such as *planet/planetarium, vicious/vice,* and *apart/apartment.* Nagy and Anderson hypothesized that if children knew or learned how to interpret morphological relationships, they would know six or seven words for every basic word. To move children along in their decoding and spelling abilities in the upper grades, instruction needs to focus on morphemes—prefixes, suffixes, and roots—and how they help us decode, spell, and gain meaning for polysyllabic words.

# chapter 5

# Building Vivid, Vital, and Valuable Vocabularies

R ead each of these three words, and think about what comes immediately to mind:

plastic    purple    racket

What did you think of for *plastic?* Did you image the multitude of plastic objects that make up everyday life? Did you experience negative feelings, such as "I hate using plastic knives, forks, and spoons," while simultaneously realizing that our current world would be very different if it weren't for the omnipresence of plastic? Did you worry because plastic biodegrades so slowly and is not good for the environment? Did you recall one of the most famous lines in movie history from *The Graduate?*

What did your brain do with the word *purple?* Did you picture something purple? Did you think "I hate purple" or "Purple is one of my favorite colors?" Did you imagine different shades of purple—orchid, lavender, lilac? Perhaps the word *purple* made you think immediately of someone you know who was in the military and earned a Purple Heart, and you wondered how this medal came to be associated with the color purple.

Did you picture a tennis or badminton racket for the word *racket?* Or did you think of all the racket being made by the construction across the street? Perhaps you were reminded about the shenanigans of your local government and thought, "It's all a racket!"

When we see or hear words, our brains make all kinds of connections with those words, depending on our past experiences. These connections include images and scenes from our own lives as well as from movies and television. We have emotional reactions to words. Words make us worry, celebrate, appreciate, and wonder.

What our minds don't do when they see or hear a word is think of a definition. Look up *plastic, purple,* and *racket* in any standard dictionary, and you will find definitions such as these:

> **plastic**—any of a large group of synthetic organic compounds molded by heat pressure into a variety of forms

> **purple**—a color made by mixing red and blue

> **racket**—a loud noise; a scheme for getting money illegally; an oval strung frame with a long handle used for hitting balls

When you see or hear words, your brain makes connections to those words. Your brain does not think of definitions.

Now think back to your elementary school days and recall your associations with the word *vocabulary.* Do you remember looking up words and copying their definitions? If a word had several definitions, did you copy the first one or the shortest one? Did you ever look up a word and still not know what it meant because you did not understand the meanings of the other words in the definition? Did you copy that definition and memorize it for the test, in spite of not understanding it? Do you remember weekly vocabulary tests, in which you had to write definitions for words and use those words in sentences?

Copying and memorizing definitions has been and remains the most common vocabulary activity in schools. It is done at all levels and in all subjects. This definition copying and memorizing continues in spite of research that shows definitional approaches to vocabulary instruction increase children's ability to define words but have no effect on reading comprehension (Bauman, Kame'enui, & Ash, 2003).

Vocabulary is critical to reading comprehension. If you are reading or listening to something in which you can instantly access the appropriate meanings for the words, you are well on your way to understanding. But when you are reading or listening to something and you don't have meanings for a lot of the words, your comprehension is severely impaired. Vocabulary is also crucial for writing. We all know that one of the challenges of writing well and clearly is "choosing just the right word."

Helping children build vivid and vital vocabularies is a crucial goal in helping all children become the very best readers and writers they can be. Vocabulary is one of the most valuable tools for literacy. In the next two chapters, we will describe specific strategies teachers use for teaching students to comprehend and to write clearly. A schoolwide, day-in-day-out vocabulary-building component in the curriculum provides the foundation on which specific comprehension and writing skills can be built.

## *How Do We Learn All the Words We Know?*

How many words do you know?

5,000?
10,000?
20,000?
50,000?
100,000?

If you found it difficult to estimate the size of your vocabulary, you should be comforted to know that this seemingly simple question is a difficult one to answer. The first question is, of course, "What do you mean by *know?*" Is it enough to know that *anthropoids* are some kind of apes, or do you have to know the specific information that anthropoids are apes without tails, such as chimpanzees, gorillas, orangutans, and gibbons? The next question is, "How many meanings of the word do you have to know?" If you know the sports meaning of *coach,* do you also have to know the motorbus and "coach class" meanings to count this word in your meaning vocabulary? The other complication in counting the words you have meanings for is how to count the various forms of a single word. If *play, plays, playing, played, playful, replay,* and *player* count as separate words, your vocabulary is much larger than if these words count as one word, all related to the root word *play.*

In spite of the difficulties of estimating vocabulary size, it is important for teachers to have an idea of what the meaning vocabulary development goal is. Most linguists estimate that college graduates have reasonably deep meanings for at least 20,000 root words. Root words include words such as *play* and any easily understood derivatives. Thus, all your common *play* words only count for one root word. Biemiller (2004) estimates that the average grade 12 student knows about 15,000 root words. Entering kindergartners have meanings for an average of 3,500 root words, and that number increases to 6,000 root words by the end of second grade. On average, children add approximately 1,000 root words to their meaning vocabulary stores each year—or about 3 words per day for 365 days!

Children differ greatly, however, in the sizes of their meaning vocabularies at school entrance and as they continue through the grades. Children who enter school with small vocabularies tend to add fewer words each year than children who enter with larger vocabularies. Since vocabulary size is so closely related to children's comprehension as they move through school, there is a sense of urgency about intensifying efforts to build more and deeper word meaning stores for all children.

To help you understand how we add words to our meaning vocabulary stores, consider the analogy that learning word meanings is a lot like getting to know people. As with words, you know some people extremely well, you are well acquainted with others, you have only vague ideas of still others, and so on. Your knowledge of people depends on the experiences you have with them. You know some people, such as family members and close friends, extremely well because you have spent most of your life in their company. You have participated with them regularly in situations that have been intense and emotional as well as routine. At the other extreme, think of people that you have only heard about as well as historical figures, such as Charles Darwin and Catherine the Great, and current public figures, such as politicians and entertainers. You have heard of them and seen pictures and videos of them, but these people are known to you only through the secondhand reports of others. Your knowledge of people that you know indirectly through secondhand information is limited in comparison to your knowledge of those you know directly through firsthand experience. Learning words—like coming to know people—varies according to how much time you spend with them and the types of experiences you share.

Now think of how you make new friends. Social gatherings, such as parties and meetings, are excellent opportunities for getting to know others. When you move through a gathering on your own, you strike up conversations and get to know new people, in part as a function of your motivation and your social skills. However, having a host, hostess, friend, or group of friends introduce you to people tends to expedite the process. And once you have made new contacts, you might get to know them better as you meet again in other settings. And don't forget the power of social networking: The more people you know, the more opportunities you have for helping each other out and meeting even more people.

The levels of knowledge about people and the dynamics of getting to know them are comparable in many ways to learning words. When given the opportunity, students learn new words on their own, depending on their motivation and literacy skills. Students also benefit from direct introductions to and intensive interactions with a few new words.

As students learn new words, their opportunities for learning additional words increase exponentially.

Literacy experts all agree on the need for vocabulary building for all students at all grades. They disagree, however, about the best way to provide students with the valuable vocabulary tools they need. We know that you can teach specific vocabulary and that learning new words will improve the comprehension of text containing those words. But the teaching must be quite thorough and across several days and weeks, and thus, the number of words any teacher can directly teach is limited. Many of the words children add to their vocabularies each year are learned through reading. Thus, wide reading is often recommended for vocabulary development.

When you meet a word in your reading, you have two sources of information to help you figure out the meaning of that word. Consider the following sentence:

I wish I understood how they can colorize old movies.

If you had never heard the word *colorize* before, you probably figured out what it meant using the context of the sentence and your morphemic knowledge about the root *color* and the suffix *ize.* Since you know that when you *modernize* something, you make it more modern; when you *categorize* things, you put them into categories; and when you *rationalize* something you have done, you make it rational (even if it really wasn't!); you quickly realize that to *colorize* something is to make it have color. Of course, you know that old movies were black and white, and thus you can read the sentence, immediately understand the meaning of *colorize,* and wonder how they do that! Because we know that wide reading is associated with large vocabularies and that the clues available when you come to a new word in your reading are context and morphemes, some experts argue that the best way to help students build vocabulary is to promote wide reading and teach the use of context and morphemes.

Since we know that words can be directly taught and that wide reading—supported by context and morpheme detection—are both valuable ways of building vocabulary, the wise thing for most teachers to do is to "hedge their bets" and tackle the vocabulary challenge from "both fronts." In the remainder of this chapter, we will describe a variety of ways teachers can help all their students build vivid, vital, and valuable vocabularies.

## *Provide as Much Real Experience as Possible*

We all learn best when we have real, direct experience with whatever we are learning. Most of the vocabulary learning children do before they come to school is based on real things and real experiences. Children first learn to name things—*table, chair, cat, dog.*

Two-year-olds delight in pointing to the objects they can see and naming them. Put them in a new environment, such as the beach or the doctor's office, and they will almost immediately begin to point to things and ask, "What's that?" It is not only nouns that children learn through direct experience. Every young child knows the meanings of *run* and *walk* and has probably been told many times that you can't run in the parking lot! Children also learn emotion words through real experiences:

> "I know you feel sad that your friend moved away.
> I would be sad too if that happened."

The words we know best and remember longest are those we have had real, direct experience with. Teachers who want to build students' vocabularies are always looking for ways to introduce words with "real things."

## Bring Real Things into the Classroom and Anchor Words to Them

Look around your house or apartment, and identify common objects your students might not know the names of—even if they have the same objects in their houses or apartments! Here are some of the objects one teacher brought to school for Show and Talk:

- Vases in assorted sizes, colors, and shapes
- Balls—tennis, baseball, basketball, football, golf, volleyball, beachball
- Art—watercolors, oils, photographs in frames of different colors, materials, and sizes
- Kitchen implements—turkey baster, strainer, spatula, whisk, zester
- Tools—hammer, screwdriver, nails, screws, drill, wrench

In addition to the names of objects, of course, lots of descriptive words are used in talking about the objects and lots of verbs are used in talking about what you do with the objects. You may want to teach children a simple version of the game 20 Questions, in which you think of one of the objects, and the children see how many questions they have to ask you to narrow down which one it is.

## "Mine" Your School Environment for Real Things

In addition to gathering objects from home and carting them to school, look around your school environment and think about what objects your students might not know the names for. They probably know the words *door* and *window,* but can they tell you that what goes around the door and window is the *frame?* Can they tell you that the things that allow the door to open and close are the *hinges* and that the thing you grab to open and close the door is the *knob?* They can turn the water in the sink off and on, but do they know that they use *faucets* to do that? Is your playground covered with *asphalt? Gravel? Grass? Sand?* What kind of *equipment* do you have in your *gymnasium,* and what can you do with it?

## Seize Upon Unexpected Events as Opportunities for Vocabulary Development

Clever teachers seize every opportunity to turn classroom occurrences into opportunities for vocabulary development. The misfortune suffered by a child who breaks his leg and arrives at school with his leg in a cast and walking on crutches can be "mined" for vocabulary development opportunities. The clever teacher will encourage the children to ask questions and share their own experiences with broken bones. He or she might take a photo of the child with the broken leg and write a few sentences summarizing that experience:

> Michael slipped on the ice and broke his leg. He went to the hospital in the ambulance. The doctor set the bone and put a cast on his leg. He has to walk with crutches and can't move very quickly.

## Look for Real-Thing Connections for New Vocabulary Words

When you are reading to or with children and new words occur, think first of how you might connect those new words with things in their environment. When reading about a mountain ledge, the teacher might point out the window ledge and table ledge as examples of other kinds of ledges right there in our classroom. The word *pierce* can be connected with students' pierced ears. When encountering the word *unexpected,* the teacher can remind children of something unexpected that happened in the classroom.

## Introduce Science and Social Studies Units with Real Things

As you are planning to introduce a new science or social studies topic, begin by collecting objects that are even vaguely related to that topic. Some museums have crates of objects related to commonly studied topics. Some school media centers collect and store things that many teachers need. In some schools, teachers take responsibility for gathering objects related to a particular topic and then teach those topics at different times so that everyone can use the same objects.

● · · · · · · · · · · · · · · · · · · · · · · · · · · · · · · · · · · · · · · · · · · · · · · · · · · · · · · · · · · · · · · · · · · · · · · · · · · · · · · · · · · · · · · · · · · · · · · · · · · · · · ·

**94**

## Send Students Looking for Real Things in Their Home Environments

Many of the objects you bring to school or identify in school to build vocabularies can also be found in the home environments of your students. Get in the habit of posing questions that will send students looking for and identifying similar objects in their homes:

> "Do you have tools (kitchen implements, balls, vases, picture frames, etc.) in your house? What do they look like? What do you use them for?"
>
> "How many faucets (hinges, knobs, ledges, door frames, etc.) do you have in your house? Count them and bring in the number tomorrow. We will add up all the numbers at the beginning of math."
>
> "Is there gravel (asphalt, grass, sand, etc.) anywhere in your neighborhood?"
>
> "Is there a playground or park near your house? What kind of equipment does it have?"

In addition to having children identify common objects in their home environments, encourage them to talk with family members about those objects. Children can tell them that they have the same things at school, too, and explain what they are for. Children can tell their families about how they are using batteries—like the ones they have at home—to learn about electricity in school.

Teachers are always looking for opportunities to make home–school connections. Having children take new vocabulary words they are learning into their home environments helps make school learning more relevant and extends each child's opportunities for vocabulary development.

## Take Advantage of Media and Technology

Many young children have a concept for *mountain* even if they have never seen a real mountain. Most young children can recognize zebras, elephants, and monkeys even though they have never been to a zoo, circus, or other place with these animals. Many children who have never sailed or been in a canoe know what sailboats and canoes are. How did this learning occur? Did someone explain to them what a mountain was? Was the dictionary definition of the word *monkey* read to them? Did some adult attempt to explain or define a *canoe?* In most cases, when children have concepts for objects and realities they have never directly experienced, they have seen these objects or realities portrayed on television, in movies or videos, or in pictures or picture books.

The Internet makes providing visual images and simulated experiences a daily possibility in every classroom. Through the Internet, you can follow the progress of the latest space probe, find images of all the major deserts of the world, and see and hear Winston Churchill as he rallies the people of London during World War II. You and your children can take virtual field trips all over the world and back in time.

The saying "A picture is worth a thousand words" is definitely true when it comes to vocabulary. When you can't provide the real thing in your classroom, looking to the media for visual and auditory images is definitely the next best thing.

## Go on Scavenger Hunts

Have you ever been on a scavenger hunt? Everyone has a list of things to find and a limited amount of time in which to find them, and the team that finds the most things wins. You can adapt the scavenger hunt notion to help your children expand their vocabularies. Choose a topic that you are about to study or a book you are about to read. As you think about what the children will be reading and learning, select words for which you would like to develop meanings and for which children could scavenge for pictures and/or objects.

For the topic *weather,* for example, a teacher decided that pictures and/or objects could be found to represent:

| | | | |
|---|---|---|---|
| cirrus clouds | thermometer | hurricane | rainbow |
| cumulus clouds | cyclone | lightning | meteorologist |
| stratus clouds | tornado | fog | wind vane |
| barometer | blizzard | frost | rain gauge |

She made a list of these words and distributed the list to teams of children in her class. She then explained that the class was going to have a scavenger hunt. Each team had one week to collect as many objects and/or pictures as they could to represent the words on the list. They could bring one object and one picture for each word and would get two points for an object and one point for a picture. The teacher then let the teams meet for a few minutes and discuss what the words meant and who thought they could find what objects. When the children protested about not being able to bring in a hurricane, she responded, "No, but perhaps you could bring in a picture of a hurricane." When the children said, "I don't even know what a rain gauge is," she said, "Well, maybe you had better look it up in the dictionary or on the Internet, if you want your team to win the scavenger hunt."

Each day for a week, the teacher let the teams meet briefly to discuss what they had found and what they still needed. She stressed that they should whisper and keep their finds very secret because they did not want the other teams to figure out where they were finding things. When asked if drawings of the objects were allowed, she responded that they were, as long as they were well drawn and actually looked like the object being represented. Later, someone asked if they could bring "something like the object, but smaller, like a model of it." The teacher responded, "If the model or smaller thing really represented the real thing, it would count as an object."

On the designated final day, the children came with the "scavenged" objects and pictures. Each team gathered and laid out their finds. Most teams had pictures—drawn, found, or copied—of almost everything. There was also a surprising number of real objects, including a handmade rain gauge and one of those small, glass balls with a scene inside that becomes a "blizzard" when you turn it upside down! The team who had thought of this was particularly pleased with their cleverness, and the other teams did have to admit that it was "kind of like a model of a blizzard."

The winning team was rewarded for its efforts. They got to create the *weather* bulletin board! They put up all the words and then made a collage of the pictures brought in by all the teams. They labeled the objects and put them on a nearby table. They then signed all their names and put in big letters:

WEATHER BULLETIN BOARD CREATED BY WINNERS OF WEATHER SCAVENGER HUNT

## Simulate Real Experiences with Dramatization

Using word dramatizations is a powerful way to help students build vivid word meanings. Both skits and pantomimes can be used to help students "get into words." To prepare your students to do vocabulary skits, select six words and write them on index cards. Tell your students that in a few minutes, their group will plan a skit—a quick little play—to demonstrate the word they have been given. Choose a few students to work with you and model for them how to plan a skit. Talk with your group as the rest of the class listens in. Plan a scene in which you can use the word several times. When you have a plan, act out your skit using the target word as many times as possible. Have one member of your group hold up a sign containing the word every time it occurs in the skit.

Imagine, for example, that the word your group is acting out is *curious.* You decide that the skit will involve a dad and his 2-year-old son walking to the post office. The dad and the 2-year-old meet several people on their walk, and each time, the 2-year-old stops, points to the stranger, and asks these questions:

"What's your name?"
"Where are you going?"
"What's that?"
"What are you doing?"
"What's in the bag?"
"Why are you wearing that funny hat?"

The dad smiles each time and explains to the stranger that his son is curious about everything. The strangers answer the boy's questions and then remark, "He's the most curious kid I ever saw" as they walk on.

Perform the skit as the class watches. At the end of the skit, have the people in the skit ask the audience how the skit showed that the little boy was curious. Finally, you should ask if anyone in the audience has a story to share about a curious person.

Next, divide the class into five groups, putting one of the children who helped you in the skit in each of the groups. Give each group a card on which the word they will dramatize is written. Today, you are focusing on adjectives and give the groups the words *nervous, frantic, impatient, jubilant,* and *serene.* Help the groups plan their skits by circulating around and coaching them. Encourage the child in each group who helped in the original skit to take a leadership role and help boost the group's confidence that they can do this.

Each skit is acted out with one person in each group holding up the card each time the word is used. The group then asks the audience what they saw in the skit that made the word "come alive." You should ask if anyone in the class wants to share a personal experience with the target word. After the last skit, place the six word cards with others on a board labeled

> GET YOUR ADJECTIVES HERE: COOL DESCRIBING WORDS TO
> SPICE UP YOUR TALK AND WRITING

Pantomime is another form of dramatization that is particularly useful when the words you want to teach are emotions or actions. Imagine that you want to introduce the emotional adjectives *confused, disappointed, furious,* and *frightened.* Assign a pair of students to each word. Have the rest of the class watch the pairs pantomiming the words and try to guess which pair is acting out each word. The same kind of pantomime can be done with actions such as *swaggered, crept, sauntered,* and *scurried.* Adverbs are also fun to pantomime. Imagine four pairs of students walking to school: One pair walks *briskly.* One pair walks *cautiously.* One pair walks *proudly.* One pair walks *forlornly.*

For any kind of dramatization, it is important to conclude the activity by asking all the students to relate the word that was acted out to their own experience:

> "When have you been *confused? Disappointed? Furious? Frantic?*"
> "When have you *swaggered? Crept? Sauntered? Scurried?*"
> "When would you walk *briskly? Cautiously? Proudly? Forlornly?*"

Acting out words in skits and pantomimes provides students with real experience with many words. They will remember these words because of this real experience and because they enjoyed acting and watching their friends act. Keep a list of words your class encounters that could be acted out in skits or pantomimes, and schedule 20 minutes for vocabulary drama each week. You will be amazed at how students' vocabularies and enthusiasm for words will grow.

# *Increase Meaning Vocabularies through Reading*

Reading is one of the major opportunities for vocabulary learning. Many words occur much more frequently in written text than in spoken language. As children listen to text being read aloud by the teacher and read independently, they will have lots of opportunities to add words to their meaning vocabularies. Unfortunately, many children do not pay a lot of attention to the new words they meet while reading, and thus, they miss many opportunities to increase the sizes of their vocabularies. Here are ways to help all children increase their meaning vocabularies through reading.

## Teach Three Words from Your Teacher Read-Aloud

Teacher read-aloud is one of the major opportunities for children to learn new word meanings. Several studies have demonstrated the power of focused read-alouds on fostering vocabulary growth (Beck, McKeown, & Kucan, 2002; Juel, Biancarosa, Coker, & Deffes, 2003). In each of these studies, the teachers went beyond just reading books aloud to children. Before they read a book aloud, they selected a few words that they felt many children would not know the meanings of. After the book had been read aloud and discussed, the teachers returned to those selected words and focused student attention on them. Use the following Three Read-Aloud Words activity to promote more vocabulary learning from your teacher read-aloud.

*Using "Goldilocks" Words in Teacher Read-Alouds*   Any good book is going to have many words you could focus your attention on. Narrowing the number of words you are going to teach to a reasonable number will increase the chances that all your children will learn them. Beck, McKeown, and Kucan (2002 ) divide vocabulary into three tiers. The first tier includes words generally known by almost all children. *Boy, girl, jump, sad, laugh,* and *late* are examples of tier-one words. The third tier includes uncommon, obscure, and technical words. *Languid, thrush, oblique,* and *catamaran* are examples of tier-three words. Tier-two words are words many students don't know but will need to know. *Despair, exhausted, catastrophe,* and *proceeded* are tier-two words. Beck and other experts suggests that teachers focus their time and energy on vocabulary development in teaching these words. Some people refer to these tier-two words as "Goldilocks" words because they are not too well known, not too obscure, but hopefully "just right" for children.

As you look at the book you are going to read aloud to choose your three Goldilocks words, you will probably find a lot more than three possibilities. Narrow the selection down to three by considering the usefulness and appeal of each word to your children and how well the word is defined by the context and pictures in the book. If you have more than three words that are useful, appealing, and well defined, consider how many times each word occurs. Your best choices for three words are useful, appealing, well-defined words that are central to the text and that occur many times.

Once you have chosen the three words, write them on index cards. Then follow these steps:

- *Read the text the first time, making no reference to the three chosen words.* The first time you read anything aloud should always be for enjoyment and information. Read the book to your children as you normally would, stopping from time to time to ask questions of your children that will engage them in the text but not doing anything particular about your chosen words.

- *Show the three words to your children.* After reading and enjoying the text, show your children the words one at a time. You may want to give a very brief meaning or sentence for each word—but don't do a lot of elaborate meaning building because you want the text to help you do that.

- *Reread the text and have children stop you when you read each of the words.* Put the index cards with your three chosen words where your children can clearly see them, and read the text to them again. On this second reading, do not stop to discuss pictures or engage the children with questions. When you come to one of the chosen words, some of your children will be sure to notice and signal you. Stop reading and use the pictures and context to explain each word. If the word is used more than once, let the children stop you each time and see if any new information is added to their understanding of the word.

- *Help children connect their own experiences to the three words.* Once you have finished reading the book, stopping each time one of the chosen words has occurred, focus again on each word and ask a question that helps children connect their own experiences to the text. Ask questions such as:

  "When have you felt . . . ?"
  "Have you ever experienced a . . . ?"
  "Where would you see a . . . ?"

- *Reread and have children retell, using the three words in their retelling.* On the next day after you did the first and second readings of the text, show the children the words once more and tell them that you are going to read the book to them one more time. This time, they are to listen to everything that happens in the text—paying special attention to the order in which things happen and to the three words. Tell them that after they read, they will try to retell the information to a partner and use the three words in their retelling. Reread the piece without stopping. Partner up the children and have them jointly try to retell the information, using the three words in their retelling.

- *Display the title and the three word cards somewhere in the room.* Once you have introduced these three words in the rich context of the book, helped your children connect these words to their own experiences, and given your children an opportunity to use these

words to retell the text, display these words someplace in the room. You may want to copy the cover of the book and display the three index cards next to it. Tell your children that you and they are all going to be on the lookout for these words in books and conversations and trying to use the words at school and at home. Every time someone hears, reads, or uses one of these words, he or she can put a tally mark next to the word. The word with the most tally marks at the end of one week is the winning word! (Kids love competitions, especially if they cannot possibly be the loser!) Once you do this, contrive to use these words in your conversations with your children over the next several days. Congratulate them when they notice one of the words, and allow them to put a tally mark next to the word. Soon, you will notice your children trying to sneak these words into their talk—exactly what you are aiming for! Once the children are alert to these words, ask them to listen for them and to try to use them in their home environments. Have children report any instances of these words in their home environments, and add tally marks to the appropriate words.

When reading chapter books to your students, pick three words from the first chapter that occur again in the second chapter. Read the first chapter and show students the words, and then have them signal you when they hear these words in the second chapter. Just as with picture books, stop and talk about how the words are used in the book and how students connect them to their experiences. Continue to add words as you proceed through the book—particularly words that recur in future chapters.

## Use "Picture Walks" to Build Vocabulary

One resource constantly available to elementary teachers to build students' vocabularies is the variety of pictures in the books and magazines teachers read aloud and in the texts that students read. Get in the habit of taking your students on a "picture walk" before you read to them or they read to themselves, and you will find lots of opportunities to build meanings for words.

When you picture walk a text, do not stop on every page or take a long time to develop meanings. Children are going to read or listen to the text soon, and they will build more meanings for words as they read or listen. Your purpose before reading is only to alert children to the words and get them in the habit of "mining" the pictures for all the information they can.

## Read and Create Alphabet Books

While all books contain numerous possibilities for vocabulary building, one particular kind of book is a "gold mine" for vocabulary development. Alphabet books are written on all kinds of topics, including animals, foods, and the ocean. Captivating pictures make real the words students are unfamiliar with and add depth to words they already know a little about. Reading and rereading alphabet books with young children can help them develop their letter name and sound knowledge and help build their vocabularies at the same time.

If you are reading lots of alphabet books, you may want your children to create their own alphabet books—individually or as a class. Of course, you will have to brainstorm possible words for each letter of the alphabet. Just think of all the vocabulary development that will occur during that brainstorming!

## Alert Children to New Words
## They Meet in Their Reading

If you are doing the Three Read-Aloud Words activity and taking your students on picture walks before reading, you are already doing a lot to help them be alert to new words in their own reading. Your students will be in the habit of looking at the pictures and thinking about what words in the text those pictures relate to. They will know how the context of what you are reading often makes clear the meaning of a word and that each time you meet the same word, the additional context often adds to or clarifies your meaning for that word.

If you want to give children an additional nudge, however, to use what they know about learning word meanings from their reading, designate one day each week as a "Sticky-Note New Word Day." At the beginning of independent reading time, give each child one sticky note on which to write one word. Ask the children to be on the lookout for words that are relatively new to them and that they figure out the meanings based on the context and the pictures. Explain to them how you pick your three read-aloud words by looking for words that many of them don't know but that are useful and interesting words. Tell them that you also try to choose words where the context and pictures make the meanings and that are used more than once.

Ask each child to look for the perfect word to teach to the class in their reading and to write that word on the sticky note and place it on the sentence in which the word first occurs. When the time for independent reading is over, gather your students together and let four or five volunteers tell their words and read the context and/or share the pictures that helped them with the meanings of their words. Do not let all your children share their words because this would take more time than you have and you want your students to be excited about finding new words—not bored with having to listen to 25 explanations! Assure your students that you will give them more sticky notes next Thursday and that you will let other children share their finds with the class.

If you designate one day each week as "Sticky-Note New Word Day," your children will get in the habit of looking for interesting new words and using the pictures and context to figure out those words. Soon, they will be doing this in all their reading—even when they do not have blank sticky notes staring

**What They Look Like:** These frogs have bumpy skin that looks like moss.
**Habitat:** They live on mountains and in wet cav
**Froggy F** find these fu: Camouflage in their ha blend in with the moss around them! Blending in like this is called **camouflage** (cam-uh-flaj).

at them—and they will be on their way to adding exponentially to their vocabularies every time they read!

Another simple way to keep students alert for new words is to designate some space in your room as a vocabulary board. Supply your students with lots of colorful index cards and markers, and encourage them to add new words they find in their reading to the board. Each student should initial the card on which he or she writes the word so everyone can tell who found which words. Take a few minutes each day to note new additions to the vocabulary board and ask students where they found the words, what they mean, and why they thought everyone would want to learn these words.

"Great Words"

underground PC

scurried PD | marsh PH | creepy TW | despair

hilarious KC | persistent RH | bullfrogs CM | exhausted AMA

tadpoles PC | Camouflage JD | Catastrophe SB | reflection SAM

## Teach Morphemes, Context, and the Dictionary to Learn New Words

The activities already described in this chapter will help all your children build vivid, vital, and valuable vocabularies. Once your students are on the lookout for new words and convinced that words are wonderful, you can teach them some specific strategies to help figure out the meanings for new words. Good readers use morphemes, context, and the dictionary to help them refine the meanings of words.

## Morphemes

You learned in the previous chapter that *morphemes* are prefixes, roots, and suffixes, which are meaningful parts of words. Look again at the Nifty-Thrifty-Fifty list on page 82. This list has an example word for each of the common prefixes and suffixes. You may want to teach students these words or help them collect other words from their reading that have these helpful parts.

Four prefixes—*un, re, in,* and *dis*—are the most common, and knowing them will help students figure out the meaning of over 1,500 words. Graves (2004) suggests teaching these prefixes to all elementary students. You may want to focus on each of these prefixes for a few weeks. Begin a chart with some *un* words your students are familiar with, such as *unhappy, unlucky,* and *unlocked.* Help students notice the prefix *un* and that it changes the meaning of the root word to the opposite meaning. Encourage your students to be on the lookout for words in their reading in which *un* changes a word to the opposite meaning, and add these to the chart.

After a few weeks, make a chart for *re,* with the meaning of "back" or "again," and add such common words as *return, reboot,* and *replay.* The prefix *in,* which means "the opposite," can be spelled *in, im, il,* or *ir,* so you may want to start the *in* chart with the key words *insane, impossible, illegal,* and *irregular.* Your *dis* chart might begin with common words such as *dishonest* and *disagree.*

One problem with teaching students to look for prefixes and use them as clues to meaning is that many words start with *un*—such as *uncle, understand,* and *uniform*—but *un* is not the prefix and does not have the meaning of opposite. Graves (2004) provides the practical solution that for these simple prefixes, elementary children can be taught that a letter combination is not a prefix if removing it leaves a nonsense word. Thus, *un* is not the prefix in *uncle, understand,* and *uniform* because *cle, derstand,* and *iform* are not words.

When teaching morphemes to help students build meanings for words, it is probably best to begin with these four common prefixes because students will encounter many words in which these prefixes have these predictable meanings. Once students are comfortable with these prefixes, you may want to add some of the less common and less transparent ones from the Nifty-Thrifty-Fifty list.

Elementary students can also learn to notice base or root words and think about how words with the same roots are related. Again, you should start with the most common and predictable root or base words. The word *play* occurs in such related words as *replay, playground,* and *playoffs. Work* is part of many words, including *workers, workout,* and *workstation. Place* is another common base word, and students often know the meaning of *placemats, replace,* and *workplace.* Beginning a chart with common words and asking students to be on the lookout for other words containing those words will help them become attuned to root and base words in their reading.

Vocabulary experts disagree about teaching students Latin and Greek roots. While it is true that these roots do contain clues to meaning, the meaning relationships are often hard to figure out, and students might get discouraged if they cannot "ferret out" the meaning of a word based on the meaning of the root. Perhaps the most sensible way for elementary teachers to approach Greek and Latin roots is to be aware of them and to point out relationships when they think these will be understandable to most of their children. When encountering the word *spectacle,* for example, the teacher might point out that a *spectacle* is something you see that is quite striking or unusual. Furthermore, the teacher might point out that the root *spect* means "to watch" and invite the students to think about how words they know, such as *inspection* and *spectators,* are related to this meaning. The word *constructive* might be explained as "helpful" or "building up," as opposed to *destructive,* which is "unhelpful" or "tearing down." Students might be told that the root *struct* means "build" and asked to think about how other words they know, such as *structure* and *reconstruction,* are related to this meaning.

## Context

If you are doing the Three Read-Aloud Words activity regularly and having students share how they figured out the meanings of sticky-note words in their own reading one day each week, then you are teaching them to use context to figure out the meanings of unfamiliar words. If you are taking your students on regular picture walks before reading, then you are teaching them how new words are often brought to life by the pictures in the text. This regular attention to how context and pictures make word meanings clear is probably the best instruction you can do so that your students get in the habit of and know how to use pictures and context.

One caution you may need to point out to students is that context does not always directly reveal the meaning of an unfamiliar word and can sometimes be misleading. Imagine that the only reference in the text to the word *incredulously* is in this sentence:

Her dad listened incredulously.

This context does not provide much of a clue to the meaning of this new word. On the other hand, the text might continue with a much richer context:

> Her dad listened incredulously. "I find what you are telling me really hard to believe," he admitted when she had finished explaining how the accident had happened.

How much context helps with meaning varies greatly. If a word is important and the context is slim, students need to use the dictionary to figure out the meaning that might make sense in the context of what they are reading.

Context can sometimes mislead you about a word's meaning. One student had put a sticky note on the word *grimaced* and explained that the word meant "yelled." The sentence in which the student had read the word was

> The waiter in the crowded restaurant grimaced as the tray slid to the floor.

The teacher explained to the student that "yelled" would make sense here but that the waiter could have done many things and there really wasn't enough context to decide exactly what the waiter did. The child quickly looked up the word *grimaced* in the dictionary and shared its meaning with the class. The teacher had the whole class twist their faces into the grimaces they might make if they had just dropped a whole tray of food in a crowded restaurant.

As children are sharing their sticky-note words, you will have many opportunities to show them both how the context can be extremely helpful and how it can lead them astray. You can also model how a dictionary is best used—to clarify meaning and let you know if the meaning you inferred from the context is indeed the right one.

## Use the Dictionary Strategically

This chapter began with a discussion of unproductive dictionary use—looking up words and copying and memorizing definitions. There are, however, a variety of ways to promote active use of the dictionary to help students broaden their concepts and also teach them what a valuable resource the dictionary is. Students should learn to turn to the dictionary to find out about an unfamiliar word on a scavenger hunt list. The teacher should regularly ask one child to consult the dictionary when a new word occurs and the meaning of that word is unclear. A teacher who regularly says "Let's see what the dictionary can tell us about this word" and sends one child to look it up is modeling the way adults who use the dictionary actually use it. (Did you ever see an adult look up a word to copy and memorize the definition? Maybe the reason so few adults use the dictionary is because that is the only way they have ever seen anyone use it!) If you have a dictionary on your classroom

computers, model how useful this is by asking a child to "See what our computer dictionary has to say about this word."

In many classrooms, helpers are appointed to jobs each week. Someone greets
visitors, and someone else waters the plants. Why not appoint a weekly "Dictionary
Disciple"? This person gets possession of "the Book" and is always ready to be dispatched
to the farthest corners of the wide world of words to seek and share facts about them.

## Develop Vocabulary in Science and Social Studies

Two areas of the elementary curriculum "cry out for" vocabulary development. The content areas of science and social studies both have their own special vocabularies that students must understand and use if they are to read and write well in these subjects. Most of
the ideas already described in this chapter can be used not only during language arts time
but also during science and social studies. You do not need to develop a whole new set of
activities for teaching content-area vocabulary. All you have to do is remember to use the
same activities even when your schedule says science or social studies.

To develop vivid, vital, and valuable science and social studies vocabularies:

- Use real things both from the school environment and collected from various places.
- Take advantage of media and technology—especially Internet images and
  simulations.
- Use pictures and picture walks—even from textbooks that may be too hard to read
  all the text but that contain illustrations and diagrams for important concepts.
- Have students go on scavenger hunts for objects and pictures related to an upcoming
  unit.
- Use dramatization, especially in social studies, where many of the concepts involve
  interactions among various groups of people.
- Do the Three Read-Aloud Words activity with informational books related to your
  science and social studies topics.
- Provide topic-related materials for students to choose to read independently.
- Read and develop alphabet books related to topics being studied.
- Have students use context and pictures to figure out meanings of unfamiliar words
  in science and social studies materials.
- Point out morphemes in science and social studies vocabulary—for instance,
  *international, reconstruction, translucent, transparent.*

- Create class science and social studies dictionaries with illustrations and examples of key terms.

- Once words have been introduced, display them in some way to keep them in front of your students and to remind you and them to use them and notice these words.

## Teach Children to Monitor Their Vocabulary Knowledge

One of the first steps in learning anything is recognizing that you don't already know it. Children need to notice when they come to words they don't have meanings for. Sometimes, young children get so focused on pronouncing a new word that they fail to realize they don't know what it means. Children can be taught to self-assess their vocabulary knowledge using a simple scale like this one:

> 1 = I never heard of that word.
> 2 = I heard the word but I don't know what it means.
> 3 = I think I know what that word means.
> 4 = I'm sure I know what that word means.
> 5 = I can make a good sentence with that word.

This scale could be used with any of the activities for teaching vocabulary. To make this quick and easy, consider using a five-finger, every-pupil-response system. Say the word you are focusing on, and ask everyone to show you the appropriate number of fingers. When you are focusing on a word for the first time, be sure that you positively acknowledge all the responses so that children do not get in the habit of showing you five fingers just so they "look good." Try acknowledging their vocabulary self-assessment with comments such as these:

> "I see lots of one and two fingers. That makes me happy because I know I chose a word you need when I chose *desperate*. *Desperate* is an important word and lots of you don't know it yet."

> "Some of you think you know the meaning of *desperate,* and some of you are sure you do. Can someone tell me what you think it means?"

> "I see someone with five fingers up. Todd, tell me your sentence that shows the meaning of *desperate.*"

After you have worked with the new vocabulary words for several days, ask children again to show you how well they know the meanings of these words and comment on how many people are showing four or five fingers. Many teachers display a chart, such as the one on page 108, to help children remember the five-finger vocabulary self-assessment system.

"I never heard
of that word."

"I heard the word but I don't
know what it means."

"I think I know what
that word means."

"I'm sure I know what
that word means."

"I can make a good sentence
with that word."

## *Promote Word Wonder*

Enthusiasm is contagious! Teachers who are enthusiastic about words project that enthusiasm by conveying their eagerness to learn unfamiliar words and by sharing fascinating words they encounter outside the classroom. Young children are usually enthusiastic about new words, repeating them over and over, enjoying the sound of language, and marveling at the meanings being expressed. Encourage the continuation of this natural enthusiasm. Open your class to wondering about words, to asking spontaneous questions about unfamiliar words, to making judgments about the sounds and values of words.

We hope this chapter has increased your "word wonder" and that you see that the activities described are all intended to transmit the "Words are wonderful" message. In addition to the ideas already described, here are a few more "tricks of the trade" for turning all your students into "word wizards."

## Display Words in Various Ways

Displaying words enhances learning by calling attention to particular terms and signaling the importance of learning them. We have already suggested some ways of displaying words in your classroom. The three read-aloud words can be displayed along with the cover of the book, and the children can add tally marks as they hear, read, or sneak these words into conversations at school and at home. The scavenger hunt words, along with their objects and pictures, can be displayed on a bulletin board created by the winning team. Words that are dramatized can be added to lists of other words dramatized in the past. Class books can be made both for general words and for specific science and social studies words. Vocabulary boards are effective tools for calling attention to words and their meanings. Words can be displayed on a word wall or bulletin board so that all students can see them. Once the words are up, students can visit and revisit them to learn their meanings.

Many teachers like students to keep vocabulary notebooks. If you do this, make sure your students see themselves as word collectors, rather than definition copiers. In fact, most teachers do not allow students to copy any definitions into their notebooks. Rather, the students include the sentences in which they found the words and note their personal connections with the words. Students often enjoy illustrating the words in their collections with pictures and diagrams. Some older word sleuths like to include information about the words' origins.

## Read Books about Words to Your Students

Some books for children call special attention to words by presenting them in humorous or unusual ways. Countless children have delighted in Amelia Bedelia's literal attempts to dress a chicken and draw the drapes. Sharing books with children that celebrate and play with words is just one more way to show your students you are a serious word lover.

## Designate Wednesday (or Another Day) as "Words Are Wonderful Day"

**RECOMMENDED resources**

Lots of books highlight words and word play. Here are some of our recent favorites:

*Brian Wildsmith's Amazing World of Words,* by Brian Wildsmith

*Double Trouble in Walla Walla,* by Andrew Clements

*Night Knight,* by Harriet Ziefert

*Tangle Town,* by Kurt Cyrus

Pick a day of the week and designate it as "Words Are Wonderful Day." Do a variety of things to celebrate words that day. Read a wonderful word play book during your teacher read-aloud. Share a new word that you have come across in the last week. Find a crossword puzzle your children would enjoy, and let them work in teams to complete it.

Culminate this day by picking "One Wonderful Word." Let students nominate various words that have been highlighted throughout the past week, and let everyone vote for the most wonderful word. Display this word on some kind of trophy chart along with all the other wonderful words chosen in previous weeks.

# *Summary*

As we try to close the achievement gap and make high levels of literacy possible for all children, we must pay renewed attention to the issue of meaning vocabulary. In 1977, Becker identified lack of vocabulary as a crucial factor underlying the failure of many economically disadvantaged students. In 1995, Hart and Risley described a relationship between growing up in poverty and having a restricted vocabulary. In 2001, Biemiller and Slonim cited evidence that lack of vocabulary is a key component underlying school failure for disadvantaged students. More and more of the children in U.S. schools are English language learners. The limited English vocabularies of many of these children is one of the major factors impeding their literacy development.

The size of the average child's meaning vocabulary is difficult to estimate because of the issue of what it means to know a word. Regardless, children's vocabulary growth in the preschool and elementary school years occurs daily and amazes everyone who observes it. Elementary school children acquire approximately 1,000 new root word meanings each year. The staggering number of new word meanings cannot be attributed to direct teaching of those words.

Researchers now agree that most meaning vocabulary is learned indirectly, probably through teacher read-aloud and independent reading. Research supports both the direct teaching of some words and the teaching of vocabulary learning strategies (Baumann, Kame'enui, & Ash, 2003; Blachowicz & Fisher, 2000; Graves & Watts-Taffe, 2002; NRP, 2000). All experts indicate that the number of words directly taught must be kept to a minimum because the words need to be thoroughly taught and students need to meet them in a number of different contexts across some span of time. The need for children to actively encounter the words in different contexts over an extended period of time led the NRP to recommend choosing many of the words for direct teaching from content-area subjects. In addition to the direct teaching of a limited number of useful, frequently occurring words, research supports teaching children word-learning strategies, including using context and morphemic clues to determine word meanings and learning to use dictionaries and other word resources.

The activities described in this chapter are designed to teach children some vocabulary directly and to maximize their learning of words from teacher read-aloud and their own independent reading. In addition, children will learn how context and morphemes give them clues to words and how to use dictionaries to clarify the meanings of words. Equally important, in vocabulary-rich classrooms, children learn how to assess their own vocabulary knowledge and develop a sense of word wonder that will propel them to continue to develop vivid, vital, and valuable vocabularies.

# Developing Thoughtful Comprehenders

A myth about children who have difficulty with reading comprehension is that they "just can't think!" In reality, everybody thinks all the time, and some struggling readers who must take care of themselves (and often younger brothers and sisters) are especially good thinkers and problem solvers. If children can "predict" that the ball game will be canceled when they see the sky darkening up and can "conclude" that the coach is mad about something when he walks in with a scowl on his face, then they can and do engage in higher-level thinking processes. The real problem is not that they cannot think but that they do not think while they read. Why don't they think while they read?

Some children do not think while they read because they do not really know that they should! Imagine an extreme case of a child who had never been read to and had never heard people talking about what they read. Imagine that this child goes to a school in which beginning reading is taught in a "learn the letters and sounds" and "read the words aloud perfectly" way. This child would learn to read words just as you would read this nonsensical sentence:

He bocked the piffle with a gid daft.

You can read all the "words" correctly, and you can even read with expression, but you get no meaning. In your case, of course, you get no meaning because there is no meaning there to get.

For children who have limited literacy experience and who are taught to read in a rigid, phonics-first method with texts that make little sense (*Nan can fan a man*), the real danger is that they will not learn that thinking is the goal. The goal, to them, is sounding out all the words, which is what they try to do. Ask them what reading is, and they are apt to look at you as if you are a complete fool and tell you that reading is saying all the words right! The ability to decode is critical, but when we overemphasize accurate word pronunciation and only provide beginning reading materials in which all the words are "decodable," we can create readers who not only misread the purpose of reading but also do not comprehend the story.

Some struggling readers are unaware that they should be thinking while they are reading, and many have inadequate background knowledge for understanding the books and curriculum materials in their schools. Read the next two sentences and think about the implications for your teaching:

> Current models do not allow expectancy-based processing to influence feature extraction from words. Indeed, most current models largely restrict expectancy-based processing and hypothesis-testing mechanisms to the postlexical level. (Stanovich, 1991, p. 419)

You are probably wondering why we would waste book space (and your time) on these two nonsensical sentences. In reality, these sentences are not nonsensical. They actually have meaning, and if you are a research psychologist, you can think and talk intelligently about them! For most of us, however, we can say these words, but we cannot really read them because we are unable to think as we say them. Background knowledge, which includes topically related vocabulary, is one of the major determinants of reading comprehension.

In addition to specific knowledge about the topic, knowledge about the type of text about to be read is called up as well. When a reader begins to read a story or a novel, a whole set of expectations based on other stories that have been heard or read are called up.

The reader does not know who the characters are but does expect to find characters. The reader also knows that the story is set in a particular time and place (setting) and that goals will be achieved or problems will be resolved. In short, the reader has a story structure in her or his head that allows her or him to fit what is read into an overall organization.

Imagine that you are going to read a *Consumer Guide* article on the newest car models. Again, you do not know what specific information you will learn, but you do have expectations about the type of information and how it will be related. You expect to find charts comparing the cars on different features and to find judgments about which cars appear to be the best buys.

Now imagine that you are about to read a travel magazine article about North Carolina. You have never been there and do not know anyone who has, so you do not know too many specifics. However, you do have expectations about what you will learn and about how that information will be organized. You expect to learn some facts about the history of North Carolina, along with some descriptions of historical regions and locations in the state. You also expect to find information about places tourists like to visit, such as the coast and the mountains. You would not be surprised to find a summary of the cultural and sporting events that are unique to North Carolina. Information about the climate and the best times to visit different parts of the state, as well as some information on how to get there and places to stay, would also be expected. As you begin to read, you may create a mental outline or web, which helps you understand and organize topic and subtopic information.

The different ways in which various reading materials are organized are referred to as text structures and genres. To comprehend what we are reading, we must be familiar with the way in which the information is organized. The fact that most children can understand and remember stories much better than informational text is probably because they have listened to and have read many more stories and thus know what to expect and how to organize the story information. If we want to create readers who think about what they read, we must help them become familiar with a variety of ways that authors organize ideas in their writing.

Even with a clear understanding that reading is primarily thinking, sufficient background knowledge, and a familiarity with the kind of text structure being read, you cannot think about what you read unless you can identify a majority of the words. Try to make sense of this next sentence, in which all words of three of more syllables have been replaced by blanks:

The _____ _____ fresh ideas for action and _____ new
_____ that will help the _____ _____ and the _____
meet the challenge of _____ adult and _____ _____
worldwide.

Now read the same sentence but put the words *conference, provided, generated, partner-ships, literacy, community, association, promoting, adolescent,* and *literacy* in the blanks. To learn to think while you read, you must

1. Be able to identify almost all the words
2. Have sufficient background knowledge that you call up and try to connect to the new information
3. Be familiar with the type of text and be able to see how the author has organized the ideas
4. Have a mindset that reading is thinking and know how to apply your thinking in comprehension strategies

## Comprehension Strategies

The different kinds of thinking that we do as we read are referred to as *comprehension strategies.* Because thinking is complex and happens inside your mind, little agreement exists concerning exactly what or how many strategies there are. Many teachers use a local or state curriculum guide to determine which strategies are deemed critical in their school or grade level. Teacher's manuals also provide teachers with lists and suggestions for teaching important comprehension strategies.

In considering which strategies to focus on, the teacher considers both the demands of the text that children are about to read and the needs and abilities of the children. Readers need to use some strategies on almost all texts, including

- Calling up and connecting relevant background knowledge
- Predicting what will be learned and what will happen
- Making mental pictures, or "seeing it in your mind"
- Self-monitoring and self-correction
- Using fix-up strategies such as rereading, pictures, and asking for help when you cannot make sense of what you read
- Determining the most important ideas and events and seeing how they are related
- Drawing conclusions and inferences based on what is read
- Deciding "what you think": Did you like it? Did you agree? Was it funny? Could it really happen?
- Comparing and contrasting what you read to what you already know
- Summarizing what has been read

In addition to these "generic" strategies that we use regardless of what we are reading, particular texts cause us to use other strategies as well. These strategies are too numerous to list completely, but a few examples include

- Understanding figurative language and using it to build clear images
- Following the plot of a story and figuring out what happened to whom and why
- Determining character traits and deciding why certain characters behave as they do
- Extracting information from charts, graphs, maps, and other visuals
- Determining the objectivity or bias of an author

In planning a comprehension lesson, we decide which thinking strategies will help students make sense of the text they are reading today and be better—more strategic—readers when they are reading on their own. Most comprehension lessons involve some kind of modeling, demonstrating, explaining, and/or brainstorming before students begin to read and some follow-up after reading. If the text is particularly difficult, the teacher may give additional support during the reading.

Many different, engaging, and research-supported ways can be used to carry out comprehension lessons. There are three compelling reasons to use a large variety of types of comprehension lessons. First, comprehension is primarily thinking, and thinking involves many complex processes, so no one type of comprehension lesson can teach all the different kinds of thinking. Second, comprehension of story text and informational text require different kinds of mental organizing. Third, children differ on all kinds of dimensions, including the types of comprehension lessons that engage their attention and help them learn how to think while reading.

We organize our comprehension lessons into four categories: literate conversations, think-alouds, informational text lessons, and story text lessons. We hope you find opportunities throughout the year to use some of each type as you teach your curriculum and teach your students to think their way through all kinds of text.

## *Literate Conversations*

Asking students questions after reading may provide teachers with a quick assessment of student understanding, but traditional question and answer sessions do not offer much in the way of improving students' understanding of texts they have read. When students engage in conversations about what they have read, their understanding improves (Fall, Webb, & Cudowsky, 2000). Effective classrooms provide a balance of question and answer sessions and conversation about the texts students read (Allington & Johnston, 2001). So how do you get good conversations going in your classroom?

A good first step is to modify the questions you do ask so that you are asking more open-ended questions. *Open-ended questions* are those that can have multiple correct responses. For instance, after reading you might ask:

> Is there anything you want to know more about?
>
> Is there anything you are wondering about?
>
> Does this story/book remind you of anything else you have read?
>
> What did you think about . . . ?
>
> Has anything like this ever happened to you?
>
> What was happening in this part of the story/book?
>
> Were you surprised by anything in this story/book?
>
> Did anyone in the story remind you of someone you know?

Each of these open-ended questions allows for a range of responses, all potentially correct. Such questions serve to begin a conversation about the material read. In many respects the goal is to create the kind of conversation that adults typically engage in when discussing something they have read. Adults do not interrogate each other. They do not ask each other the types of questions that teachers typically have asked. Instead, they discuss, they converse. The goal is to share understandings and through this to gain an even better understanding of the material read.

One way to think about creating classroom conversations is provided by Keene and Zimmerman (1997). The framework they provide focuses on helping children think about three types of connections:

- Text to self (Do any of you have a pet that is creating problems like the one in the story?)
- Text to text (What other book have we read where a child was brave?)
- Text to world (Has anyone ever ridden on a subway? Tell us what it was like.)

It is just these kinds of connections that good readers make as they actively read a story or book. It is these kinds of connections we make as we discuss something we have read with someone else.

Some students find responding to open-ended questions easier than others do. Some find it easier to make connections to a story. We need to help all students develop and refine their ability to engage in literate conversations. Initially, a teacher might simply begin to model such responses after a read-aloud activity. In other words, after a read-aloud the teacher might say, "This story reminds me of *The Little Engine That Could* because the boy in the story just wouldn't give up." Of course, in this case, the children must be familiar with the book *The Little Engine That Could* before the connection can make any sense. The teacher might then discuss a personal incident of persistence and ask the children to make the same connections. Such demonstrations are designed to help all children learn to engage in literate conversations.

In some cases, especially with older students lacking experience talking about what they have read, it may help for the teacher to model and then to provide a minute or so for kids to jot their responses into a notebook. After a minute or two, the teacher can initiate the conversation by calling on kids to tell what they wrote. This "quickwrite" procedure provides a bit of thinking time for all kids as well as an interlude for those students who need a short time to generate a connection.

Although whole-class discussions are useful, increasing evidence shows that literature circles offer even greater benefits for improving comprehension. The typical literature group has three to seven members, all reading the same text on a common schedule. The texts that each group is reading may reflect a selected theme (families), genre (biography), or curricular topic (the Civil War). Day and her colleagues note that the smaller groups involved in literature circles better promote discussion because smaller groups foster the following (Day, Spiegel, McLellan, & Brown, 2002):

- Greater opportunities for children to talk
- More natural context for conversation
- Ability to find texts all members of the group can and want to read
- Greater choice of books for all students
- Cooperation and collaboration
- Personal responsibility

In addition to giving students multiple opportunities to develop thoughtful literacy by engaging them in conversations guided by higher-level questions—the kind of conversations adults often hold about their own reading—teachers can initiate two other types of activities to help children engage in conversations. In Questioning The Author, the teacher and children raise questions that they would like to discuss with the author. In the "Oprah Winfrey" strategy, teachers and children become interviewers—like Oprah—and the people they interview are characters from books.

## Questioning The Author (QTA)

When we read, we do not just understand what the author is saying; rather, we figure out what the author means. This might sound like a picky distinction, but helping struggling readers put this distinction into practice as they read makes a huge difference in their comprehension. If you have ever taught students who read a passage carefully and then tell you they cannot answer the questions because the passage "didn't say!" you have experienced the reason students need to have their reading guided by a constructivist strategy such as Questioning The Author (QTA).

The word *constructivist* is currently in danger of death from overuse, but it names a simple and powerful concept. When we read, we use the author's words to construct meaning. The meaning is more than what the author has written. Authors cannot tell us everything. They assume we know some things that we will connect to what they are telling us. They assume that we will form some opinions based on what they tell us and what we know. Our initial assertion—that reading, at its heart, is thinking—means that reading is a constructive activity. Readers construct meaning by understanding what the author is saying, figuring out what the author means, and forming opinions based on the author's meaning and what the reader already knows. This description of QTA is based on an excellent book by Isabel Beck, Margaret McKeown, Rebecca Hamilton, and Linda Kucan (1997) that gives detailed examples of QTA lessons, suggestions for planning and implementing QTA lessons, and results of QTA use in several classrooms. If our brief description intrigues you, we highly recommend you read their practical and clearly written book.

Several things distinguish QTAs from other comprehension-fostering formats. The most important differences to us are that the instruction goes on not before students read or after students read but as students are reading, and that the teacher's job is to pose queries that foster meaning construction, not to ask questions to assess if that meaning construction took place. To plan a QTA lesson, the teacher carefully reads the text and decides (1) what the important ideas are and what problems students might have figuring out these ideas; (2) how much of the text to read in each segment before stopping for discussion; and (3) what queries to pose that might help students construct meaning from the text. A clear distinction is made between *queries,* which lead the students to think and construct, and *questions,* which usually assess whether students have been able to think or construct. The teacher's job in a QTA is to pose the types of queries that can help students use what they know and figure out what the author means. Having decided on important ideas and segmented the texts, teachers plan both initiating and follow-up queries. The following example is adapted from Beck and her colleagues as students are about to read and construct meaning for a social studies passage on how Pennsylvania was formed.

The teacher and students are seated in a circle or horseshoe shape so that they can all see each other. They all have copies of the book open. For this lesson, the teacher has decided that the first segment to be read is just the first sentence. She tells the students to read the first sentence to themselves:

The shape of the land in North America has changed over millions of years. (p. 51)

And then she poses a typical initiating query:

> "What do you think the author is telling us?"

Initially, students may want to respond by just reading the sentence aloud, but the teacher responds by saying,

> "Yes, that's what the author says, but what is the author trying to tell us?"

The teacher then poses the follow-up query designed to help them connect information learned in previous chapters.

> "What have we already learned about the different kinds of shapes land can have that we need to connect here?"

The second segment contained many sentences and ended the paragraph. It is important to note that the segment division is not determined by paragraphs but by ideas. (Sometimes you want to make sure students are constructing meaning from a single sentence, and sometimes you may want them to read several paragraphs.) The teacher segments the text so that students stop at points where they need to construct important meanings. This segment developed the concept of glaciers, and after students had read this segment to themselves, the teacher initiated the query:

> "What is the author telling us about snow and ice and glaciers?"

The QTA continued with the teacher telling the students how much to read and posing both initiating and follow-up queries until students had worked together to construct meaning for this difficult and complex text.

Children often think that authors are infallible! In doing QTAs with children, teachers point out that authors are not perfect! Sometimes they do not write clearly. Sometimes they assume we know lots of things that we do not know, and they leave out important facts. Children who engage in regular QTAs learn that when you are reading, you try to figure out what the author means—not just remember what the author says. They are then on the path to constructing meaning and active reading.

## The "Oprah Winfrey" Strategy

This is another technique that fosters involvement. To use it, several children must be reading the same book. You play the role of Oprah (initially) and interview them about their lives and roles. For instance, after reading *Anastasia at Your Service* (Lois Lowry), assign students the roles of Anastasia, Mrs. Bellingham, and her granddaughter, Daphne. (We could also add Mr. and Mrs. Krupnik, Sam, and perhaps the surgeon or the maid.) Now, just like Oprah, invite the students to appear on your "show." Arrange chairs alongside your desk, facing the rest of the class. Seat the "guests," with Anastasia next to your desk, and welcome them.

Begin with broad questions: "Tell me a bit about yourself, Anastasia." "What seemed to be the problem?" Then move to other characters for verification: "Do you agree with her, Daphne?" "What else would you add, Mrs. Bellingham?" You might even turn to the audience for questions, especially if some members have not read the book. Basically, like Oprah, you let your guests tell their stories. Ideally, readers transform themselves into the characters, taking on mannerisms and speech patterns that seem appropriate. You may want to model this transformation yourself by letting a student take Oprah's role while you become Mrs. Bellingham or another character. This activity can be brief (3–5 minutes is all most guests get on talk shows!) and takes little time to set up after the initial exposure. The activity provokes thought about the characters and their motives, attitudes, and personalities. In short, it is a wonderfully innovative way to foster thinking and involvement while reading.

### Literate Conversations

Literate conversations mimic the conversations real readers in the real world have about real books they really want to talk about! The key to good literate conversations is to help the children learn to ask and think about the questions real readers ask each other and friends who have read the book. Real readers do not interrogate each other about books. They do not ask "Who were the main characters?" or "What year did the conflict break out?" Rather, they ask and converse about the big ideas—and particularly their reactions to and feelings about what they have read. To promote literate conversations in your room:

1. Conduct your discussions with your readers as conversations—not interrogations. Ask them higher-level questions that require reactions and responses—questions to which you don't know the answer because there isn't one right answer.

2. Model for your students the types of connections readers make—text to self, text to text, and text to world. Your comments and questions should regularly focus them on these connections so they get in the habit of making these connections when reading on their own.

3. Arrange for students to have literate conversations in small groups. Literature circles is one format for organizing small-group conversations.

4. For variety, use Questioning The Author and the "Oprah Winfrey" strategy to increase the number of people with whom your students can have conversations.

## *Think-Alouds*

Think-alouds are a way of modeling or "making public" the thinking that goes on inside your head as you read. To explain think-alouds to young children, we tell them that two voices are really speaking as we read. The voice you can usually hear is your voice reading the words but inside your brain is another voice telling you what it thinks about the material you are reading. We use think-alouds to demonstrate for children how we think as we read.

Thinking as we read takes many different forms. We make connections—to ourselves, to other things we have read, and to the world. Teachers use sentence starters to think aloud about the connections they are making:

> "This reminds me of . . ."
> "I remember something like this happened to me when . . ."
> "I read another book where the character . . ."
> "This is like in our school when . . ."
> "Our country doesn't have that holiday, but we have . . ."

We predict and anticipate what will happen next:

> "I wonder if . . ."
> "I wonder who . . ."
> "I think I know what is coming next . . ."
> "He will be in trouble if . . ."
> "I think we will learn how . . ."

We summarize what has happened so far and draw conclusions not stated by the author:

> "The most important thing I've learned so far is . . ."
> "It didn't say why she did that, but I bet . . ."
> "I know he must be feeling . . ."
> "So far in our story . . ."
> "So far I have learned that . . ."

We question what is happening and monitor our own comprehension:

> "I wonder what it means when . . ."
> "I don't understand . . ."
> "It didn't make sense when . . ."
> "I'm going to reread that because it didn't make sense that . . ."

We imagine and infer and enter into the world the author is describing:

> "Even though it isn't in the picture, I can see the . . ."
> "Mmm, I can almost taste the . . ."
> "That sent chills down my spine when it said . . ."
> "For a minute I thought I could smell . . ."
> "I could hear the . . ."
> "I can imagine what it is like to . . ."
> "I can picture the . . ."

We make evaluations and form opinions and decide how we think and feel about things:

> "My favorite part in this chapter was . . ."
> "I really liked how the author . . ."
> "What I don't like about this part is . . ."
> "It was really interesting to learn that . . ."
> "I am going to try this out when I . . ."
> "I wish I could . . ."
> "If I were her, I would . . ."

**RECOMMENDED resources**

Two wonderful sources just full of examples to teach children to think and share their thinking are *Strategies That Work* (Harvey & Goudvis, 2000) and *Mosaic of Thought* (Keene & Zimmerman, 1997).

Teachers use think-alouds in a variety of ways, but the most efficient and effective use of time is probably to read and think-aloud the first quarter or third of a selection the children are about to read. In addition to hearing you think your way through the text, children get introduced to the selection, including characters, setting, type of writing, and important vocabulary. After listening to you think-aloud your way through the first part of the text, children collaborate in small groups, finish reading the selection, and share the thinking voices inside their brains.

The following example of a think-aloud is based on the first part of *Missing: One Stuffed Rabbit* by Maryann Cocca-Leffler (1999). The think-aloud begins with the cover of the book. The teacher reads aloud the title, *Missing: One Stuffed Rabbit,* and looks at the picture saying something like what follows:

> "This is an intriguing illustration on the cover of the book. A girl is reading from a notebook labeled Coco, and she looks very unhappy. The two children listening look surprised and upset. Because the title of the book is *Missing: One Stuffed Rabbit,* I bet the unhappy and surprised looks have something to do with the lost rabbit. I wonder who lost the rabbit and who the rabbit is and what the notebook has to do with it?"

The teacher turns the page and thinks aloud about the picture on the first two pages:

> "I see a teacher holding a stuffed rabbit and reaching into a fishbowl to pull
> out a slip of paper. The children in the class are all watching her. They all
> look happy and excited. In the other picture is the stuffed rabbit and the
> notebook labeled Coco. I bet Coco is the name of the stuffed rabbit."

The teacher then reads aloud the text on these two pages, which explains that Coco is indeed the stuffed rabbit and that the teacher is pulling the name of one student who will get to take Coco home for the weekend. She pulls out a slip of paper and the lucky winner is Janine!

> "I bet Janine is the girl in the front in the glasses. She is also the unhappy-
> looking girl on the cover, reading from Coco's notebook."

The teacher turns the page and thinks aloud first about the pictures.

> "There's Janine looking very happy and hugging Coco and his notebook."

The teacher reads the text aloud and we discover that the notebook is Coco's diary. Each student gets to take Coco home overnight and write Coco's thoughts about the adventure in his diary.

> "I used to have a diary when I was younger. I wrote in it every night."

The next two pages have some of the diary entries written by children who have already taken Coco home and helped him write about his adventures. We learn that Coco fell off the monkey bars while playing with Danny, went to Matthew's soccer game and cheered when Matthew got a goal, and went to the skating rink with Christina. The teacher makes these comments:

> "I love how the author showed the diary pages. I can tell different children
> wrote them because you can see the different handwriting. I can't wait to see
> what Janine does with Coco and what she writes in the diary."

The pictures and text on the next two pages show Janine and Coco being picked up by Janine's mom and heading home. The following pages show Janine and Coco having a good time together. Janine reads Coco a bedtime story and rides him on the back of her bike. After reading these four pages, the teacher comments:

> "They seem to be having such a good time. But I am worried. I remember
> how unhappy Janine looked on the cover, and the title of the book says a
> stuffed rabbit is missing. I hope Janine is not going to let Coco get lost!"

The next four pages show the family shopping at the mall and, sure enough, as they are having lunch, Janine realizes that she cannot find Coco! She thought she put him in one of the bags, but he is not there. Coco is missing!

> "I can just imagine how Janine must be feeling. She looks like she is going to cry, and I feel like crying too! How could she have lost him? Will she find him? What will the other kids—and the teacher!—say if she doesn't find him?"

At this point in the book, the teacher stops reading and thinking aloud and turns to the children, asking them what they think will happen. They share some ideas and the looks on their faces show how concerned they are. The teacher quickly reviews the pages read and reminds the children that she shared her thinking with them about the pictures and the words. Next the teacher forms small groups of three or four students and tells them that it is now their turn to read and share their thinking. She chooses one group to model for the others what they will do, and, with the teacher's help, this group shares their thinking about the pictures and words on the next two-page spread. The teacher tells them that when they read, little voices inside their heads tell them what their brains are thinking. When we do think-alouds, we let that little voice talk out loud so that we can hear what all our different brains are thinking.

The groups form and begin reading. The teacher circulates to the various groups and helps them to take turns and to verbalize their thinking. She also writes down some of the

### Think-Alouds

The goal of comprehension instruction is that children learn how to think as they read on their own. Think-alouds help children see what good comprehenders do. If you do your think-aloud based on the first part of the selection they are going to read, you give them a "jumpstart" into the selection. To do think-alouds,

1. Choose a selection that truly causes you to think.

2. Decide how much of that selection you will read aloud.

3. Look at the pictures and read the selection before you do the think-aloud. Look for places where you actually use different thinking strategies—connect, predict, conclude, self-monitor, image, infer, evaluate. Think about how you will explain your thinking to your children. Mark these places with sticky notes and cryptic comments if this helps you remember.

4. Do the think-aloud as the "invisible" children watch and listen. Comment on pictures first; then read the text, stopping at appropriate places, and comment.

5. Provide a structure for your children to get in tune with and share their thinking as they finish the selection or read another selection.

most interesting thoughts to share with the whole group when they reconvene after reading to react to the story and "debrief" their thinking.

Many teachers, when they first hear about think-alouds, are afraid to do them because they do not know exactly what they are supposed to think! We hope that our example shows you that your brain is thinking as you read, and if you tune into that thinking and learn how to communicate your thinking to children, think-alouds are not difficult to do. It is important to read the selection and plan what you are going to say as you think aloud. Many teachers find it helpful to attach sticky notes with reminders to the appropriate pages. We try to use as many different ways of expressing our thinking as we can and try to have it match as closely as we can the thinking actually engendered by the text.

Although we normally invite participation, it is important not to let the children "chime in" as you are thinking. If you use the procedure of beginning the selection with your think-aloud and finishing the selection with the children sharing their think-alouds, they are usually willing to let you have your turn! Some teachers tell the children that they are to pretend to be invisible while the teacher is reading and thinking. They get to hear the teacher thinking, but they are invisible and should not let the teacher know they are there! You want to signal the children when you are reading and when you are thinking. Many teachers look at the book when they are reading and then look away from the book—perhaps up toward the ceiling—when they are thinking. Other teachers use a different voice to signal their thinking. They read in their "reading voice" and think in their "thinking voice."

### Bookmarks, Sticky Notes, and Highlighters

When we adults read, we often mark things we want to go back to with bookmarks, sticky notes, or highlighters. Children read more purposefully when they use one of these markers.

1. Decide if students would read more purposefully if they could mark the text with a bookmark, sticky note, or highlighter.

2. Give them the bookmarks, sticky notes, or highlighters, and make sure they know what they are going to mark with them.

3. Limit the number of bookmarks or sticky notes each child can have. It is better for a child to use the ones he or she has and wish for more than to wonder how he or she will ever use them all!

4. Use the bookmarks, sticky notes, or highlighted text to guide the after-reading activity.

5. Once children know how to use bookmarks, sticky notes, and highlighters to note things they want to contribute to the after-reading activity, consider having them use these markers occasionally for words they have successfully decoded or that have stumped them.

## *Informational Text Lessons*

Most readers are much better at comprehending stories than at comprehending informational text. Elementary children need a better balance between information and story text in their reading instruction. Because many children have difficulty with informational text, they approach reading informational text with less confidence and enthusiasm. Children who engage in KWL lessons and who learn how to construct a variety of graphic organizers become better and more enthusiastic readers of informational text.

## KWL

One of the most flexible and popular ways of guiding students' thinking is KWL (Carr & Ogle, 1987; Ogle, 1986). The letters stand for what we *know,* what we *want* to find out, and what we have *learned.* This strategy works especially well with informational text.

Imagine that the teacher is planning to have the class read about Washington, D.C. The teacher might begin the lesson by finding Washington, D.C., on a map and asking which students have been there. A chart such as the following would then be started:

| Washington, D.C. | | |
|---|---|---|
| **What we know** | **What we want to find out** | **What we learned** |
| | | |

The students brainstorm what they know about Washington, D.C., and the teacher writes their responses in the first column. When the children have brainstormed all their prior knowledge, the chart might look like this:

| Washington, D.C. | | |
|---|---|---|
| **What we know** | **What we want to find out** | **What we learned** |
| Capitol<br>White House<br>president lives there<br>lots of drugs<br>azaleas in spring<br>cold in winter<br>near Virginia<br>near Maryland | | |

Next, the teacher would direct the students' attention to the second column and ask them what they would like to find out about Washington, D.C. Their questions would be listed in the second column:

| Washington, D.C. | | |
|---|---|---|
| **What we know** | **What we want to find out** | **What we learned** |
| Capitol<br>White House<br>president lives there<br>lots of drugs<br>azaleas in spring<br>cold in winter<br>near Virginia<br>near Maryland | How old is it?<br>How big is the White House?<br>What else is in D.C.?<br>Where is the FBI?<br>What kind of government does D.C. have?<br>Why do so many people visit D.C.?<br>How many people live there?<br>What do the people do who aren't in the government? | |

Once the questions are listed, students read to find out which questions were answered and to find other interesting "tidbits" they think are important. After reading, the teacher begins by seeing which questions were answered and then leads the students to add other interesting facts. This information is recorded in the third column. All members of the class are encouraged to contribute to this group task, and no one looks back at the book until all initial responses are shared. Disputed or unclear information is marked with question marks.

When all the initial recalls are recorded, children go back to the text to clarify, prove, or fill in gaps. The teacher encourages the children to read the relevant part aloud and helps them explain their thinking. When the information on the chart is complete and accurate, the teacher points out how much was learned and how efficiently the chart helped to record it. Inevitably, some questions are not answered in the reading. A natural follow-up to this lesson is to help the children use additional resources to locate the answers to these questions.

## Graphic Organizers

Another popular format for a guided reading lesson involves having the students construct or fill in a graphic organizer. Webs are the most commonly used graphic organizer at the elementary level. They are wonderful ways of helping readers organize information when their reading gives lots of topic and subtopic information.

Imagine that your class is going to read an informational selection about birds. You might begin a web to help them organize the information they will be learning:

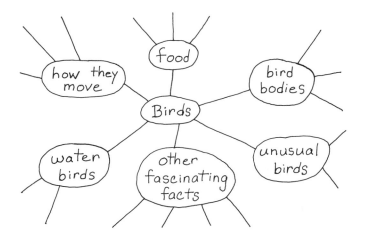

As you set up each spoke of the web, you can discuss with the children what they might expect to find out: "What are some ways you already know that birds move? What do you already know that birds eat? What body parts do birds have?" Children then read to find out more about birds. After reading, the children reconvene and complete the web.

Webs are efficient graphic organizers for topic and subtopic information, but many other ways to show types of relationships exist. A feature matrix helps children organize information about several members of a category when they are reading. Imagine that the children are reading a selection that compares and contrasts many different types of birds. This information would be better organized in a feature matrix than in a web. Here is what that feature matrix skeleton might look like:

| Birds | | | | | | |
|---|---|---|---|---|---|---|
| | fly | swim | build nests | lay eggs | have feathers | molt |
| robins | | | | | | |
| whippoorwills | | | | | | |
| penguins | | | | | | |
| ostriches | | | | | | |
| | | | | | | |

Before reading, the teacher and the children talk about the birds listed and about the categories. Children make predictions based on what they know about which birds fly, swim, build nests, and so forth. The teacher then points out the four blank lines and tells the children that in addition to robins, whippoorwills, penguins, and ostriches, four other birds will be described. The children read to decide which features apply to the four birds listed on the matrix and to the four other birds they will add after reading. Once the children have read the selection, the teacher leads them to fill in a yes/no or a +/– for each feature.

Feature matrices are infinitely adaptable. *Semantic Feature Analysis: Classroom Applications* (Pittelman, Heinlich, Berglund, & French, 1991) is full of wonderful variations. One suggestion adapted from this book (p. 40) that we particularly like includes having kindergartners classify fruit using happy and sad faces, like this:

| | Fruits | | | | | | | |
|---|---|---|---|---|---|---|---|---|
| | **round** | **has peel** | **bumpy peel** | **orange** | **red** | **eat peel** | **smooth peel** | **eat seeds** |
| orange | ☺ | ☺ | ☺ | ☺ | ☹ | | | |
| apple | | | | | | | | |
| banana | | | | | | | | |

We also like their suggestion that some things do not break down into neat yes/no classifications. They suggest that feature matrices can become much more useful if you consider using an A/S/N (Always/Sometimes/Never) classification scheme.

Data charts are another way of helping children organize information that compares and contrasts members of the same category. Rather than indicate whether something has a feature, children fill in particular facts. Here is a data chart used in a science classroom:

| Planets in Our Solar System | | | |
|---|---|---|---|
| **Name** | **Size (1 = biggest)** | **Distance from sun** | **Earth days in year** |
| Earth | 6 | 92,960,000 mi. | 365 |
| Mars | | | |
| | 1 | | |
| | | 3,660,000,000 mi. | |
| | | | 60,188 |
| | | | |
| | | | |
| | | | |
| | | | |

●  ......................................................................................................................

**130**

To begin this chart, you might partially fill in the chart for the students, talking as you write about what is needed in each column:

> "Earth is the sixth-largest planet. Its mean distance from the sun is 92,960,000 miles. The year is the number of days it takes a planet to orbit the sun, and the earth year is 365 days."

Now you point to the second row and have students explain what they will try to put in each column about Mars. For the third row, help them notice that because you put a 1 in the size column, this planet has to be the biggest planet. The fourth row must be completed for the planet that is 3,660,000,000 miles from the sun. The planet that takes 60,188 earth days to orbit the sun goes in the fifth row. The remaining four rows are filled in with the remaining four planets.

Webs, feature matrices, and data charts are the most popular graphic organizers used in elementary classrooms, but they are not the only possibilities. Here are two other types of graphic organizers:

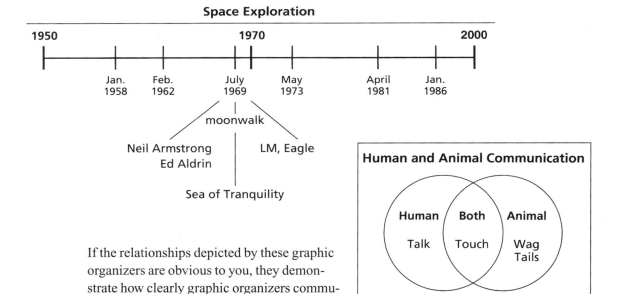

If the relationships depicted by these graphic organizers are obvious to you, they demonstrate how clearly graphic organizers communicate and how well they help students see important relationships in the information they are reading. In the Venn diagram, which we and children like to call a "double bubble," children compare and contrast how animals and humans communicate. The time line is an excellent device to use when order or sequence is important, for instance, in history, historical fiction, and biography. Students fill in the important space exploration events that occurred on each date and a few details about each. A variation is to give students a time line of events and have them fill in the dates.

## Informational Text Lessons

### KWL

KWLs help children connect what they know to new information. They are particularly helpful to children as ways to guide their reading with science and social studies texts.

1. Before beginning the chart, lead a general discussion of children's experiences with the topic. By letting children discuss these experiences (e.g., "My uncle lives in Washington"; "We're going to go to Washington some summer"), you avoid having to put these "experiences" in the known column.

2. After the discussion of experiences, ask children what they know about the topic and list these in the K (known) column. If children disagree about a fact, put it in the W (want) column with a question mark. ("Washington is in Virginia." "No, it's not!" Record this exchange as *Is Washington in Virginia?*)

3. When you have all the known facts recorded, show them what they will read and ask them to come up with questions they think that text will answer. If their questions are too specific, help make them broader.

4. After reading, begin with the questions first and add answers to the L (learned) column. Then add other important facts.

5. If they are going to continue reading about the topic for another day, ask them whether what they have read so far has helped them think of more questions that the remaining part might answer. Add these to the W column.

## Graphic Organizers

Graphic organizers help children organize and summarize information. They are often used as the prewriting activity for focused-writing lessons.

1. Look at the text and decide how the information can best be organized. If the text structure is topic/subtopic/details, you probably want a web or data chart. If the text compares two or more things, a feature matrix, data chart, or Venn diagram works well. Time lines help children focus on sequence.

2. Let the children see you construct the graphic organizer skeleton. Use this time to discuss the words you are putting there because these are apt to be key vocabulary from the selection.

3. Have students read to find information to add to the organizer.

4. Complete the organizer together.

5. You may want to do a focused-writing lesson in which you help children use the information from the organizer to write summaries or reports.

6. When children understand and can complete the various organizers, have them preview the text and decide what kind of graphic organizer works best, and have them help you construct the skeleton.

## *Story Text Lessons*

Children understand stories better than informational text, but they still need instruction in story comprehension. Story maps, the Beach Ball, and "doing" the book are three activities that help children understand story structure and develop independent story comprehension strategies.

### Story Maps

Story maps are a popular and effective device to guide students' thinking when they are about to read a story. There are many different ways of creating story maps, but all help children follow the story by drawing their attention to the elements that all good stories share. Stories have characters and happen in a particular place and time, which we call the *setting*. In most stories, the characters have some goal they want to achieve or some problem that they need to resolve. The events in the story lead to some kind of solution or resolution. Sometimes stories have implicit morals or themes from which we hope children learn. The story map here is based on a model created by Isabel Beck (Macon, Bewell, & Vogt, 1991). Here is the story map filled in for *The Three Little Pigs*:

| Story Map |
|---|
| **Main Characters:** |
| **Setting (Time and Place):** |
| **Problem or Goals:** |
| **Event 1:** |
| **Event 2:** |
| **Event 3:** |
| **Event 4:** |
| **Event 5:** |
| **Solution:** |
| **Story Theme or Moral:** |

| Story Map |
|---|
| **Main Characters:** Mother Pig, three little pigs, Big Bad Wolf |
| **Setting (Time and Place):** Woods, make-believe time and place |
| **Problem or Goals:** Pigs wanted to be independent and have own house. |
| **Event 1:** Mother Pig sends three little pigs out to build their own houses. |
| **Event 2:** First little pig gets some straw and builds a straw house. Big Bad Wolf blows the straw house down. |
| **Event 3:** Second little pig gets some sticks and builds a stick house. Big Bad Wolf blows the stick house down. |
| **Event 4:** Third little pig gets some bricks and builds a brick house. Big Bad Wolf cannot blow the brick house down. |
| **Event 5:** Big Bad Wolf runs off into woods (or gets scalded coming down the chimney, depending on how violent the version of the story is). |
| **Solution:** Pigs live happily ever after in strong brick house. |
| **Story Theme or Moral:** Hard work pays off in the end! |

When using story maps to develop a sense of story structure, the teacher must work through several of them with the children first. For readers who are having trouble comprehending, it is not enough to distribute story maps for them to complete. After reading a story, display the story map on an overhead projector. As you complete the map, think aloud so the thought processes you use are audible to children. Teacher think-alouds provide the expert model many struggling readers need to develop the thinking strategies that underlie good comprehension.

Once children understand the elements and how to fill them in, they can complete story maps in small groups and then independently. It is important to have children read the whole story before completing the map and to help children see that the map is a device that helps them determine and remember important elements in a story.

The Beach Ball is not a story map activity, but using this format helps children develop all the important concepts and can lead to the development of written story maps. The beach ball has a question written in black permanent marker on each colored stripe of the ball:

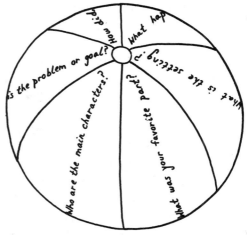

Who are the main characters?
What is the setting?
What happened in the beginning?
What happened in the middle?
How did it end?
What was your favorite part?

After reading a story, the teacher and children form a large circle. The teacher begins by tossing the ball to one of the students. The first student to catch the ball can answer any question on the ball. The teacher then tosses the ball to another student. The next student can add to the answer given by the first student or answer another question. The ball continues to be thrown to various students until all the questions have been thoroughly answered. Some questions, such as, *What happened in the story?* and *What was your favorite part?* have many different answers.

The Beach Ball is a favorite comprehension follow-up for children in all the classrooms in which it is used, including intermediate-aged children. In classrooms in which the teacher regularly uses the Beach Ball to follow up story reading, children begin, as they read, to anticipate the answers they will give to the questions on various stripes. These children have developed a clear sense of story structure, and their comprehension (and memory) increases as they organize what they are reading and thinking around those colored beach ball stripes.

## Doing the Book

Children who "do" the book become more active readers. Characters, setting, events, dialogue, conclusions, mood, and motivation become important, and children pay more attention to them when they have to interpret and re-create the drama. Doing the book greatly increases story comprehension. Doing the book can take a variety of forms, from performing a play, to acting out stories, to concentrating on re-creating a single scene of a play.

*Do a Play*   Children of all ages enjoy being in a play, and some wonderful stories for children are already written in play format. Recasting a story as a play can also be a powerful reading/writing activity, especially if the children create the script and stage directions from the original story. Not only do children write, but they also must read carefully to transform ideas into action.

Most basal readers have at least one or two plays. Children's magazines, including *My Weekly Reader* and *Sprint* (Scholastic), often contain plays for children to do. *Take Part Starters, Grades 2–3* and *Take Part Plays, Grades 3–6* (Sundance) are play versions of favorite tales and stories, including *The Clever Little Tailor, Robin Hood, Treasure Island,* and many others. Curriculum Associates publishes some plays, including fables, fairy tales, and others, in the Primary Reader's Theatre series. Rigby produces a set of PM readers called *Traditional Tales and Plays*. These include familiar tales—*Robin Hood, The City Mouse and the Country Mouse, The Three Billy Goats Gruff,* and more—at different reading levels. The first part of each book tells the tale and the last pages of each book contain a play version of that tale—ready to be read and done.

When having struggling readers do a play, remember that doing repeated readings is a powerful way to help children develop oral reading fluency and an understanding of characters. It helps their reading more if they do not memorize lines but rather read and reread their parts until they can read them fluently.

Some teachers do not do plays because there are not enough parts for everyone, or they do not know what to do with the children who are not in the play while the players are preparing. Most children enjoy preparing to do the play and then watching each other do it. If you have a play that requires seven actors and you have 24 children in your class, divide your class into three groups of eight, putting a director and seven actors in each group. Let all three groups prepare and practice the play simultaneously. Then let each "cast" put on the play for the others.

If you have children do plays, remember that the purpose of this activity is for them to become more active readers, to visualize characters, to do some repeated readings, and to transfer their enjoyment from being in the play to reading. "Doing it" is what matters, not how professionally it is done. Props, costumes, and scenery should be nonexistent or very simple. Take the "process attitude" that the play helps develop important reading processes, not a "product attitude," and you will develop a new appreciation for plays.

Some teachers find that letting children make a simple mask to hide behind (using a paper plate and Popsicle stick) can help diminish shyness and stage fright. This is especially true for ESL children, who are less self-conscious about their language ability when they have something to hide behind!

***Act Out a Story***    Acting out a story is another way to help children think actively and to visualize as they read. The best stories for acting out are the ones that you can visualize as plays. Everyone should have a part, as they did in the plays. Many teachers write down on little slips of paper the characters' names along with a number to designate acting cast:

| | | |
|---|---|---|
| First Little Pig 1 | First Little Pig 2 | First Little Pig 3 |
| Second Little Pig 1 | Second Little Pig 2 | Second Little Pig 3 |
| Third Little Pig 1 | Third Little Pig 2 | Third Little Pig 3 |
| Mama Pig 1 | Mama Pig 2 | Mama Pig 3 |
| Wolf 1 | Wolf 2 | Wolf 3 |
| Man with sticks 1 | Man with sticks 2 | Man with sticks 3 |
| Man with straw 1 | Man with straw 2 | Man with straw 3 |
| Man with bricks 1 | Man with bricks 2 | Man with bricks 3 |
| Director 1 | Director 2 | Director 3 |

The teacher then explains to the students that three groups will be acting out the story and that they will all have parts. She explains what the parts are and that she will pass out the slips after the story is read to determine what parts they will have. She encourages them to think about what all the characters do and feel because they might end up with any of the parts.

After the story is read and discussed, the teacher hands a slip of paper to each child randomly. (This procedure of letting chance determine who gets starring roles and who gets bit parts is readily accepted by the children and easier on the teacher, who will not have to try to decide who should and could do what. Sometimes, the most unlikely children are cast into starring roles and astonish everyone—including themselves!) The children then form three groups and whoever gets the director slip in each group helps them act out the story. The teacher circulates among the groups, giving help and encouragement as needed. After 10–15 minutes of practice, each group performs their act while the other groups watch. Just as they enjoy doing a play, children generally enjoy acting out a story. Teachers who keep their focus on the process children go through as they read and act out stories enjoy this activity and do not worry too much about the product. Acting out stories is designed to turn the children into avid readers, not accomplished actors.

*Make a Scene!*   Whereas full-blown plays may seem a bit daunting for children and teachers (and take time), a variation on this theme is often easier for children and can be quickly incorporated into many lessons. Rather than acting out a full play, have the children re-create a single scene. Scenes can be done by individuals, pairs, or small groups. They simply require the readers to select a scene, transform it into a script (not necessarily written out), briefly rehearse it, and then present it—no props, no costumes, just reenactment! The scene can be as short as a single exchange between characters or can even be a single sentence delivered in the appropriate voice. Children who can literally become Richard Best from *The Beast in Ms. Rooney's Room* (Pat Reilly Giff) or the sassy little brother in *Island of the Blue Dolphins* (Scott O'Dell) demonstrate an understanding of the story and the characters.

## Summary

Comprehension—thinking about and responding to what you are reading—is "what it's all about!" Comprehension is the reason and prime motivator for engaging in reading. What comprehension is, how comprehension occurs, and how comprehension should be taught have driven hundreds of research studies in the last 30 years. Reading comprehension—and how to teach it—is probably the area of literacy about which we have the most knowledge and the most consensus. It is also probably the area that gets the least attention in the classroom.

In 1979, Delores Durkin published a landmark study demonstrating that little, if any, reading comprehension instruction happened in most classrooms and that the little bit that did occur was "mentioning," rather than teaching. Having children answer comprehension questions to assess their reading comprehension was the activity most often seen. This finding shocked the reading community and probably propelled much of the reading comprehension research that has occurred since. Unfortunately, more recent research (Beck, McKeown, & Gromoll, 1989; Pressley & Wharton-McDonald, 1998) has indicated that reading comprehension instruction is still rare in most elementary classrooms.

Duke and Pearson (2002) have reviewed the research and identified six research-based comprehension strategies:

1. Prediction/activation of prior knowledge
2. Think-alouds (which includes monitoring comprehension)
3. Using text structure
4. Using/constructing visual representations (including graphic organizers and imagery)
5. Summarization
6. Answering questions/questioning

### Story Text Lessons

The goal of comprehension instruction is to have children learn how to independently do the strategies as they read on their own. How to follow story structure and how to summarize stories are two important comprehension strategies. Story maps, the Beach Ball, and "doing" the book activities all help children develop story structure and learn to summarize and conclude.

**Story Maps**

1. Decide on a story map skeleton that will work best for your children.
2. Talk about the slots on the map, and make sure children understand their purpose for reading.
3. Have them read in whatever format you choose.
4. Have them complete the story map as a class or in small groups.

**The Beach Ball**

1. Decide on the questions and write them with permanent marker on a beach ball.
2. Talk about the questions on the stripes, and make sure children understand their purpose for reading.
3. Have them read in whatever format you choose.
4. Toss the beach ball and answer the questions.

**Doing the Book**

1. Include plays in your reading repertoire. Have children read and do plays, and have older children turn stories into plays by writing scripts for them.
2. Have children do some impromptu acting out of stories—no scripts, props, or costumes needed. Children should read the story several times, parts should be chosen, and children should "do their thing." To include more children, have several casts performing the same story.
3. Have children act out scenes from longer stories. Let small groups pick different scenes; then have each group perform in order of scenes. All the groups not in a particular scene become the audience for that scene.

Duke and Pearson have also summarized what good readers do. Good readers:

- Are active and have clear goals in mind
- Preview text before reading, make predictions, and read selectively to meet their goals
- Construct, revise, and question the meanings they are making as they read

- Try to determine the meanings of unfamiliar words and concepts
- Draw from, compare, and integrate their prior knowledge with what they are reading
- Monitor their understanding and make adjustments as needed
- Think about the author of the text and evaluate the text's quality and value
- Read different kinds of text differently, paying attention to characters and settings when reading narratives and constructing and revising summaries in their minds when reading expository text

Previous chapters of this book have described a variety of activities for building word identification, fluency, and vocabulary, all of which are required for comprehension. This chapter describes a variety of activities designed to teach children how to think as they read and how different kinds of text require different kinds of thinking.

# chapter 7

# Developing
## Ready, Willing, and Able Writers

I magine that you come upon someone sitting pen in hand or with fingertips poised over a keyboard, staring at a blank page or blank screen. When you ask "What are you doing?" the person will often respond "I'm *thinking!*" Continue to observe, and you will see the person move into the writing phase eventually, but this writing will not be continuous. There will be constant pauses. If you are rude enough to interrupt during one of these pauses to ask "What are you doing?" the writer will again probably respond "I'm *thinking!!!*"

Eventually, the writer will finish the writing, or rather the first draft of the writing. The writer may put the writing away for awhile or may ask someone to "Take a look at this and tell me what you think." Later, the writer will return to writing to revise and edit. Words will be changed, and paragraphs will be added, moved, or deleted. Again, the writer will pause from time to time during this after-writing phase. If you ask what the writer is doing during this phase, you will get the familiar response "*I'm thinking!*"

We offer this common scenario as proof that the essence of writing is thinking and that even the most naive writer knows this basic truth. Because writing is thinking and because learning requires thinking, students who write as they learn will think more and thus will learn more.

In addition to the fact that writing is thinking, writing is hard! It is complex. There are many things to think about at the same time. There are such big issues as:

- What do I want to say?
- How can I say it so that people will believe it?
- How can I say it so that people will want to read it?

In addition to these big issues, there are a host of smaller but still important issues:

- How can I begin my writing in a way that sets up my ideas and grabs the reader's attention?
- Which words will best communicate these feelings and thoughts?
- What examples can I use?
- Do I need to clarify here or include more details?
- How can I end it?
- Now, I have to think of a good title!

As if these grand and less grand issues are not enough, there are also a number of small details to worry about. Sometimes, these are taken care of during the after-writing phase, but often writers think about them as they write. Some examples include:

- I wonder if this sentence should begin a new paragraph?
- Do I capitalize the word *state* when it refers to North Carolina?
- How do you spell *Beijing?*
- Does the comma go inside or outside the quotation mark?

We do not offer this sampling of a few of the "balls" writers have to keep in the air as they perform the difficult "juggling" act of writing in order to discourage you. Rather, we offer them to convince you that students need instruction, guidance, support, encouragement, and acceptance if they are going to be willing and able participants in writing.

To become the very best writers, children need two kinds of writing instruction. First, all children need to engage in some writing in which they select the topics and decide how they will write about those topics. Most teachers organize their classrooms in a Writer's Workshop fashion to provide children with opportunities to write on their self-selected topics and help them learn how to write, edit, revise, and publish. Children also need to know how to write particular forms and genres, including letters, reports, descriptions, and narratives. To teach children how to write these forms and genres, teachers carry out focused writing lessons, in which all the children are writing on the same topic and/or in the same form or genre. The remainder of this chapter will describe ways successful teachers organize their instruction to do both Writer's Workshop and focused writing.

## Starting the Year with Writer's Workshop

*Writer's Workshop* (Calkins, 1994; Graves, 1995) is the term most commonly used to describe the process of children choosing their own topics and then writing, revising, editing, and publishing. In Writer's Workshop, teachers try to simulate as closely as possible the atmosphere in which real writers write and to help children see themselves as "real authors."

Writer's Workshop usually begins with a minilesson during which the teacher writes. Next, the children write. As the children write, the teacher conferences with children, coaching them on how to revise, edit, and publish. Writer's Workshop usually concludes with an Author's Chair, in which children read their writing and get responses from the other "writers" in the room.

Writer's Workshop can be done in all elementary grades. While the basic principles are the same, the focus for the minilessons and the amount of revising, editing, and publishing will be quite different. Regardless of grade, if you want to create willing writers, you must begin the year by emphasizing meaning and deemphasizing mechanics and perfection. Because writing is hard and complex, children who see the goal as producing a certain number of perfect sentences will not write willingly and will only do the bare minimum needed to get by.

You want to establish in the first few weeks of school that the most important thing about writing in your classroom is what the writing says—not how perfectly it says it. So, most teachers begin the year by doing minilessons in which they focus on how you choose a topic and how you write the first draft as best you can. After the 8- to 10-minute minilesson in which the teacher writes what he or she "wants to tell," the teacher asks the students to write "what they want to tell." As the children write, the teacher circulates and encourages them by making comments such as:

- "Did you really go to camp this summer? I went to camp every summer when I was your age. I think I will write about that one day soon."
- "Oh, you are interested in dinosaurs. I bet lots of the other students like dinosaurs, too. They will be eager to hear what you have learned about them."
- "I watched that TV program last night, too. It is one of my favorites."

When a child is found having written one sentence and an "I wrote a sentence. That's all I know" attitude, the teacher barrages him or her with questions related to the sentence. If the child has written

I got a dog.

The teacher might ask:

- "Do you really have a dog?"
- "Is your dog a male or a female?"
- "What's her name?"
- "Is she a big dog or a little dog?"
- "What color is she?"
- "Do you take her for walks?"
- "Where did you get her?"

Let the child tell you the answers to these questions, but do not wait for the child to write them. Just leave the child by saying something like:

"You sure have a lot to tell about your dog. I bet other kids will wish they had thought of writing about their dog."

As you circulate, remember the message you are trying to convey to your students:

"The most important thing about writing in this classroom is *what* you write. I am eager to hear what you are telling me in your writing. Your classmates will also want to know about what you are writing."

Inevitably, as you circulate, someone will ask you to spell a word. How you respond to this request will determine the progress you can make in your Writer's Workshop for the rest of the year. If you spell words for children now, you will never be able to pull away from them and use the time while they are writing to hold conferences with individuals and groups about their writing. Consider the following responses to the "Can you spell *dinosaurs?*" request:

- "Yes, I can now, but I couldn't when I was your age and I don't want you to get too hung up on spelling when you're doing your first-draft writing. I want you to write what you want to tell—not just what you can spell. Let's stretch out *dinosaurs* together and put down the letters you think are there. You will be able to read it, and that's all that matters now. In a few weeks, we will start publishing some of our best pieces, and then we will fix up all the spelling to make them easy for everyone to read."
- "I'm sorry, but teachers aren't allowed to spell words for kids when they are first drafting, but I can help you stretch it out."
- "Dinosaurs—hmmm . . . I think I see the word *dinosaurs* in the title of that book over there."

However you accomplish it, make it clear to your students that you will help them stretch out words and point them to places in the room where they can find words, but on first draft, you cannot spell words for them. At the same time, assure them that if these are pieces they choose to publish, you will enthusiastically help them "fix" the spelling.

Limit the amount of time your children write for the first few weeks of school. Eventually, you want them writing for 15 to 20 minutes, but it is better to start with a smaller amount of time, perhaps 6 or 7 minutes, so that they do not get too discouraged and bored if they are not particularly good writers. Some teachers use a timer and increase the amount of time in one-minute intervals as the children become more able to sustain their writing.

When the time is up, circle your students and ask who wants to read or tell about what they have written. You may want to single out some of the children with affirming statements such as:

- "Carl has a big dog named Tammy. Carl, tell us more about Tammy."
- "Josh is a big dinosaur fan. He hasn't finished writing all he wants to about dinosaurs, but perhaps he will tell or read what he has written so far."
- "Terry and I like the same TV show. I wonder how many of you like it, too."

Be sure you let your students read or tell what they are writing. Some children do not like to write but they almost all like to "tell," and soon they will be writing eagerly so they have a chance to tell during the sharing time. Again, keep in mind your goal for getting Writer's Workshop off to a successful start. You want the children to look forward to the writing time (which does not last too long!), and you want them to see writing as a way of telling about themselves and the things that are important to them.

Make a point of asking some children to share writing they have not finished yet. Tell them that during Writer's Workshop, we do not usually start writing a new piece every day

### Tips for Starting the Year with Writer's Workshop

**The Minilesson**

Begin each Writer's Workshop with a 8- to 10-minute minilesson in which you write and the children watch. Include minilessons in which you model and think aloud about how you decide what to write about:

- "When I saw Todd writing about his dog Tammy, it reminded me of the dog I had when I was your age. I think I will write about Serena today."

- "Yesterday, we were reading about the pioneers. I am going to write what I think it would have been like to be a pioneer."

- "In science yesterday, we did that experiment with balloons. I think I will write about that."

- "Just before the busses came yesterday, we had that huge thunderstorm. My cat hates thunderstorms. I will tell you what my cat does when it thunders."

- "I went to the football game at Wake this weekend. I saw several of you there. I am going to tell you what I liked best about the game."

- "I have a lot of things I want to tell you about, and I think I might forget some of them. Today, instead of writing about one thing, I am going to make a list of all the things I might want to write about." (Refer to your "Things I want to write about list" over the next several weeks before you write, and add to it when you get good ideas from what your students are writing. Encourage your students to make their own lists, if they want to.)

Also model for students what you do about spelling:

- Look up at your word wall periodically, and model how using it helps you spell.

    "*Because* is a tricky word. I am glad we have *because* on the word wall."

    "*Brook* rhymes with *look,* so I can use *look* to help me spell it."

    "*Talked* is our word wall word *talk* with *ed* on the end."

- Use other print in the room to spell words.

    "I can spell *Wednesday* by looking at the calendar."

    "*Hydrogen* is on our science board."

    "*Pioneers* is on the cover of the book I read to you this morning."

- Stop and stretch out a word, putting down the letters you think are there.

    "I can spell *ridiculous* now, but let me show you how I would have stretched it out when I was your age."

Model for students how you add on to a piece you have not finished:

    "Yesterday, I was telling you about my two grandmothers, and I only had time to describe my mama's mother. I am going to reread what I wrote yesterday to get my thoughts back and then tell you about my dad's mother."

"This is the third day I have been writing about our trip to the museum. I am going to reread what I wrote the first two days and hope I can finish this up today."

**The Students Write**

- Increase the time gradually, starting with a small amount of time that all your students can handle. Many teachers use a timer and increase writing one minute at a time.

- Circulate and encourage your writers by "oohing" and "aahing" about their topics. Ask questions of students who have just written a sentence or two. Comment regularly that they have "given you a good idea for your writing." If you are keeping a writing topics list, go right over and add it to your list.

- Do not spell words for students but help them stretch them out and use the word wall and other print in the room to find words.

**The Students Share**

- Let volunteers tell or read what they have written.

- Spotlight some children who you interacted with as they were writing.

- Let children ask questions of their fellow writers.

- Point out children who are going to be "adding on" to their writing tomorrow.

- Encourage children to find writing topics during this sharing by asking questions of one another. How many of them have dogs? Grandmas? Went to the football game? Ever broke a bone?

- Add topics to your writing list, inspired by what they share.

and that sometimes it takes a week or more to finish a piece if we are writing about something we really care about or know a lot about.

## Adding Editing to Writer's Workshop

Early in the year at every grade level, we have three major writing goals we want to accomplish. We want children to get in the habit of writing each day and coming up with their own topics, based on what they want to tell. We want them to learn to use the supports for spelling words displayed in the classroom and how to stretch out the big words they need to be able to write what they really want to tell. Finally, we want them to realize that they can take several days to write a piece if they have a lot to tell and that in order to add on, they need to read what they have already written.

When all the children are writing willingly, if not well, we begin teaching them how to edit their writing. Here is how one teacher described the first editing lesson.

## One Teacher's First Editing Lesson

As I was getting ready to write one morning, I told the children that soon we would be publishing some of their best pieces and before we did so, we needed to know how to edit. I then wrote on a sheet of chartpaper:

**Our Editor's Checklist**
1. Do all my sentences make sense?

I explained to the children that one thing editors always read for is to make sure that all the sentences make sense. Sometimes, writers leave out words or forget to finish a sentence, and then the sentences don't make sense. I told the children, "Each day, after I write my piece, you can be my editors and help me decide if all my sentences make sense." I then wrote a piece and purposely left out a word. The children who were, as always, reading along as I wrote and often anticipating my next word, noticed my mistake immediately. When I finished writing, I said, "Now let's read my piece together and see if all my sentences make sense. Give me a 'thumbs up' if my sentence makes sense." The children and I read one sentence at a time, and when we got to the sentence where I had left out a word, we decided that the sentence didn't make sense because my mind had gotten ahead of my marker and I had left out a word. I wrote the word in with a different-colored marker and thanked the children for their good editing help.

After I wrote my piece, the children all went off to do their own writing. As they wrote, I circulated around and encouraged them. When the writing time was up, I pointed to the editor's checklist we had just begun. I said, "Be your own editor now. Read your paper and give yourself a 'thumbs up' if each sentence make sense. If you didn't finish a sentence or left a word out, take your red pen and fix it." I watched as the children did their best to see if their sentences made sense and noticed a few children writing things with their red pens.

Every day after that when I wrote, I left a word out or didn't finish a sentence. The children delighted in being my editor and helping me make all my sentences make sense. Every day when their writing time was up, I pointed to the checklist and they read their own sentences for sense. They didn't find every problem, but they all knew what they were trying to do. After a few weeks, I noticed almost everyone picking up their red pens and glancing up at the checklist as soon as the writing time ended.

Now, I am about to add to our checklist a second thing to read for. I will add:

2. Do all my sentences have ending punc? . ? !

From now on, the children will read my sentences and give me a thumbs up if the sentence makes sense and another thumbs up if it has punc (more fun to say than punctuation!) at the end. When the writing time is up, I will remind them that we are at the "two thumbs up" editing stage and that they should read their sentences for sense and ending punc just as they read mine.

## Build Your Editor's Checklist Gradually

The items on the editor's checklist are not just there so that children will find them as they edit. The goal is that by focusing on the checklist items as children check the teacher's writing at the end of minilessons and by asking children to do a quick self-edit of their own writing each day, children will begin to incorporate these conventions as they write their first drafts. The question of when to add another item to the checklist can be answered by observing the first-draft writing of the children. If most of the children, most of the time apply the current checklist items as they write their first drafts, it is time to add another item to the checklist.

Developing your editor's checklist is easy if you let your observations of children's first-draft writing determine what is added, the order in which it is added, and the speed with which it is added. Here are two examples of editors' checklists—one for primary and one for intermediate grades:

### Our Editor's Checklist

1. Do all my sentences make sense?
2. Do all my sentences have ending punc? . ? !
3. Do all my sentences start with caps?
4. Are the words I need to check for spelling circled?
5. Do names and places start with caps?
6. Do all my sentences stay on topic?

### Editor's Checklist

1. Do all the sentences make sense and stay on topic?
2. Do all the sentences start with caps and end with correct punc?
3. Are the words I need to check for spelling circled?
4. Do names and places start with caps?
5. Do words in series have commas?
6. Do quotes have correct punc?
7. Is there a beginning, middle, and end?

## Teach Children to Peer Edit

Once children have had lots of experience editing the teacher's piece each day, they can learn how to edit with partners. You can introduce this by choosing a child to be your partner and role-playing how he or she will help with the editing. Here is how one teacher taught students to peer edit.

## A Peer-Editing Minilesson

I began by telling the class that we would soon start choosing some of their best pieces to publish and that once they had each chosen a piece, the first step in the publishing process would be to choose a friend to help with the editing:

> "Boys and girls, we are going to pretend today that I am one of the children in the class. I am getting ready to publish a piece, and I will choose one of you to be my editor."

I then wrote a short piece on the overhead as the children watched. Instead of letting the whole class read the sentences aloud and do "thumbs up or down," as we had been doing, I chose one child to be my editor. As the children watched, my editor and I read my sentences one at a time and edited for the four things on the checklist. As we read each sentence, we decided if it made sense and had ending punc and a beginning cap. Next, we looked at the words and decided if any of them needed to be circled because we thought they were not spelled correctly. Here is what the edited piece looked like:

---

### Polar Bears

Polar bears live in the arctic which is one of the coldest places on earth. Polar bears are the largest bears. Male polar bears are about 10 feet tall and weigh 1,100 pounds. Polar bears are fast movers. they can run 30 miles and hour. They are good swimmers to. Polar bears have a lot of fur and blubber to keep them warm. Polar bears eat fish, seals, careboo berrys and seaweed. People used to hunt polar bears. they wer almost extink. only about 5,000 were left. Now, there are laws against hunting polar bears and there are about 40,000. Polar bears are amazeing animals.

---

**Editing Tips: Editing = Fixing Up Your Writing**

- Don't begin editing instruction until children are writing willingly and fluently—if not well!

- Observe children's writing to decide what mechanics and conventions they can do automatically and what things you need to focus on.

- Begin your checklist with one item. Let children edit your piece for this one item every day.

- When the writing time is up, ask students to be their own editors. Praise their efforts at self-editing, but don't expect them to find everything.

- Add a second item when most of your students do the first item correctly most of the time. In your minilesson, sometimes make a #1 error and sometimes a #2 error—but do not make more than two errors total.

- Continue to add items gradually, using the same procedure to teach each.

- Teach children to peer edit by role-playing, and then provide supervised practice as children peer edit with writers of similar ability.

For the next several days, I followed the procedure of choosing a child to be my editor and doing the partner editing in front of the children. When I thought most of the children understood how to help each other edit for the items on the checklist, I partnered them up, assigning partners of similar writing ability to work together, and had each pair choose a piece and edit it together. I had several more peer-editing practice sessions before turning the children loose to peer edit without my supervision.

## Adding Conferencing, Publishing, and Author's Chair to Writer's Workshop

Once your students understand how to edit and partner edit with an editing checklist and are writing for about 15 minutes each day, you may want to add conferencing, publishing, and Author's Chair to your Writer's Workshop. (You should not wait until the editor's checklist is complete before beginning this, and, in fact, you will continue to add items to the checklist and do minilessons on editing conventions all year long.) Once publishing begins, you will spend the writing time holding conferences with your students to help them get their pieces ready to publish. (Since you cannot be in two places at one time, this means you will no longer be circulating and encouraging children as they write. Do not begin publishing until almost all your children are coming up with topics, spelling words for themselves, and writing willingly.)

## Author's Chair

When children begin publishing, most teachers also shift from the informal circle sharing that has been happening each day at the end of Writer's Workshop to an Author's Chair format. One-fifth of the children share each day. They can share anything they have written since their last day in the Author's Chair. Of course, when they have published a piece, they share that. But they can also share a first draft or work in progress. After each child has read, he or she calls on class members to tell things they liked about the piece. The author can also ask if anyone has any questions and elicit suggestions to make the piece better. During Author's Chair, the focus is exclusively on the message that the author is trying to convey.

Here again, the role of the teacher model is extremely important. Useful comments include:

- "I love the way you described . . ."
- "I wondered why the character . . ."
- "Your ending really surprised me."
- "The way you began your story was . . ."
- "I could just imagine . . ."
- "I thought this was a true story until . . ."

When assigning children to days to share in the Author's Chair, you may want to assign one of your best and one of your most struggling writers to each day. The best writer might get an extra minute to share because these children often write longer, more complex pieces. Take a minute before Author's Chair each day to check in with your struggling writer and make sure he or she has selected something to share and is prepared to read or tell about it.

## Publishing

Most elementary teachers tell children that they can choose a piece to publish when they have written three or four good pieces. They then teach minilessons in which they role-play and model picking a piece to publish and taking it through the process. Once the publishing part of the Writer's Workshop has been established, students will be at all different stages of the writing process each day. Those children who have just finished publishing a piece will be working to produce new first drafts, from which they will pick another one to publish. Other children will have picked a piece to publish and will be editing it with a friend. Some children will be having a writing conference with the teacher. Other children will have had their piece "fixed" during the writing conference and will be busy copying, typing, and illustrated the final product.

Since you can't help everyone publish at the same time, you may want to begin the publishing cycle by choosing five or six children to publish. This will allow you to conference with these children while the others continue to produce first drafts. Once these children are at the copying/typing/illustrating stage, you can continue to choose more children to begin the publishing process, until all the children have published something. From then on, the children will know that they can choose a piece to publish when they have three or four good first drafts. Many teachers post a chart like this to remind children of the publishing steps:

### Steps for Publishing

1. Pick one piece that you want to publish.
2. Choose a friend and partner edit your piece for the items on the checklist.
3. Sign up for a writing conference.
4. Work with your teacher in a conference to edit your piece and fix spelling.
5. Copy or type your piece, making all the corrections.
6. Illustrate your piece.

## The Writing Conference

Be sure that each child edits his or her piece with a friend before signing up for a writing conference with you. Children, of course, are at all different stages of understanding about writing and how to edit, and some children are much better editors than others. Peer editing for the checklist items is not perfect, and teachers often find things that should have been changed that weren't (and things that were changed that shouldn't have been!). But all the children become much better at being editors of their friends' and their own pieces as the year goes on, and they get in the habit of trying to edit before they publish and not leaving all the work for the teacher.

Once the piece has been edited with a friend using the checklist, you should hold an individual conference with the writer and "fix everything!" Your goal in publishing is to have children experience the pride of being authors and having others read and enjoy their writing. This cannot happen if the final piece is not very readable. So, before the child goes to the publishing phase, sit down with that child and do a final edit. Fix the spellings of words, add punctuation and capitalization, clarify sentences that do not make sense, delete sentences that are totally off the topic, and do whatever else is necessary to help the child produce a "masterpiece" of writing!

You can generally do the "fixing" right on the first draft with a different-colored pen. To make this easier, have children write all their first drafts using every other line on the paper, leaving blank lines so that editing can occur. (Of course, some children can't write on every other line but most can, and they all get better at it as the year goes on.) If something must be inserted and cannot be clearly written between the lines, write it on a separate piece of paper and mark the insertion point. You should read each edited piece with each child, making sure he or she can read anything inserted and stopping to notice where to add punctuation, change spelling, and make other needed changes.

*Adding Conferencing, Publishing, and Author's Chair to Writer's Workshop*

## Give Additional Support to Your Most Struggling Writers

In almost every class, once you begin publishing, you will have a few children whose writing is really not "editable." (Like love, this is hard to describe, but you will recognize it when you see it!) You generally should not begin publishing until almost all of the children are writing something "readable"—but *almost all* leaves a few children whose pieces are collections of letters with a few recognizable words and very few spaces to help you decipher the letters from the words! You might say these children just aren't ready to publish and that they should just continue producing first drafts. But the message that these children will get from being left out of the publishing process is that, just as they thought, they "can't write!" Once you begin publishing, you need to include everyone in the process. Some children will publish more pieces that others. Some authors are more prolific than others! The goal is not for everyone to have the same number—and in fact, you should not count or let the children count. The goal is, however, for everyone to feel like a real writer because he or she has some published pieces.

Once you begin publishing, you should work with the most avid writers first, but when most of them have pieces published and are on their second rounds of first drafts, you should gather together the children who have not yet published anything. Help them choose pieces they want to publish and then give them the option of reading or telling what they want to say. Then, sit down individually with these children and help them construct their pieces. Get them to tell you again what they want to say. As they tell, write down their sentences by hand and later type them on the computer. Once these children's sentences have been written, read the sentences with them several times to make sure they know what they have said. Then cut the sentences apart and have the children illustrate each one and put them all together into a book! They are now—like everyone else—real published authors, and they will approach their second round of first-draft writing with renewed vigor—confident that they, too, can write!

It is important to note here that you would not give this kind of support to the majority of your children. If more than a few children need this support, you are not ready to pull away during their writing time to hold individual and group conferences. But when most are ready and only a few lag behind, the solution just suggested works quite well in most classrooms and provides a big boost for your most struggling writers.

## Keep the Publishing Process Simple

There are lots of different ways to publish, but you don't want to spend too much of your or your children's time in publishing. In many schools, groups of volunteers create "skeleton books" for children to publish in. They cut sheets of paper in half and staple or bind them with bright-colored covers into books of varying numbers of pages. Children write (or type on the computer and cut and tape) their sentences on the pages and add illustrations. In other classrooms, the pieces are typed on the computer (by the child or an assistant/volunteer) and then illustrated (with drawings, photos, or clip art) and displayed on the writing bulletin board. A variety of computer programs are available that make the publishing process a much less onerous one and help children produce professional-looking products. In many classrooms, children publish their pieces on the Web to share with the larger world.

## *Adding Revising to Writer's Workshop*

*Editing* is "fixing" your writing. *Revising* is making good writing *even* better! Because learning to do some basic editing is easier than learning to revise, teachers usually teach some editing rules first and then teach some revising strategies. Once teachers have taught some revising strategies, students should revise their pieces before editing.

When you begin to teach revising, make sure your students understand that revising is not editing. *Editing* is fixing mistakes and making the writing easy for the reader to read. *Revising* is making the writing better—clearer—more interesting—more dramatic—more informative—more persuasive—more *something!* When a writer revises, he or she looks again at the writing, asking the essential question:

*"How can I make this piece of writing even better?"*

The word *even* in this question is important because it implies that the writing is good but can be even better! Using the phrase *even better* is part of the attitude adjustment your students may need to make about revising, since many children think that having to revise means you did not do a good job to begin with. All successful writers revise, and all published writing has been revised. Writers always begin revising by rereading their writing and thinking about how to make it *even* better.

Once they decide what is needed to make the meaning or clarity of their drafts even better, writers make revisions by adding, replacing, removing, or reordering. Sometimes they add, replace, or remove one or more words or phrases, or they reorder some words or phrases. Sometimes they add, replace, or remove one or more sentences or paragraphs, or they reorder some sentences or paragraphs. Occasionally, a writer will add, replace, or remove an entire section or reorder the sections that are already there.

To teach children how to revise, use the general revising strategies of adding, replacing, removing, and reordering. This will help them to understand what revision is, how it is different from editing, and where to begin when trying to make the meaning of a selected piece of writing even better. Just as with editing, begin your revising instruction by teaching minilessons in which you pick one of your writing pieces and revise it in front of the children. Of course, you want students to learn how to help each other revise, so you should teach some minilessons in which you pick a student to be your revising helper and role-play this peer revising as the other students watch. Next, partner up children with writers of similar ability and give them practice peer revising.

Just as with editing, revising strategies should be taught gradually, and when students have been taught only one strategy, they should be expected to use only that one strategy. As you conference with children getting ready to publish, remind them of the revising strategies you have taught so far and give them help implementing some of these with their pieces.

### Steps for Publishing (Including Revising)

1. Pick one piece that you want to publish.
2. Choose a friend to help you revise.
3. Check your revisions with your teacher.
4. Partner edit your piece for the items on the checklist.
5. Have a conference with your teacher to do a final edit.
6. Copy or type your piece, making all the corrections.
7. Illustrate your piece.

# Teaching the Adding Revising Strategy

*Adding* is the easiest revising strategy, and thus you should teach it first. Children are often impressed with themselves when they write a long piece—and adding makes it even longer and more impressive! By starting with the adding revising strategy, you can capitalize on your students' affinity for length and start them off with a positive attitude toward revising.

If you have been writing on every other line on your transparency or chart and having your children write on every other line on their first drafts, adding just a word, phrase, or sentence will be easy to do and seen right on the original piece. Adding longer sections will require cutting and taping—something children love to do and that also helps improve their attitude toward revising.

For your first adding minilesson, you may want to show students how adding words or phrases can make the meanings of their pieces clearer and more vivid. To do this mini-lesson, choose a piece you wrote recently and pull it back out. Tell the children that you want to revise this piece before you publish it and that one way to revise is to add a few words or phrases that will make the meaning clearer. Use a bright-colored marker and show children how you put a ^ and then insert a word or phrase in the empty line above at two or three different places to make what you have written better. Over the next several days, demonstrate adding words or phrases to revise with a few more of your pieces.

When you have done enough minilessons to be sure that most of your children understand how to revise by adding words or phrases, partner them up so that children of relatively equal ability are working together. Ask each pair to choose pieces of their own writing and suggest words or phrases to each other that will make their writing clearer and more vivid. Give them brightly colored pens and christen them "our revising pens." Collect the pens when children have finished revising their two papers and reserve them only for revising. The children will

**Walking My Puppy**

Today, I went ^straight home from school to see my new

puppy. He came up to me and licked my ^whole face.

I ^quickly put his leash on and we went outside. We

saw a ^big, black dog. My puppy ran after the dog. The

dog ran away. Next he ran after a ^tiny squirrel.

The squirrel ran up a ^tall tree. Finally, he saw a

^gray cat. He ran after the cat. My dog ^just wanted to

play with the other animals but they all ^just ran

away.

enjoy using these special pens, and this, too, will have a positive effect on their attitude toward revising.

As the children revise, go around and help the partners who seem to be having trouble adding words and phrases, as you have taught them in your minilessons. As you move around the room, monitoring and helping the partners, be on the lookout for particularly good additions. At the beginning of Author's Chair, take a few minutes and share some of the best revisions you have noticed.

Another way of making writing clearer and more vivid by adding is to add dialogue. Again, take one of your pieces and use it as the first example. (You might want to plan ahead and write a piece with no dialogue but that would be improved by a few exact words so that you have a good example to use.) Tell the children that you want to revise this piece because after you wrote it, you realized that adding some dialogue—the words people or characters actually said—will make it "come alive." Use the same procedure that you used with adding words and phrases, and include a brief explanation of how quotations are punctuated.

Depending on the age and writing levels of your children, you may want to teach them how to revise by adding a missing part. To do this, write a first draft in which you purposely leave out some important information. Bring that piece out on the following day, and explain to the students that you realized you failed to include some very important information. As the students watch, cut your transparency, write the new part on another transparency, and then tape it between the two parts of the original transparency. Students of all ages will be intrigued by this idea that you can cut your writing piece and tape in a missing part. Encourage them to look at their own first drafts and find one that would be "even better" if it had more information. Then turn them loose with scissors and tape!

## Teaching the Replacing Revising Strategy

*Replacing* is another revising strategy all writers use. While the adding strategy makes writing better by making it more elaborate and complete, the replacing strategy makes writing better by improving the quality of what is already there. As with adding, you can replace words or phrases, sentences, or a whole chunk of text. When replacing a small amount of text, use the special revising pens to cross out the text you want to improve and then write the new text clearly above it. When replacing large chunks in order to improve them, use the cut-and-tape procedure.

To prepare for your first replacing minilesson, write a first draft in which you purposely use as many "boring, tired, and common" words as you can. Don't tell the children your intent ahead of time. Just write it as you normally write during a minilesson. When you finish, have the class read it with you, and ask if they can think of any ways you can make your writing even better. Since you have already taught several minilessons on revising by adding, children may suggest some words or phrases for you to add. It is all right to

quickly add a few of the words suggested, but if no one also suggests replacing some of your "overused" words, you will need to suggest it yourself in order to move your minilesson from the adding to the replacing strategy:

> "I notice that I have some common words here that don't create very vivid pictures. *Good*, for example, doesn't even begin to describe how wonderful the cookies were. I think I will cross out *good* and replace it with *scrumptious*."

Continue replacing some of your boring, overused, or inexact words, eliciting suggestions from your students about which words need replacing and what you can replace them with.

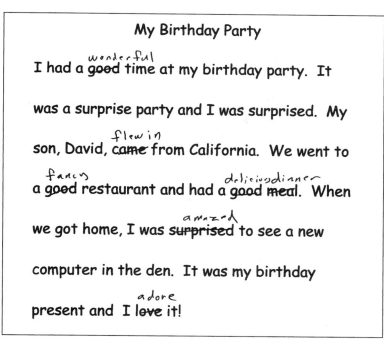

Just as with revising by adding, you probably will need to do several minilessons on replacing words or phrases before asking your students to use this strategy in their own papers. Again, when students try to apply this strategy to their own writing, have them work with partners as you move around helping individuals who are having trouble. Look for good examples of revision to share with everyone afterward.

"Show, don't tell" is a basic guideline for good writing. Unfortunately, many children (and adults!) are not sure what this guideline means. To teach your students what it means, you have to practice what you preach and *show* them how to "Show, don't tell," instead of taking the far easier road of *telling* them to "Show, don't tell!"

To teach children to replace *telling* words with words and sentences that *show,* you can use many of the procedures already described in this chapter. Write pieces in which you purposely tell rather than show, and then revise these pieces in minilessons with the children's help. You can also use paragraphs from the children's favorite authors as examples and rewrite them in minilessons by replacing the showing words with telling words and sentences. After identifying the places where the children wish the writer had shown them rather than told them, read the original and compare the telling version with the showing version. After several minilessons, partner children up and ask them to help each other find examples in their writing where they could make the writing come alive by replacing some of their telling words with showing words and sentences.

> When my Grandpa died, I ~~was sad~~ *moped around for a week.* One day,
>
> my mom asked me to take my Grandpa's dog
>
> for a walk. He ~~was happy to see me~~ *jumped up and wagged his tail when he saw me.* We went
>
> for a long walk and ended up at the river. I
>
> threw sticks into the river and he swam in
>
> after them. When I took him back home,
>
> Grandma ~~was happy~~ *smiled and thanked me.* I took Champ for a walk
>
> every day *and I felt better.* Walking Champ
> *made me feel better and was*
> ~~was fun and~~ something I could do for Grandpa!

Once children understand how to replace boring and telling words with more interesting and showing words, you may want to teach them how to replace whole parts of their pieces. For most children, the first revision they do that replaces a chunk of text is when they make the beginning of that piece noticeably better. Your students need to understand that many authors routinely revise the beginning of a piece because once they have written the middle and ending, they realize what the beginning lacked.

> **Tips for Revising Beginnings and Endings**
>
> **How to Make Your Beginning** *Even Better*
>
> • Include the background knowledge needed to understand the middle and end.
> • If your piece is a story, be sure to describe the setting—time and place.
> • Grab your reader's attention with an interesting question.
> • Start with a real-life example.
>
> **How to Make Your Ending** *Even Better*
>
> • Answer any questions you posed in the beginning.
> • Tie up all the "loose ends."
> • Pose a question for your reader to think about.
> • End with a surprise—but one that fits the rest of your piece.

Any writer can tell you that a good ending is hard to write! Children often solve the problem by stopping when they can't think of anything else to say and writing "The End." Teaching students to revise by replacing the ending will help almost all of them to write better and more interesting endings.

To teach students to revise by changing the ending or beginning, you should once again contrive to write a piece in your minilesson that has a boring or noninformative beginning or ending. For the next day's minilesson, pull out your piece again, and tell your students that after writing the piece, you realized how you needed to begin it—or you thought of a much better ending. Let them watch as you reread your ending or beginning, write a replacement, and then cut and tape the new part to the original piece. (If you are fortunate enough to teach in a classroom in which you can write on the computer and have it projected on the screen, use the "Cut" and "Paste" functions on your computer to show your students how easy it is to replace with the help of a word-processing program!)

## Teaching the Reordering and Removing Revising Strategies

Revising by *reordering* should not be taught until students can revise by adding and revise by replacing. Moreover, children cannot learn to revise by reordering until they have a firm sense of sequence and logical order, which many children do not develop until third grade.

Just as children like to add because it makes their pieces longer, they don't like to remove anything because they worked hard to write it and doing so shortens their pieces. Students are usually more willing to replace something than just remove it. This is the reason that *removing* is the last of the four general revising strategies you should teach.

### RECOMMENDED
## resources

Specific grade-level lessons and ideas for writing can be found in *Writing the Four Blocks Way* (Cunningham, Cunningham, Hall, & Moore, 2005), *Writing Minilessons for Kindergarten* (Hall & Williams, 2003), *Writing Minilessons for First Grade* (Hall, Cunningham, & Boger, 2002), *Writing Minilessons for Second Grade* (Hall, Cunningham, & Smith, 2002), *Writing Minilessons for Third Grade* (Sigmon & Ford, 2002), and *Writing Minilessons for Upper Grades* (Hall, Cunningham, & Arens, 2003).

Often, however, when we finish writing something, we realize that something we included does not really add anything to our writing or distracts the reader from the point we are trying to make. None of us likes to delete the wonderful words we have written, but deleting or removing off-topic and distracting sentences or paragraphs is an essential revising strategy.

When your students are comfortable with revising by adding and replacing, you can teach reordering and removing just as you taught adding and replacing. Write some first drafts in which you purposely arrange things not in their logical sequence or include some extraneous information. Let students watch as you cut and reorder or remove sentences or paragraphs. Send them on a hunt for places in their writing they could make even better by reordering and removing, and provide guided practice with partners in using these strategies.

Revision is not an easy skill to learn, and while you want to teach children to revise and make sure they know how, you shouldn't expect a great deal of revision—particularly from first- and second-graders. The goal of revising should be to have children understand that meaning comes first—that authors often add, delete, or change things to make their writing more interesting, clear, or dramatic and that they should make whatever meaning changes they are going to make before they edit.

### Revising Tips: Making Your Writing *Even Better*

- Look again at your writing. Pick a friend to look with you.
- Use special revising pens or cut and tape.
- Add:   Words that make the writing more vivid or clearer
         Dialogue that makes the writing come alive
         Missing information
- Replace:   Boring words
            Telling with showing
            Beginnings that don't set up your piece or don't grab the reader's attention
            Endings that don't provide closure or are not very engaging
- Remove:   Sentences or paragraphs that don't stay on topic or distract the reader
- Reorder:   Sentences or paragraphs that are not in the right sequence

# *Focused Writing*

During Writer's Workshop, children choose their own topics as well as the type of writing they want to do. They come to think of themselves as writers and develop writing fluency and confidence. You do, however, need to teach children how to write specific forms. In addition to stories, children need to learn how to write short reports, business and friendly letters, and essays. Many children enjoy writing poetry, and many types of poetry do not have to rhyme. In many states, children are tested on their ability to do specific writing—narrative, descriptive, persuasive, and so on—at specific grade levels.

Demonstration is once again the most effective teaching strategy for teaching children specific forms. The following section is a sample focused writing lesson in which children learn to write a friendly letter.

## Modeling and Demonstration

The teacher of this class has a good friend who is teaching in a faraway state. The two teachers talk regularly on the phone and have both been concerned about giving their students "real" reasons to write. One of them remembers having a pen pal whom he never met but with whom he corresponded for years. The two teachers decide that, although this is a rather old-fashioned idea, their children may still enjoy having their own pen pals. The class is indeed excited about the idea; this is their first letter-writing experience. The teacher wants them to learn the correct form for a letter while also making sure the emphasis is kept on the message to be communicated.

The lesson begins with the teacher asking the children what they would like to know about their pen pals. He records these questions on large index cards:

How old is he/she?

What is school like there?

Do they have a gym?

Do they have a lot of homework?

Do they have a soccer team?

Does he/she play soccer?

Does he/she play baseball? football? other sports?

Is it cold all the time?

Does everybody ski?

What does he/she like to eat?

Do they have video games?

Do they have a mall?

It is clear that the children would like to know many things about their new pen pals. The teacher then helps them organize their questions by beginning a web like the following:

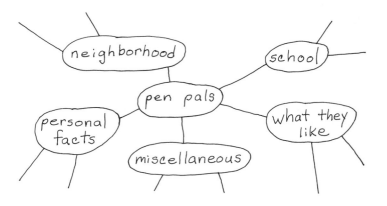

The children help decide where their questions should go and then come up with more questions that also are written on index cards and put in the correct places.

On the following day, the teacher and the children review the web, and the teacher points out that the things they would like to know about their pen pals are probably also the things their pen pals are wondering about them. He explains that they cannot possibly include all this information in the first letter but that they will be writing back and forth all year. As the year goes on, they will share and learn about these things and many things they have not even thought of yet.

The teacher then goes to the overhead and leads the children through the process of writing the first letter. He explains that the letter will be read not only by their pen pals but also, probably, by many other people, so each letter must be as correct and readable as possible. Today's task is to begin a good first draft that they can edit and recopy or type later. The teacher then explains and models for the children how and where they put the inside address, date, and greeting. The children watch as he does each step at the overhead. They then do the same on their papers.

Once these formalities are covered, the teacher leads them to look at the web and decide what to write about in the first paragraph. The class decides they should write about their personal facts. The teacher agrees and has them put their pencils down to watch as he writes a paragraph that communicates some personal facts about himself.

## Editing as You Go

After writing this first paragraph, the teacher reads it aloud, changing a word and adding another word, to model for the children that when we write, we read and change as we go along. He points out the paragraph indentation and that his paragraph has four sentences. The teacher then instructs the children to write their own first paragraphs, telling some personal facts about themselves. He reminds them that we always write first drafts on every other line so that we have space to add or change things later.

## The Children Write

The children begin to write their paragraphs. As they write, they glance at the web on the board and at the teacher's letter on the overhead. Even though these children are not very sophisticated writers, the demonstration they have observed along with the displayed web and letter clearly provide the support they need to write the first draft of a paragraph.

When most students have finished their paragraphs, the teacher reminds them that good writers stop occasionally and read what they have written before moving on. He then waits another minute while each child reads what he or she has written. He is encouraged to see them making a few changes/additions they have noticed in their own rereading.

The process of the teacher writing a paragraph, reading it aloud, making changes and additions, and then giving the children time to write their own paragraphs continues that day and the next as the teacher and the children construct paragraphs with information from the categories on the web. After each paragraph, the children are reminded to reread and make any changes or additions they think are needed. The teacher is encouraged to notice that when they get to the fifth paragraph, many children are automatically rereading and changing without being reminded to do so. Finally, the teacher suggests possible closings and shows the children where to put the closing. As they watch, he writes a closing on his letter; then they write closings on theirs. This completes the first drafts of the letters.

## Revising to Publish

The next day, the teacher helps them polish their letters. He puts them into sharing groups of four children and has each child read her or his letter to the others. Just as they do for Author's Chair, this sharing is totally focused on the message. Listeners tell the author something they liked, and the author asks them whether anything is not clear or whether they have suggestions for making it better. When everyone in the group has had a chance to share, they make whatever additions and revisions they choose. Children can be seen crossing things out and inserting additional information. As they do this, it becomes apparent why writing the first draft on every other line is useful.

## A Final Edit

Now that the letters are revised and the children are satisfied with their messages, it is time to do a final edit. During Writer's Workshop, the children are accustomed to choosing a friend to help them edit a draft that they are going to publish, so they just tailor this process to letters. They refer to the editing checklist displayed in the classroom and decide that the editing items are still valid, but that they need to add an item to correspond with letter editing. They add "Address, date, greeting, closing." The children then pair up with a friend and read for each item on the checklist together. When they have finished helping each other edit, they conference with the teacher for a final editing.

## Publishing the Letter

On the following day, they choose some stationery from a motley collection (contributed by parents or purchased from bargain bins) and copy the letters in their most legible handwriting. Finally, the teacher demonstrates how to put the address and the return address on the envelope. (Even though he intends to mail them all to the pen pals' school in one big envelope, he wants children to learn how to address an envelope and knows the pen pals will feel they are getting real letters when they come sealed in real envelopes.) The letters are mailed, and the writers eagerly await their replies. Next week, in a faraway city, this process begins again as the teacher's friend takes her class through the same steps of learning to write letters so they can write back.

The procedure just described is not difficult to carry out, but it does take time. Most classes would spend at least five 45-minute sessions going through brainstorming, webbing, modeling, first drafting, revising, and editing. When you get the letters sent off, you may think, "Never again!" But keep in mind that the first time you do anything is always the hardest—for you and the children. A month later, when the children have received their letters and are ready to write again, the process will be much easier and will go much more quickly. After three or four letters, most children know how to organize information and can write an interesting and correctly formed letter with a minimum of help. By the end of the year, they will be expert letter writers and will have gained a lot of general writing skills in the process.

## Other Examples of Focused Writing Lessons

The procedure just described for learning to write friendly letters can be used for any writing format you want children to learn. Imagine, for example, that you think they would enjoy writing cinquain poetry. Cinquains can be created in many different ways. Perhaps the easiest way for elementary children is the form shown here:

> Teachers
> Smiling, worrying
> Smart, busy, perky
> They love their children.
> Teachers

As you see, the first and last lines are the same word—the subject of the poem. On line 2, you write two -*ing* words. On line 3, you write three adjectives. On line 4, you write a four-word sentence or phrase.

To teach children how to write a cinquain, draw lines to show the form of the cinquain. Duplicate this on paper for the children and on an overhead for your use:

_____

_____        _____

_____        _____        _____

_____        _____        _____        _____

_____

Decide on a subject for the cinquain. (They make very impressive Mother's Day cards, but do expand the concept of mother to include a grandmother, an aunt, or whoever the primary female caretaker is!) Let children watch you write the noun on the first and last lines. Have them write the same noun on their first and last lines.

_Mama_

_____        _____

_____        _____        _____

_____        _____        _____        _____

_Mama_

Next, have them brainstorm words that end in -*ing* and tell what mothers do, and list these on the board:

| | | | | |
|---|---|---|---|---|
| working | talking | driving | cooking | baking |
| thinking | worrying | fussing | cleaning | singing |

Choose two of these -*ing* words and write them on your second line. Tell children to write two -*ing* words on their second line. Tell them that they can choose from the brainstormed list or can come up with any two on their own.

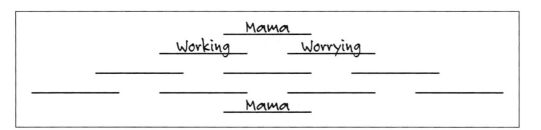

_Mama_

_Working_        _Worrying_

_____        _____        _____

_____        _____        _____        _____

_Mama_

Next, brainstorm descriptive words for line 3, and write these on the board:

| | | | | |
|---|---|---|---|---|
| busy | pretty | sweet | soft | perky |
| smart | organized | lonely | worried | careful |
| tall | short | Black | proud | perfect |

Write three descriptive words on your third line. You may want to use one or two words that are not on the brainstormed list to be sure your children understand that the list is just to give them ideas, not to limit their ideas.

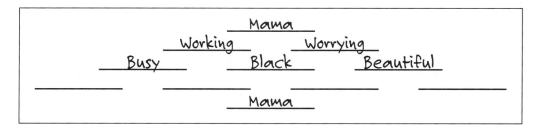

For the fourth line, have children brainstorm four-word phrases or sentences:

> She works too hard.
> She loves you best.
> My mama is best.
> I love her best.
> She makes me laugh.
> Always in the kitchen.
> Some kids have two!

Write one of these or write another four-line phrase or sentence on your fourth line and have the children write one on theirs.

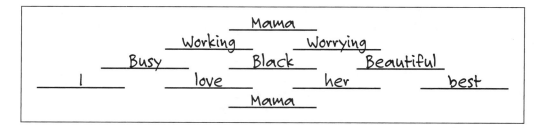

The cinquains are now complete. Let several children read theirs aloud. They will be amazed to discover that, although the topic was the same and they all worked from the same brainstormed list, each poem is different. Once children have one cinquain written, let them make up another one on the same topic. You may then want them to choose one to use as the text on a Mother's Day card. If so, have them share, revise, and edit in the usual manner.

To get reluctant writers involved, oral histories and personal memoirs are wonderful long-term writing projects because they tell about the children's families or themselves (familiar topics). To begin, you want to locate an oral history to share with the class or invite a member of the community (the principal?) to be your subject for a class oral history project. Interview the subject, tape record the interview, take notes, and have the children take notes also. After the interview, create a group summary using your notes, the children's notes, and the tape if a dispute arises. Memoirs abound in children's literature. Elizabeth Fitzgerald Howard's *Aunt Flossie's Hats (and Crabcakes Later)* and Cynthia Rylant's *When the Relatives Came* are two wonderful examples of this genre. Again, after reading and discussing these published memoirs, teachers may create their own or perhaps create a class memoir based on a collective experience. Now children can begin to plan their own memoirs.

## Focused Writing Connected to Reading

Children who write become better readers. One of the most powerful connections you can make is through reading and writing (Spivey, 1997). Children who read something knowing that they will write something are more likely to read with a clear sense of purpose. Children who use information from their reading to write produce better writing because they have more to say. Research has shown a clear benefit from connecting reading and writing (Shanahan, 1988). It has also shown that a writing program that includes instruction in specific informational text structures improves both writing and reading comprehension (Raphael, Kirschner, & Englert, 1988). In this section, we describe a variety of structures for focused writing that connect reading and writing.

*Graphic Organizers*    Chapter Six described a variety of ways to guide children's reading so they can learn how to think about different types of reading. One type of guided reading lesson involved having students construct or fill in various types of graphic organizers. The webs, charts, diagrams, time lines, and so on that you and the children constructed to organize the information learned from reading are marvelous springboards for writing. Here is a character web about Amanda.

Once the web is complete, you can have the children use the information in the web to create a character summary for Amanda. To demonstrate how you do this, choose one of the adjectives that best describes her and let the children listen and watch as you create a paragraph on the

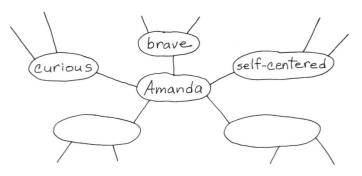

Focused Writing

*Here is a paragraph describing Amanda as a curious person. The children watched as the teacher wrote this paragraph. Using this paragraph as a model but using their own ideas, each child then chose the adjective he or she thought best described Amanda and wrote a descriptive paragraph.*

> Amanda is a very curious little girl! She always wants to know everything about Miss Morgan. One day she followed her home to find out where she lives and what her house looks like. She is also positive that Miss Morgan will marry Mr. Thompson who teaches next door. Miss Morgan isn't sure what she thinks about that! Who knows what Amanda will try and find out next!

board or on chart paper. When teachers think aloud as they model writing in front of the class, they provide powerful lessons about the writing process. After children watch you write and listen to you think aloud about how best to combine your ideas, point out to them the features of your paragraph that you want them to use:

- The paragraph is indented.
- All sentences begin with capital letters and end with a period.
- The name *Amanda* is always capitalized.
- The first sentence tells the most important idea—that Amanda is curious.
- The other sentences are details that show how curious she is.

Now each child should write a paragraph about Amanda, choosing any one of the remaining adjectives on the web (or an adjective that is not on the web that they think best describes her). Their paragraphs will all be different but should follow the form demonstrated in your paragraph.

This type of guided writing—in which children use the information they obtain from reading and record it on some type of graphic organizer and who then follow a model they watch the teacher create—is extremely effective for struggling readers. Almost all children will produce interesting, cohesive, well-written paragraphs and be proud of what they produce. With enough lessons such as this one, all children can learn how to construct paragraphs. This ability to create well-formed paragraphs is the basis for all different types of writing.

Almost any information recorded in graphic organizer fashion can be used for reading/writing lessons. In the previous chapter, you saw a web that children can use to organize the information read in an article about birds.

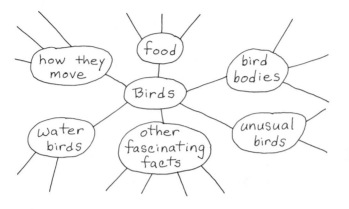

You also saw how information about birds could be recorded in a feature matrix.

Once these graphic organizers are completed, you can use them to have the children write about birds. Based on the web, the teacher would model how to write a descriptive paragraph about the different foods birds eat. Each child would then choose another one of the subtopics—bird bodies, ways birds move, and so forth—and would write a descriptive paragraph about that topic. Based on the information about particular birds from the feature matrix, the teacher would model how to write a paragraph about one of the birds and then let each child choose one of the other birds and write and illustrate a descriptive paragraph about it. After each child writes about one of the birds, the children might work in groups to revise, edit, and produce a book about birds.

| **Birds** | | | | | | |
|---|---|---|---|---|---|---|
| | fly | swim | build nests | lay eggs | have feathers | molt |
| robins | | | | | | |
| whippoorwills | | | | | | |
| penguins | | | | | | |
| ostriches | | | | | | |
| | | | | | | |
| | | | | | | |

Lessons in which graphic organizers are constructed and then used based on reading as a basis for writing are particularly important and effective for children whose first language is not English. Watching the teacher use the information from the graphic organizer to write something and then using the model they have watched the teacher write to construct their own piece of writing is an extremely powerful way for these children to increase their control of the English language. If your class contains many children whose English is limited, you should use lessons such as these on an almost daily basis.

*Response Logs*    Many teachers find that an easy and natural way to connect reading and writing is to have students keep literature response logs. Children are encouraged to take some time after reading each day and record their thoughts, feelings, and predictions. From time to time, the children can be asked to share the responses they have written. This is often a good basis for promoting a discussion of divergent responses to the same story. However, Sudduth (1990) reported that many of her third-graders did not really know what to record in their literature logs. This was especially true of those children who were finding learning to read difficult. She outlined the step-by-step instructions that she took them through:

- At first, have the students read the same book. They can read this silently, with a partner, listen to a tape recording, or listen to a teacher read aloud.
- Have specific stopping points in the reading, and help the children verbalize what they are thinking and feeling.
- On chartpaper or the overhead, record some of the students' responses and have them copy the ones they agree with into their logs. Use "frames" such as:

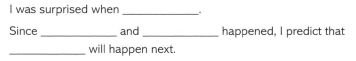

I was surprised when _____.

Since _____ and _____ happened, I predict that _____ will happen next.

The story reminds me of the time _____.

- As students understand the various open-ended ways in which they can respond to literature, move them toward independence. Continue the discussions but don't write down what they say. Rather, have them write their own personal entries following the discussions. Have the class brainstorm a list of log topics and frames, and display these so that students can refer to them when they need a "starter."
- Have students choose the books they want to read and do their own response logs. Divide the time available for self-selected reading into reading time and log-writing time, perhaps 20 minutes to read and 10 minutes to write. Once children are reading individual books, provide a time each week when they can share what they have written in a small-group format.

*Writing before Reading*  In most classrooms, writing occurs after reading and is used to help readers clarify and solidify what they have learned and to help them respond to what they have read. The reasons for having children write before they read are equally compelling. You learned in Chapter 6 that reading is primarily thinking and that although all children can think, they sometimes do not think while they read. You learned about a variety of useful guided reading formats for getting children thinking before, during, and after reading. Writing before reading is another way to get children thinking.

This writing can be a "quickwrite" such as "2-minute fast facts." Imagine that your children are going to read an informational selection about reptiles. Make sure everyone has some paper and a pencil ready, set your timer for 2 minutes, and have the children list as many facts as they can about reptiles. Stress that they should get as much down as they can in 2 minutes—in abbreviated list form, not worrying about spelling, complete sentences, and so forth. When the timer sounds at the end of 2 minutes, have students draw a line to show where they finished and have them number the facts they came up with before reading.

Next, have the students read or listen to the informational article about reptiles. Do not let them write anything while they are reading/listening, but make sure that they know they have 3 minutes to add to their list after reading. When students have finished reading, set your timer for 3 minutes and let them add to their list of reptile facts. Once the timer sounds, have the students compare lists in small groups. Each group might first list the facts most members knew before reading and second those facts most members learned from the article. Each group could then write these before- and after-fact lists on a chart and share with the class.

This very simple procedure is used most effectively when the students are going to read a topic about which they already have some prior knowledge. While making the 2-minute prereading list, they realize that they already know a lot and activate their prior knowledge to prepare them to think about the material they are going to read. They are always amazed at how much more they can list after reading. Children who use writing to tally up what they knew before and after reading soon learn that a lot can be learned from reading.

Sometimes you want students to do more extended writing before reading to sensitize them to the process of how authors create images, build suspense, flesh out characters, and so on. Writing before reading can be an especially powerful activity when used with children who have difficulty "getting into" a selection. These children typically begin reading with little or no attempt at bringing up relevant prior background knowledge, do not generate predictions or questions as they read, and passively enter the reading activity and focus on getting it over with, rather than getting involved with it. These children do better on factual questions than on responding to character motives. They can remember names of the characters but find it difficult to answer questions such as Who does Russell remind you of? (They often respond, "I don't know" or "It didn't say" or "No one"). These children find imagery difficult and do not have good mental images of what the characters look like or how they might be dressed unless the story is illustrated or is explicit on these matters. These children have not discovered what reading is all about.

Imagine that you want students to think about how authors use words to create a certain mood. You find a story in which a child is lost out in the woods at night. The fear that the child feels becomes tangible through the images that the author creates. You decide to use a writing activity in which the children write about a time that they, or someone they knew, were lost. First talk with the children about being lost and about the fears they experience. Then talk about how authors make things seem real by giving specific details and by using powerful words. Next, let them write about a real or imagined experience of being lost and have them try to make the terror become real for the reader. After writing, let them share what they have written, and notice how they used specific details, powerful words, and images.

As you show them the story you have selected for them to read, tell them that this author had the same writing task that they had. She wanted to tell about a lost child and made it so real that the readers felt like they too were lost. Have them read and compare the language and images used by this writer to the ones that they used in their stories. After they have finished reading the story, discuss specific examples of the language used and the images created by the author. Put some of the sentences on the board or on chartpaper. If they are excited by the story and the way that the author created the images of fear, they may want to revise their own stories using some of the "tricks" that were used by the author of the story they just read.

## *Summary*

Writer's Workshop is a powerful and versatile structure for teaching children to write. Beginning each day with a minilesson in which children watch you write allows you to model, demonstrate, and think aloud about all the "big" and "little" components that constitute good writing. In your minilesson, you can focus on just one aspect—choosing a topic, what to do about spelling, how to edit your writing, how to revise by replacing, or any of the other things writers must learn to do. As children write, you can encourage them in their writing or conference with them about how to make their writing better and more readable. Beginning your Writer's Workshop with only the minilesson, children writing, and sharing steps allows all children to get off to a successful start in writing. Once children are writing willingly (if not well), you can add editing to your workshop and then conferencing, publishing, and Author's Chair. Because learning to edit is easier than learning to revise, you should teach some editing rules before teaching revising strategies. Once children know some revising strategies, make sure that they revise their pieces before doing any editing.

In Writer's Workshop, children are usually writing on topics of their own choosing in whatever form or genre they choose. Once children have achieved some comfort level with Writer's Workshop, begin to include some focused writing lessons. Building on the basics required by all good writing taught in Writer's Workshop, focus your students' attention on particular topics, forms, or genres. Teach minilessons in which you model the particular kind of writing you are focusing on, and then guide children through the steps of the writing process to produce published pieces. Children who engage in both Writer's Workshop and focused writing lessons throughout their elementary years will become ready, willing, and able writers.

In reviewing the research on writing, Hillocks (1986) found that natural process writing instruction is effective and that what has been called *environmental writing instruction,* in which students engage in various writing activities designed to teach them to learn and apply specific writing strategies and skills, is more effective still. The key to teaching writing, including the conventions of writing, appears to include being consistent with a developmental sequence that recognizes the commonalties of children as they move from early emergence to sophisticated ability (Dyson & Freedman, 2003; Farnan & Dahl, 2003; Hodges, 2003). Effective writing programs will look very different grade by grade and will have expectations for children at each grade that are appropriate to their development as writers. The best writing instruction teaches students how to plan, compose, revise, and edit their own pieces of writing, all within the context of inquiry, self-assessment, and self-regulation fostered by interaction with teachers and peers.

# chapter 8

# *Multilevel*
## *Instruction*

Perhaps the biggest challenge every teacher faces is providing instruction that moves all children along in their literacy development—when the children all start at different places and learn at different rates. Children differ—and they differ on any dimension you can think of. The average height of 7-year-olds is about 4 feet. Many 7-year-olds are 3½ feet tall; many others are 4½ feet tall; a few are only 3 feet tall; and a few are as tall as 5 feet. The average height of children has increased in the last century, presumably due to better nutrition and other health factors. Today's tall children are much taller than the tall children of a century ago. Today's short children are taller too, but they are still short compared to the average. Parents and doctors who monitor the health of children do not try to get all children to be average height (even though we know that short people—especially short boys—are disadvantaged in many arenas). Parents and doctors do expect children to grow, and they monitor and document this growth to make sure it is happening. The growth does not happen in equal monthly increments, however. Most children who are 4 feet tall when they turn 7 years of age will be 3 inches taller when they turn 8 years old, but they do not grow a quarter of an inch each month. Some months they grow very little. Other months they "shoot up."

What does this height example have to do with literacy? Simply put, children will always vary in their reading levels. Some children will read at grade level, some a little above or below grade level, and a few will read way above or way below grade level. The goal of having all children read at grade level is not a reasonable goal (and getting the above-level children back down to being just average readers would take massive amounts of truly terrible experiences!). What is reasonable is the expectation that all children grow in their reading ability. With good instruction, we can also expect all children to read better.

The average readers in a school with a good, balanced literacy program read better than average readers in schools with similar populations but less effective instruction. Struggling readers in a school with a good, balanced literacy program read better than struggling readers in a school with less effective instruction even though they may not read as well as average readers. Just as with height, we need to measure children's beginning reading point and periodically monitor and document their progress. We need to demonstrate that all children, whether struggling, average, or accelerated, are growing in the level of material they can read and understand. This growth, like increases in height, often does not occur at the same rate. Children reach plateaus in their development for a few months and then spurt forward. With good instruction, most children can make 10 months of progress in reading across 10 months of instruction, but they often do not demonstrate one-tenth of that growth each month.

If this information seems so obvious to you that it is not worth the paper it is printed on, consider some regulations and legislation being passed and implemented in school districts across the country. Many states have legislated that all children come to school ready to learn. Still more states have decreed that children must be at least average in reading and math to be promoted to the next grade. We think some remedial mathematics needs to be provided to help lawmakers understand why getting everyone to be at least average is a mathematical impossibility!

Children differ on all kinds of variables, including their current reading level and how rapidly and how far they can rise above that level. With good instruction, all children can read at higher levels, and the progress of all children can be accelerated. But our classrooms will always contain a variety of literacy levels. What kind of instruction can

**Those Who Do Not Learn from History Are Doomed to Repeat It!**

Providing instruction for children at all different levels is not a new challenge! Schools across the decades have tried a variety of solutions, none of which has shown good long-term results. In the early days of U.S. schooling, children were promoted to the next level based on end-of-year tests. Some children never did get promoted, and seeing a 6-foot-tall 12-year-old sitting in a tiny desk at the back of a room filled with 6- and 7-year-old children was a common sight.

Reading groups based on reading level were common in most elementary classrooms for much of our recent history. Data indicate that children who were placed in the low group almost never moved up to a higher group and that very few of these children ever reached grade level in reading. Some schools have tracked children by reading level, putting all the low readers in one class, average readers in another class, and above-average readers in another class. This tracking was abandoned in the 1970s because of its failure to accelerate the reading progress of the low-track students.

Retention, leveled-reading groups, and tracking are all failed solutions of the past but are once again being implemented in the hope that they work this time around. We see no reason to believe they will!

teachers reasonably be expected to provide to help all children, regardless of beginning point, make progress? We have been working on and worrying about this issue for the better part of the past 15 years. We do not have all the answers, but we do know a lot more than we did 15 years ago. We call instruction with a wide range of learning possibilities *multilevel instruction.* In this chapter, we provide many examples of ways in which teachers make their literacy instruction multilevel.

## *Multilevel Self-Selected Reading, Writing, and Words*

A balanced reading program is like a balanced diet. Just as a variety of different foods are essential for the development of healthy bodies, many components are necessary for the development of able, avid, thoughtful readers and writers. These components have all been described in the first seven chapters of this book. Perhaps the most critical component of a balanced reading program is engaging all children in self-selected reading and writing. Simultaneously, children need to learn to read and spell high-frequency words automatically and to use word patterns to decode and spell thousands of words. While doing self-selected reading and writing and while building their word fluency, children need to engage in a variety of comprehension lessons so that they learn how to think their way through all different kinds of text and in focused writing lessons so that they learn how to write different kinds of texts for different purposes.

The lessons and activities described in the first four chapters of this book comprise what we see as a balanced reading program. Some activities in this balanced reading program—self-selected reading and writing—are by their nature multilevel. Others—word instruction and comprehension lessons—are much more difficult to make multilevel. In the remainder of the section, we describe how to maximize the multilevel possibilities of self-selected reading, writing, and word instruction. The bulk of this chapter is devoted to the difficult task of making guided reading multilevel.

## Self-Selected Reading

*Self-selected reading* is that part of a balanced literacy program in which children get to choose what they want to read and which parts of their reading they want to respond to. Opportunities are provided for children to share and respond to what is read. Teachers hold conferences with children about their books. The goals of self-selected reading follow:

- To introduce children to all types of literature through teacher read-alouds
- To encourage children's reading interests
- To provide instructional-level reading
- To build intrinsic motivation for reading

Self-selected reading is multilevel because children choose what they want to read. They choose from a wide variety of easily accessible materials in a variety of genres and with a wide range of reading levels. During weekly conferences, teachers support children's choices and help children choose books for the next week that they can read and will enjoy. If you follow the guidelines and suggestions set out in Chapter 2, you can create a truly multilevel self-selected reading component.

## Writing

Writing should include both self-selected writing, in which children choose their topics, and focused writing, in which children learn how to write particular forms and on particular topics. During the writing component, teachers model all the things writers do. Children write many first drafts and choose from these drafts pieces they want to revise, edit, and publish. Children share their writing with others and get feedback and help from their peers. While the children write, the teacher conferences with individual children, helping them revise, edit, and publish and providing instruction for each child on just the right level. The goals of the writing component are:

- To have children view writing as a way of telling about things
- To develop fluent writing for all children
- To teach children to apply grammar and mechanics in their own writing
- To teach particular writing forms
- To allow students to learn to read through writing

Writing is always multilevel. All of us—children and adults alike—can only write on our own level. (Perhaps that is why most of us find writing hard!) When we allow children to choose their own topics, accept whatever level of first-draft writing each child can accomplish, and allow them to work on their pieces as many days as needed, all children can succeed in writing. As teachers conference with children, they have the opportunity to truly individualize their teaching. Looking at the writing of the child usually reveals both what the child needs to move forward and what the child is ready to understand. The writing conference provides the "teachable moment" in which both advanced and struggling writers can be nudged forward in their literacy development.

## Words

As you read in Chapter Four, a wide variety of activities can help us meet our word goals:

- To learn to read and spell high-frequency words
- To learn how to decode and spell unknown words using patterns from known words
- To use phonics and spelling patterns automatically and fluently while reading and writing

Word activities are multilevel in a variety of ways. A few examples relate to the activities described in Chapters Three and Four. When we focus on the names of children, other concrete words, and the daily word wall practice, some children who have learned to read the words begin to learn to spell them. Other children who require lots of practice with words begin to learn to read them. When we read and make alphabet books to help children learn letter names and sounds, children who did not know many letter names and sounds begin to learn them. Children who already knew a lot of letters and sounds often learn to read all the words in the books we read and make!

During Guess the Covered Word activities, the words are always read in the context of a sentence or paragraph. Children learn how to use word length, all the beginning letters, and known words to make really good guesses about unknown words. In every Guess the Covered Word lesson, beginning sounds are reviewed for children who need more practice with beginning sounds. Advanced readers often learn to read all the words in the sentences used in Guess the Covered Word activities—greatly increasing the number of words they can read.

Each Making Words lesson begins with short, easy words and progresses to longer, more complex words. Children who still need to develop phonemic awareness can do this as they "stretch out" words while making them and as they decide which words rhyme while sorting them. Each lesson includes sorting words into patterns and using those patterns to read and spell new words.

During Reading/Writing Rhymes lessons, children blend together the beginning letters and the rhyme to produce the word. This blending is an important component of phonemic awareness. Beginning sounds are reviewed every time the deck of beginning letter cards is distributed. Homophones are taught by writing *plain* and *plane* in both columns of the *ain/ane* chart and their different meanings are explained. Of course, when children write silly sentences using the rhyming words, they are incorporating these words into writing at their own level.

Word activities are not as inherently multilevel as self-selected reading and writing are. But by carefully orchestrating each activity, we have found many ways to broaden the

### Doing Self-Selected Reading, Writing, and Word Activities at Centers

To make time to work with many small, leveled groups during guided reading, some teachers set up their classrooms so children do their self-selected reading, writing, and word activities in centers. To determine how successful this is in moving all children forward, we have to assess what the struggling readers and the advanced readers are doing in those centers. Most children who read and write above grade level happily read, write, and do word activities in the centers. Unfortunately, they rarely work up to the level they are capable of working on. Struggling students, on the other hand, rarely do much reading and writing in centers and often cannot complete the word activities.

When the teacher is available to conference with individual children while the rest of the class engages in self-selected reading and writing, the teacher can monitor and provide instruction that is right for each child's level. Clever teachers notice when advanced readers are always reading books that are too easy for them and entice them into reading wonderful books that are closer to their level. Likewise, clever teachers spend extra time conferencing with struggling readers and helping them choose books they can actually read and get started reading. Individual conferences are also critical for making writing multilevel. Looking at a child's writing can tell you just what that child needs to learn to move forward, and you can provide that instruction as it is needed. The teacher is essential to making word activities multilevel by leading children through a lesson that is planned to include review and challenges. Center activities can provide needed practice, but only a teacher can stretch instruction to fit all the children.

range of understanding and applications included in each. The word activities described in Chapters 3 and 4 provide lots of review for struggling readers and some challenges for advanced readers.

## *Providing Multilevel Guided Reading*

Historically, *guided reading* (sometimes called *directed reading*) was instruction provided by the teacher to help children improve their oral reading fluency and silent reading comprehension as they read different kinds of texts. Today, some people use the term *guided reading* in a narrower sense to refer only to the guidance the teacher gives to a small group of readers as they read material at their level. We, however, use the term in its broader sense. For us, guided reading occurs when a teacher guides some students—whether a whole group, small group, or individual—through an activity designed to help them apply their word identification and comprehension strategies. Chapter Six described a variety of activities that help children learn to think as they read. In all these activities—literate conversations, think-alouds, story maps, the Beach Ball, doing the book, KWLs, and graphic organizers—the teacher guides the thinking of the children so that they become better comprehenders.

To do a guided reading activity, you need children who need instruction (plentiful in all classrooms!), a comprehension strategy to focus on and a way to draw children's attention to that strategy, and something for the children to read. The "something for the children to read" is the problem! Remember that your children all read at different levels. Nothing you find for your children to read will be just right for everyone. What is just right for half your children will be too hard for some, too easy for some, and much too hard and much too easy for a few! What does a hard-working, smart, well-intentioned teacher do in this situation? How do you provide guided reading instruction when your children all read at different levels?

Remember the solutions of the past: retaining children until they got to grade level, putting children in reading groups according to level, and tracking children to different classrooms according to reading level. None of these produced the desired goal of getting all children on grade level. How do you do guided reading instruction with a class full of children reading at different levels? We do not have a perfect solution, but we do have a lot of doable options for you to try.

### Refine and Commit to Your Self-Selected Reading, Writing, and Word Components

We described in the previous section how self-selected reading and writing are inherently multilevel and how word activities can be "tweaked" so that they became more multilevel. In a school that has a balanced reading program, substantial amounts of time each week are devoted to these multilevel components. Guided reading lessons are only one component of this balanced reading program. Although we know the reading levels of all our children and we try to vary the materials and formats we use for guided reading, all children are not on the "just right" reading level every day during guided reading. However, they are on the right level during self-selected reading and writing, and they benefit from different activities designed to teach them to decode and spell words. Guided reading instruction is just one part of a balanced reading program. Much of the challenge for our advanced readers and success for our struggling readers is achieved through the other three components.

## Use a Variety of Materials at Different Levels for Guided Reading Lessons

Once your multilevel self-selected reading, writing, and word components are in place, you can consider materials for guided reading lessons. You want to use the widest variety of materials you can find, making sure to include materials each week that suit the average reading level of your students as well as materials that are easier than the average level. To do this, you need to know the reading levels of all your students. (This too is a complicated topic, and we tackle it next in Chapter Nine, "Assessment.")

Teachers are most successful with guided reading when they use a variety of materials:

- Grade-level basal readers (if they have them)
- Appealing selections from easier basal readers (often from old basals, taken apart and reassembled into "skinny books")
- Class sets of real books
- Books from sets of leveled readers
- Big books, including informational "big books" correlated with science and social studies
- Selections from *Weekly Reader, Time,* or *Scholastic News* magazines
- Plays and poetry typed and duplicated or written on large charts
- Selections from science and social studies sources, particularly graphs, maps, charts, and other visuals
- Reader's Theater selections duplicated from a source (including many sites on the Web) or written by the students
- Laminated selections from various sources relating to unit studies and used year after year

We teach a wide variety of comprehension lessons during guided reading to help children learn how to think about all different kinds of text. Multilevel guided reading instruction cannot be done with any single adopted reading text or a few class sets of books or a box of leveled readers. When a diversity of reading materials at different reading levels is used, guided reading becomes more enjoyable and multilevel.

## Use a Variety of Guided Reading Formats to Provide Support for All Readers

Reading level is not a static entity like height. Interest, prior knowledge, type and amount of instruction, type of support, and rereading all matter to what children can successfully read. Of course, you are limited in how readable you can make a particular text for a particular child, regardless of these other variables. A child whose reading level is at the end of first grade will not be able to read a selection written at the fifth-grade level—even if that selection is on a high-interest, high-prior-knowledge topic like dinosaurs; even if that child gets good prereading instruction; even if a partner helps the child with some words; and even if he or she is reading it for the second time. Four grade levels is just too great a leap! But most children whose measured reading level is at the end of first grade could read and understand that same selection on dinosaurs with all the same conditions if that selection were written at a late second-grade or early third-grade level.

Conversely, a student whose measured reading level is at the fifth grade but who has little knowledge of or interest in dinosaurs and minimal prereading instruction might read this fifth-grade-level text on dinosaurs individually on the first reading but not understand much of what he or she read. Many grade-level readers develop reading problems in the intermediate grades when they are faced with boring text and little instructional support. Considering whether a child is reading at his or her level during guided reading requires more than just looking at the reading level of the child and the reading level of the text. We must consider factors within the child, such as interest and prior knowledge, as well as the type and amount of instruction and support we can provide.

## *Formats for Guided Reading*

*Formats* are the various ways children read during guided reading. This section describes some formats we use to make guided reading as multilevel as possible for a wide range of children.

### Shared Reading of a "Big Book"

*Shared reading* is a term used to describe the process in which the teacher and the children read together. Typically, a book is read and reread several times. On the first reading, the teacher does most of the reading. As the children become more familiar with the book, they join in and "share" the reading.

For beginning readers, the best kind of books to use in shared reading are predictable books. *Predictable books* are books in which repeated patterns, refrains, pictures, and rhymes allow children to pretend read a book that has been read to them several times. Pretend reading is a stage most children go through with a favorite book that some patient adult has read and reread to them. Perhaps you remember pretend reading with popular predictable books such as *Goodnight Moon, Are You My Mother?* and *Brown Bear, Brown Bear, What Do You See?* Shared reading of predictable books allows all children to move successfully into the acquisition of literacy, to develop some reading and print concepts, to learn some words, and, most importantly, to develop confidence in their ability to learn to read.

Shared reading can also be used as the format to solve a common problem encountered by teachers of older children. Many children who are otherwise good readers have trouble reading science and social studies textbooks. These books often have a table of contents, illustrations with captions, diagrams with labels, maps, charts, a glossary, and an index. Many children do not know what to do when they encounter these foreign elements in their books, so they skip over them. Informational books have different structure and special features that stories don't have. Children must slow down their reading rate and pay attention to more than just the text to comprehend informational books.

Guiding children's thinking about the special features of informational books is difficult when everyone is looking at his or her own individual copy of the book. All teachers have carried out lessons in which the following sample of oral instruction pertains:

> "All turn to page 28. Look at the diagram in the top, left corner of the page. What do you see in the diagram? Look at the top arrow. Where is that arrow pointing? Follow your eyes around the arrows and see how the cycle works."

This step-by-step direction sounds simple enough, but careful observation of the students demonstrates that many eyes are not focused on the diagram and still fewer eyes are following the arrows. Moreover, even those children who are focused on the diagram may not be thinking about how this diagram graphically portrays the water cycle. (A few children may not even be on the right page!)

Informational "big books" allow us to focus our students' attention on what we are teaching them. The teacher and students can use a pointer, highlighting tape, or other attention getters to make sure everyone's eyes are in the right place! Most teachers know that students need to be taught how to use the special features of informational text and that learning to read and use these

## RECOMMENDED resources

### Informational Big Books

Many wonderful and engaging informational big books are being published today. Textbook publishers often provide some big books along with their science and social studies texts. National Geographic, Modern Curriculum Press, and Shortland Publications have a large variety of informational big books. Some magazines, including *Weekly Reader, Time for Kids,* and *Scholastic,* supply "big magazine" versions with a class subscription.

features greatly increases student confidence and comprehension of informational text. Because of the difficulty of accomplishing this when students have their own individual copies of textbooks, many teachers have quietly "given up." Shared reading of informational big books is a format that is encouraging many teachers to give informational book instruction another try!

## How Shared Reading Is Multilevel

A good shared reading lesson has something for everyone! As we read predictable books, most beginners learn basic concepts, such as how to track print and what reading actually is, while advanced readers learn many—if not all—of the words. After several rereadings of a predictable big book and some accompanying comprehension and word activities, all children feel that they really can read. A few children are just reproducing the memorized text; many other children are reading some words and filling in the rest from memory; and our most advanced readers are usually learning most of the words. As we continue to do shared reading with predictable books, more and more children move from the pretend reading stage to the real reading stage.

When we use informational books for shared reading with older students, they can learn a multitude of things. The main purpose of using these books is to teach the important comprehension strategies needed for informational text. Every reader, whether struggling or advanced, can learn how to preview informational text; how to get the maximum information from pictures, maps, charts, graphs, diagrams, and accompanying quicktext; and how to use the table of contents, index, and glossary. We choose informational big

**Tips for Reading Information**

1. Preview the text to see what it is all about and what special features it has.
2. Use the table of contents and index if you are looking for something specific.
3. See whether the text has a glossary with meanings for the important big words.
4. Make a KWL chart in your brain or on paper, and think about what you already know and what you want to learn.
5. When you begin to read, read the title first to see what the text is all about.
6. Read the pictures and all the quicktext (labels, captions, etc.) next.
7. Study the maps, charts, graphs, and diagrams and try to figure out what they tell you.
8. Read the text and see what it tells you that you did not learn from the visuals.
9. Stop and add things you are learning to the KWL chart in your brain or on paper.

books that connect to our science and social studies units, allowing every child to learn new science and social studies content and vocabulary. Of course, advanced readers learn the most—probably being able to read and have meanings for all the new words in the informational big book!

Multilevel instruction does not mean that everyone learns the same things or the same amount. Rather, multilevel activities always include a multitude of things to be learned. Multilevel activities are structured so that everyone can engage in them, learn something from them, and thus feel successful. When students experience success in an activity, they engage in that activity more energetically the next time, triggering an upward spiral: success→motivation→engagement→learning→success.

## Echo and Choral Reading

Echo and choral reading are formats we commonly use for reading plays and poetry. In *echo reading*, the teacher reads first and then children read it back, becoming the echo. As children echo read, they try to match the teacher's expression and phrasing. *Choral reading* is reading together in chorus. Children are often assigned parts, which they practice several times. Teachers often combine echo reading and choral reading. They first do an echo reading of a selection and then assign parts for choral reading.

Children seem to particularly enjoy echo and choral reading when we read plays. We first read the whole play in an echo reading format, using different voices for the different characters. Next, we assign parts to different groups and do a choral reading. We often reread the plays the following day in a play school group format in which the children read their parts in small groups.

## How Echo and Choral Reading Are Multilevel

Echo and choral reading are multilevel in much the same way that shared reading is. There are multiple things to be learned. Everyone learns how to read expressively. All children learn some new words and concepts. Advanced readers, who already know many of the simpler words and concepts, learn the biggest words and the most complex ideas! The repeated readings allow everyone to engage and to feel successful. Echo and choral reading help build reading fluency. They are an important part of a balanced reading program for elementary children of any age—and are particularly helpful if your class contains a lot of English language learners.

## ERT . . . (Everybody Read To . . . )

The practice of taking turns reading orally, commonly known as *round robin reading,* has been criticized and condemned for decades. Still, round robin reading persists in many classrooms. When teachers continue to do something despite numerous and almost unanimous criticism, they must have a reason! Perhaps the reason teachers still close their doors and do round robin reading is that sometimes they want to guide the whole class or a small group through the reading of a selection, making sure that the students are attending to certain critical concepts and that everyone is getting important information. By having the selection read orally and asking questions to make sure everyone is paying attention, the teacher feels assured that everyone is involved in some way in reading the selection.

Round robin reading is not a multilevel activity in which everyone feels successful, nor can multiple things be learned! ERT . . . , that is, Everybody Read To . . . , is a way of guiding the whole class (or a small group) through reading a selection. We use ERT (which rhymes with *hurt*) when we want students to do an initial reading on their own but also want to keep them together to provide guidance and support. Here is how we use the ERT format.

When we do ERT, we lead students through the text, setting purposes for each page or two-page spread. Some purposes are literal and some are inferential. We cue students to the type of question by asking students to *find out,* when the answer is directly stated on the page, or to *figure out,* when the answer is not directly stated but can be figured out based on what is written (the clues!). Students are asked to read to find out or figure out a variety of things. When they have found them or figured them out, they raise their hands but continue reading until they finish the page. When most hands are raised, we call on one child to tell the answer and another child to read the part where the answer was found or the clues that helped in figuring out the answer.

When children do the reading to find or figure out answers to our questions, that reading is done silently or in a "whisper voice" if children still need to hear themselves reading. We usually include one or two "two-handers" in each lesson, a purpose that has two questions. Students love these because they get to raise one hand and then the other and usually need to hold the book open with their elbows, providing a bit of a balancing challenge, a chance to stretch their muscles, and a comical image!

ERT can be used with both story and informational text. In the following sample ERT lesson, both literal and inferential purposes are set for students reading a social studies selection on Mount Vesuvius.

"Everybody read these two pages to figure out why Pompeii was a good place to live and what Vesuvius was compared to." (Students read and raise first one hand and then the other hand for this two-hander. The teacher reminds those whose hands are raised to finish reading the section and then calls on one student.)

"Who figured out why Pompeii was a good place to live? Jack, can you tell us?" (Jack gives an appropriate answer, and the teacher calls on a different student to read some of the clues.)

"Who can read some of the clues that helped Jack figure out why Pompeii was a good place to live?" (The student selected reads some clues from the text. The teacher asks the second part of the question and calls on another student to answer.)

"Who figured out what Vesuvius was compared to?" (The student chosen to answer gives an appropriate response, and the teacher asks for another volunteer to read some of the clues.)

"Who can read some of the clues you could use to figure out what Vesuvius was compared to?" (The selected student reads several clues, and the teacher sets a literal purpose for the next page.)

"On this page, I want everyone to read to find out whether the people knew what was going to happen." (Students read and many hands are raised. The teacher calls on a student.)

"Josh, did the people know what was going to happen?" (Josh answers that the people did not know, and the teacher calls on another student to read the part where Josh found the answer. That student proudly reads.) "The people did not know what was going to happen."

## How ERT Is Multilevel

An activity is multilevel if readers at all different levels can feel successful and if multiple things can be learned. ERT is a very multilevel format when you strictly follow a few rules. First, make sure that you include about equal numbers of inferential (figure out) purposes and literal (find out) purposes. Make your find-outs very literal. In the Vesuvius example, everyone was asked to "find out whether the people knew what was going to happen" and in the text can be found the sentence *The people did not know what was going to happen.* By including literal purposes, struggling readers soon discover that, although they may not be able to read the entire text, they can find the answers to many of the questions. They are happy to raise their hands and proud to give the correct answers! Remember that kids who do not try are kids who are convinced they cannot do it. When they experience obvious success, they try harder. As they listen and try to read the pages, they (and the teacher) usually discover that they can read more than they thought they could.

In addition to including some very literal questions, many teachers have students repeat the purpose before they read. As students respond that they are reading "to find out whether the people knew what was going to happen," they are attending to these words by the very act of speaking them. The probability that struggling readers will recognize those very same words as they turn their attention to reading the page is greatly increased.

In ERT, the person who gives the answer to a question is never the same person who reads the part where the answer was found or who reads the clues used to figure it out. This ensures the participation of many students in the lesson and is also important to the participation of the struggling readers. Many struggling readers can read enough to find out and figure out some answers, but their oral reading would be choppy or hesitant. Many older struggling readers would never volunteer to answer a question if they thought they would be called on to read aloud. The teacher makes it clear after a few ERT lessons that the child who gives the answer is *never* the child who reads aloud (even if that child wants to read aloud). Struggling readers quickly figure out that it is "safe" to answer questions, and they begin to participate in the activity (instead of just sitting there waiting for it to end!).

In addition to allowing all participants to feel successful, a multilevel activity must have multiple things to be learned. ERT lessons always have multiple things to be learned. The most obvious and important thing you can learn from participating in ERT lessons is that not everything you need to think about as you read is directly stated, in so many words, right on the page. Most teachers have experienced students responding to a question that requires them to make inferences by saying, "It didn't tell us that." Some students—even good students—expect the text to tell them everything directly. In reality, most comprehension requires inference. In ERT lessons, students learn that they can find the answers to some questions but that they have to figure out the answers to others. As they listen to their friends answer inferential questions and read clues, they learn how to connect what they read in the text to what they already know to understand what they are reading.

Many teachers experience so much success with ERT that they are tempted to use it every day. Resist the temptation! ERT is fun for the students if used judiciously, but any format becomes boring if you do it every day. Many teachers use ERT as the format for reading the first chapter in a book or the first part of a selection. The first part of any selection is hardest to read because it is where major characters are introduced and major concepts built. Once readers are successfully launched into a selection, consider using other formats, such as partner reading, play school groups, or coaching groups to provide students the support they need to continue experiencing success and learning from the selection.

## Partner Reading ("Two Heads Are Better Than One!")

Imagine that you and your best friend both have the same task to accomplish. Perhaps you need to learn PowerPoint to create a presentation for your graduate class. Would you be likely to get together to work on it? Would doing it together be more fun than doing it alone? Would you be able to do it better and perhaps faster together than alone (provided you did not get sidetracked by other mutual interests!)? In real life, when we have something to accomplish and someone we like has the same task, we often arrange to do it together, believing the old saying that "Two heads are better than one."

The partner reading format allows children to learn to read better and faster, and for many children doing it with a friend is just more fun! Just as you and your friend have to stay "on track" as you work, you need to structure your partner reading format so that partners spend most of their time focused on what you want them to focus on. We have worked with teachers for many years to help them make partner reading a fun, productive, successful multilevel format. We would like to share our most important "do's" for successful partner reading.

**1** *Do think about who you will partner up with whom—and who you won't!* Children whose families have been feuding for generations probably will not make good partners. The best reader in the class is probably not the best partner for the worst reader. If boys are at the stage where they "can't stand girls," same-gender partnerships are probably best. Think about your struggling readers first and who would be the best partners for them. Ask yourself "Who will be patient and not just tell them all the words?" "Who will be insightful and able to coach them and get them to talk about their reading?" In most classrooms, there are a couple of very nurturing children who would love to help some of their struggling classmates. These are the children to try out as partners for your most struggling readers.

**2** *Do make sure your partners* know *their purpose for reading.* We all work more purposefully when we know exactly what we are trying to accomplish. The purpose for reading is what students are trying to learn and what they should be ready to contribute to the after-reading activity. If the Beach Ball activity is going to be done after reading, the partners should be reading and talking about their answers to the questions on the beach ball. If they are going to add things to the KWL chart, they should be reading to find things to add. Remember that guided reading lessons are intended to teach children how to think about text—the comprehension skills and strategies. Having a clear comprehension-oriented purpose for reading helps children become good thinkers and comprehenders.

**3** *Do set a time limit for reading.* Before children begin reading, tell them exactly how much time they have to read. Make it a reasonable amount of time, but don't give them more time than most of them will need. Most behavior problems during partner reading happen when children have time to fool around. Don't give them the same amount of time each day because some selections are longer, and rereading selections can be done in less time. But set a time limit. Write it on the board and/or set a timer. When the time is up, tell them you are sorry if they didn't finish but you need them to join the group, or tell them they may finish and then join the group. The course of action you choose doesn't matter, but be consistent and enforce your time limits. You will be amazed how much more they can read and how much better they behave when the "clock is ticking."

**4** *Do make sure they have something to do if they finish before the time is up.* Always give students a "filler"—what they should do if they finish early. Relate this filler as closely as you can to the purpose for reading. If they are reading to answer the questions on the beach ball and finish early, tell them they should take turns asking each other the questions on the beach ball and come up with "awesome" answers. If they are reading to find information to add to the KWL chart and finish early, tell them they should begin to write down the information. If the after-reading activity is doing the book and they have a few minutes, tell them to decide which character they would like to be and to practice what they will say and how they will act.

Having fillers is absolutely essential for successful partner reading because some partners will rush through the reading and then create problems because they are "all done!" Children are not in such a rush to finish first when they have to think and prepare for another task. (Do not turn the filler into a class requirement that must be turned in or completed in a specified amount of time, or you will be right back in the same old bind: "They don't all finish at the same time." Also, it is probably not a good idea to use the word *filler* when speaking to the children, but it is important for you to remember that is what it is!)

(**5**) *Do teach your students how you want them to read with their partners.* Role-play and model for them what partners do, how partners help each other, how partners correct each other nicely, and how to ask good questions. Here are some of the different ways we teach partners to read, depending on their age and the purpose for reading that day:

- *Take Turns.* One partner reads the first page and the other partner reads the second page and so on. This is the most common way of partner reading—but not necessarily the most productive.

- *Read and Point.* One partner points to the words on one page while the other partner reads; then they switch reader/pointer roles on the next page. This is particularly helpful in the beginning, when print tracking is a big issue with some children. You will be surprised at how quickly some children pick up print tracking when a nurturing, helpful partner is pointing to their words and making sure the other partner points to the words correctly when it is his or her turn. We do not recommend this practice once children become more fluent, however, because it slows down children's reading and can take their focus away from the meaning.

- *Ask Questions.* Both children read each page, silently if they can or chorally if they need help. They then ask each other a "good question" about what they have read.

- *Say Something.* Say Something is also a good partner working strategy. The simple notion is that after you read a page, you "say something." If you do not have anything to say, you may have been concentrating too much on the words and not enough on the meaning. You may need to reread the page, thinking about what you might say about it. Some teachers have partners take turns—one partner reads a page and the other partner says something; then they reverse roles. On other days, partners read the page together or silently and then each says something.

- *Echo Reading.* Once children know how to echo read, they will enjoy echo reading some selections. Give the child who is the echo in each partnership something to designate his or her status, or have the children read the selection twice switching their reading and echo reading roles. For struggling readers, make sure they are the echo on the first reading.

- *Choral Whispering.* Choral whispering is a variation of choral reading. Children whisper with their partner. Children use a "whisper" voice so that their voices do not distract partners seated nearby.

- *ERT. . . .* Children love doing ERT with each other. It is particularly effective as a rereading strategy when they know what the selection is about and need a good purpose for rereading. Even children who are not very fluent readers can usually find the answer to a question and pose a good question for their partner when they have already read the selection and this is a rereading.

**6** *Do use partner reading time to assist and monitor your children's reading.* Many teachers who are accustomed to doing reading instruction in small groups worry that when they use a variety of multilevel formats, they will not have time to listen to individual children read and will not know who is getting it and who isn't. Partner reading is a wonderful opportunity for teachers to circulate around and both assist and monitor the reading of individual children. Many teachers tell the children that they will be coming around to most of the partnerships to listen to the reading and discussion that is going on.

> "When I join your partnership, I may interrupt and ask each of you to read a little aloud for me so that I can hear how well you are growing in your reading ability. I may ask you to retell or summarize what you have read so far. I will write some notes here on my clipboard so that I have a record of how well you are reading and how you are all becoming such good thinkers about your reading. If I don't get around to all the partners today, I will make a note of that too and make sure I get to listen to you read and tell about your reading next time we read in partners."

Many teachers use the partner reading format 1 or 2 days each week. They use their time while partners are reading to monitor and coach individual children on word and comprehension strategies.

## Play School Groups

Play school groups are like partnerships, except they have three to five children instead of two. One child in the play school group will play the role of the "teacher," and we vary who is the teacher, depending on what type of activity the groups are doing. The guidelines for successful partner reading also apply to play school groups. We form heterogeneous groups and think about who to assign to each group. Children in play school groups always know what their purpose is, how long they have to play, and what to do if they finish before the time is up. We circulate to see how individual children are doing.

Play school groups can do many of the types of activities that partnerships can do. They can ask questions, say something, echo and choral read selections, and do ERT. Because they are composed of more children, play school groups are the format to use for doing the book activities. Small-group discussions can also be carried out in play school groups. After completing a graphic organizer or KWL chart several times as a whole-class activity, the activity is turned over to play school groups. The children contribute ideas and one child does the writing on the chart. Finally, all charts are compared and displayed.

Play school groups always have a "teacher." One problem is making sure all the children have a chance to be teacher. Everyone does not necessarily get to be teacher the same number of times, but the same "bossy girls" cannot be teacher every time! To get around this, consider which play school formats do not require a super reader.

Imagine that the class has read a story and completed an appropriate activity with it the preceding day. Today they are going to decide what the characters are saying and doing on each page in preparation for pantomiming the book. Divide your struggling readers, one among each group, and assign them the role of "teacher." The rest of the group take turns reading the pages. Because you read it yesterday, and the struggling readers are not reading aloud, the other children should be able to fluently read their page aloud. The teacher tells everyone whose turn it is and then asks everyone, "Who was talking and how would they act?"

Struggling readers can also be the teacher when the play school group is using the choral reading format. For echo reading, on the other hand, one of your best readers needs to be the teacher. Likewise, when groups do ERT, they need a good reader to formulate the purposes for reading each page.

Play school groups are one of the children's favorite formats for reading and rereading selections. With some clever thinking, you can allow all your children to be the teacher on various days. As the children read, you can circulate and coach the children as they need help with words or with the thinking required to fulfill their purpose for reading. In addition to the teacher coaching, some teachers appoint a student word coach in each group. This child—and only this child—is allowed to help other children figure out words. The word coach and the teacher are two different people, so you have more opportunities to let the children who are not the best readers be the teacher.

**RECOMMENDED resources**

For many more ideas about and examples of all the multilevel formats described in this section, see *Guided Reading the Four Blocks Way* (Cunningham, Hall, & Cunningham, 2000).

## How Partner Reading and Play School Groups Are Multilevel

Working together on something is a natural arrangement in real life. Children are used to helping each other and teaching each other all kinds of things. Most children learn how to ride a bike and how to play a new game from their friends. When you use partner reading and play school groups, you increase the number of "teachers" in your classroom.

## Book Club Groups

In book club groups, as in literature circles, the children in the different groups do not read the same books. Children have some choice about the books they read, and they meet in groups to read and discuss the books. To do a book club group, we select four books related by author, topic, genre, or theme. In our book club groups, we have used four biographies, four mysteries, four Dr. Seuss books, four books about sea animals, and four books about friends. When selecting four books, we always include one book that is fairly easy and one that is more challenging.

Book club groups usually meet for several days or weeks to read the book. On the first day, children preview all four books and indicate to us their first, second, and third choice of which book they would most like to read. We promise everyone that they will get one of their choices, but we caution them that everyone will not get his or her first choice.

To form groups, we first look at the choices of our struggling readers. If they choose the easy book for any of their choices, we assign them to that book. (Obviously, we do not tell anyone about an "easy" book.) If a struggling reader does not choose the easy book for any of his or her choices, we usually assign that child to the first choice of book, assuming the first choice is not the challenging book! Next, we look at the choices of our advanced readers. We assign them to the challenging book if it is one of their choices. We then assign the other children, giving as many first choices as possible and making good groups that can work well together.

When everyone is assigned, the group reading the easy book contains some struggling readers and some average readers who chose that book as their first choice. The group reading the challenging book likewise contains some advanced readers and some average readers who chose that book as their first choice. The groups reading the average-difficulty books contain mostly average readers with a few struggling and advanced readers who didn't choose the book closer to their level.

The book clubs meet for as many days as you decide they need to complete the book. The comprehension purpose/focus is the same for all the groups. Groups share daily with the other children what they have learned so far. The next section is one example of how a book club group might work.

## A Book Club Group Example

The teacher decides that all the children will read and do plays and chooses four plays from the Rigby *Traditional Tales and Plays* collection, in which each book contains the tale told both in story format and in play format. The books chosen are *Goldilocks and the*

*Three Bears* and *Town Mouse and Country Mouse* (average difficulty), *The Three Billy Goats Gruff* (easier), and *Robin Hood and the Silver Trophy* (challenging). The teacher decides to spend 4 days with the children—previewing and choosing on the first day, reading the story and play in their groups for 2 days, and reading the plays in small groups and for the other groups on the final day.

*Day 1*    The teacher begins these book club groups by sharing the book covers and explaining that the books contain both a story and a play! The teacher explains that today they get to look at all the books and decide on their first, second, and third choices for which one they would most like to read. Eight books of each title have been placed in four gathering places in different corners of the room. The children circulate to the different corners and have 6 minutes to look at and talk about each book. When all the children have looked at all four books, they write down their first, second, and third choices and give these to the teacher. After school, the teacher looks at their choices and assigns children to groups, considering both their reading levels and their choices.

*Day 2*    The teacher gathers the children together and tells them that today they will spend most of their time reading the tale told in story form. Each group has 22 minutes to read the tale, and then they will gather back together and do the Beach Ball activity. The teacher quickly reviews with the children the questions on each stripe of the beach ball and the rules for Beach Ball activities. The teacher then distributes the appropriate books to members of the different groups and assigns each group a place to meet. The teacher tells the children that their group can decide how to read the story but that they must stop after every two pages and discuss their answers to the questions on the beach ball. As the children read, the teacher circulates and makes sure every group knows what to do. The teacher spends more time with the group reading *The Three Billy Goats Gruff,* coaching them on word and comprehension strategies.

   After reading the selection, they gather together again. The teacher has each group come to a circle inside the big circle, and that group answers the questions on the beach ball as the others watch and listen. The children are very interested in all four stories and pay good attention as each group shares ideas from their particular story.

*Day 3*    The activity for the third day is reading the play. Today, the teacher tells the students to read the play in two-page segments. They first read each segment in an echo reading format and then read it again with different children reading different parts. The teacher appoints a child to be the "teacher" in each group. This child teacher is the voice that all the other children will echo. The groups are instructed to take turns reading so different people read different parts. The teacher again circulates as the children read, coaching them to read with appropriate expression and settling a few disputes about who reads which part on which page.

After reading the plays in small groups, the teacher gathers the children together again, once more placing each group, in turn, in the inner circle. The teacher takes the role of narrator for each group and reads the narrator parts. Then the teacher lets all the children chorally read all the other parts. The children delight in listening to the choral reading of all the groups.

*Day 4*    Today, the children gather in their small groups once again and read the play with one person reading each part. The teacher has assigned each child a part. The child who is the narrator in each group is also given the role of "director." The children read their part and then do whatever acting is required. The teacher encourages all the groups and "rehearses" the billy goats and the troll so that they read and act with expression. After about 20 minutes of practice, the class reassembles. The members of each group read and act out their play for the other groups. Each group gets a round of applause with the loudest applause given to the big billy goat.

## Literature Circles

Literature circles are similar to book club groups in that children choose books and meet in small groups to discuss them. In literature circles, children usually have different roles and can choose the roles they want. These roles determine their purpose for reading. The roles can be divided up in a variety of ways. Some teachers designate the roles as character sketcher, author authority, plot person, conflict connector, and solution suggester. The student who likes drawing can become the character sketcher and sketch the characters in the story their group is reading. Another child in each group who knows a lot about the author can become the author authority. The plot person makes sure that everyone in the group understands what has happened in the story so far. To carry out this task, the plot person must keep track of who (somebody), what they wanted (to happen), what happened (but), and how the problem was solved (so). The conflict connector helps the group understand the conflict that exists (character versus character, character versus nature, character versus society, etc.) in the book and how the characters in the book work through the conflict. Playing these roles helps the children discuss the books they are reading and share what is happening in the stories with the whole class.

Another way of assigning roles is to give students a role sheet and model how to use it. The following is an example of the role sheets one teacher used:

- *Discussion Director:*  Your job is to develop a list of questions that your group might want to discuss about today's reading. Try to determine what is important about today's text. Focus your questions on big ideas.

- *Passage Master:*  Your job is to locate a few special sections of the reading that the group should look back on. You should help your group notice the most interesting, funny, puzzling, or important parts.

- *Vocabulary Enricher:* Your job is to be on the lookout for a few especially important words that your group needs to remember or understand. You should look for new, interesting, strange, important, or puzzling words.

- *Connector:* Your job is to find connections between the material you are reading and yourself and other students. Also look for connections to the world and to other books we have read.

- *Illustrator:* Your job is to draw some kind of picture related to the reading. It can be a sketch, diagram, flow chart, or stick figure scene.

## How Book Clubs and Literature Circles Are Multilevel

Book club groups and literature circles are two of our favorite—and most multilevel— ways to organize guided reading. By choosing books tied together in some way, we can establish a comprehension purpose and focus for everyone to work on. Including two books at the average reading level of the class—one book that is easier and one that is more challenging—allows us to come closer to matching the reading levels of most of our students. The support children get from their group and the support the teacher is able to give while circulating to the different groups (spending more time with the group reading the easy book) means that all children can have a successful reading experience.

Most teachers find that their children participate eagerly in these groups and that the books they do not get to read are the most popular selections during self-selected reading time for the next several weeks. It is not unusual for children to read all three books their group did not read. Their knowledge of the concepts and vocabulary in each book is greatly increased by the daily sharing of books that follows the small-group reading. Because they have read one of the books, including plays, biographies, mysteries, and informational books about animals, they know how that type of book is written and how to read that genre. Even struggling readers often can successfully read a book that was a little beyond their level just a few weeks ago!

## Coaching Groups

On some days, the teacher meets with a small group and coaches them to use their word and comprehension strategies. The selection of children in the coaching group changes from time to time, and although average and some advanced readers are selected each time we do a coaching group, struggling readers are included more often than advanced readers. Including some better readers guarantees that members of the coaching group and others do not view the coaching group as the "dumb readers." Including better readers also ensures that the group has some good reading models and allows everyone to learn to be a word coach.

We explain coaching groups to the children by making analogies to sports teams. Children understand that you practice various soccer moves, and then in game format the coach watches you play, stopping you from time to time to coach you to use the skills you have practiced. Before long, children learn how to coach and begin to use their coaching skills when reading with partners or in play school groups. Once they understand how to coach, we let them play the role of "word coach." We choose reading material that is at the reading level of most of the children included in this group. The children read parts of the selection to themselves first. Then someone reads aloud so that we can demonstrate what a word coach does.

## Coaching Steps

Before the children start to read, we remind them of the strategies they can use to figure out an unfamiliar word. We post a chart of steps that we review before children begin each reading lesson.

### How to Figure Out a Hard Word

1. Put your finger on the word and say all the letters.
2. Use the letters and the picture clues.
3. Look for a rhyme you know.
4. Keep your finger on the word and finish the sentence; then pretend it's the covered word.

Here is how we coach each step and why each step is important:

**(1)** *Put your finger on the word and say all the letters.* When children come to a word they do not know, we have them put their finger on the word and name all the letters. It is very important that the children name the letters. Naming the letters is not the same as pronouncing individual sounds to sound out the word. English is not a sound-it-out-letter-by-letter language, and the worst readers are the ones who try this phonetic approach. We want them to name all the letters because having them do so is the only way we know for sure that they have indeed looked at them and seen them all in the right order. We also want them to name the letters because strong evidence supports the idea that retrieval from the brain's memory store is auditory. Just looking at an arrangement of letters and searching in your brain for the word, or a rhyming word, that resembles them is apt to be a more difficult way of identifying that word than saying the letters, which goes through the brain's auditory channel.

In our experience, if children are reading at the right level and name the letters of an unfamiliar word out loud, they can sometimes immediately pronounce that word correctly, which may be proof positive that the auditory channel was needed for retrieval! After they name all the letters and successfully pronounce the word, cheer! They have scored a goal. ("See, it was in there. You just had to say it so your brain could find it!") If they still do not know the word after they name all the letters, give them one of the next three cues, depending on the word.

(2) *Use the letters and the picture clues.* Pictures often provide clues to words. The child who sees the word *raccoon* and names all the letters, then glances at the picture, may indeed see a picture of a raccoon. The picture, along with naming the letters, often allows children to decode the word. Once the child has named all the letters out loud and studied the picture, we cue them to notice the picture clue:

> "I see an animal in the picture that looks to me like a *r-a-c-c-o-o-n.*"

(3) *Look for a rhyme you know.* In our word activities, we teach children to decode and spell words based on rhyming patterns. If the unknown word has a familiar rhyming pattern, we cue the child to some of the rhyming words he or she might know:

> "We know that *w-i-l-l* is *will* and *s-t-i-l-l* is *still.* Can you make *t-h-r-i-l-l* rhyme with *will* and *still*?"

(4) *Keep your finger on the word and finish the sentence; then pretend it's the covered word.* Guess the Covered Word is an activity that helps children use beginning letters, word length, and context to figure out words. It is the "default" cue, the one we use when others do not work. If neither picture clues nor rhyming words help, we cue children to try the covered word activity. Having children read on and then go back is not the preferred method for decoding words because it interrupts their reading. Moreover, we want children to study and process unknown words as they encounter them. However, when children need the clues provided by the rest of the sentence to decode a word, we coach them to use the sentence clues.

## Coaching a Missed Word

The procedure just described is what we do when a child stops on a word. If instead of stopping, the child misreads a word, we let him or her finish the sentence and then have the child return to that misread word. Imagine, for example, that the child reads "There was not a cold in the sky" instead of reading the sentence *There was not a cloud in the sky.* At the moment the child misreads "cold" for *cloud, cold* does make sense. But by the end of the sentence, the child should realize that the sentence did not make sense and go back to try to fix the error. We let children finish the sentence to help them develop their own self-monitoring system. If, however, they do not notice any error and just continue to read, we stop them and say something like, "That didn't make sense. Let's look at this word again. Say all the letters in this word." We then give them the appropriate cue to help them figure out the word.

## When We Do Coaching Groups

Many teachers do coaching groups while those children not in the coaching group read with partners. Some teachers find time in their weekly schedule to meet with coaching groups outside the guided reading time. In some classrooms, the teacher meets daily with an "after-lunch bunch" and does coaching at that time. We include all children in the after-lunch bunch activities across the week, but we include the struggling readers almost every day and the others less frequently. In some classrooms, teachers have a center time each day and do a coaching group that we call a "Fun Reading Club" during that time. Coaching groups last only 10–15 minutes. We do not do before- and after-reading activities to teach comprehension because the children in our coaching group were also in our guided reading comprehension lessons. We do not introduce high-frequency words or teach decoding strategies because these lessons are covered during word activities. We simply choose material at the instructional level of most of the children we intend to include and begin reading it, simulating as we read what children must do during self-selected reading when they tackle text on their own. As the children read and encounter problems, we coach them to apply what they have learned when they actually need to use it.

In some classrooms, special teachers or assistants do coaching groups with children. If you have help coming and have many children that need coaching, you might schedule self-selected reading at that time and have the helping person coach children in their self-selected books. Many teachers like to schedule guided reading when they have help coming. The helping teacher can coach children through the selection, if it is close to their instructional level, or can read that selection to them and then coach them in material at their level.

Finding the time, people, and reading materials to do coaching groups is not easy. But when you add regular coaching in instructional-level material to the good instruction struggling readers receive throughout the day, you will be amazed at the rapid progress these readers can make.

## How Coaching Groups Are Multilevel

In coaching groups, we stress that all children are learning to become word coaches. We call them together and model what a word coach does. Then we let children volunteer to be word coaches and coach them on how to coach. We do include struggling readers in coaching groups more often than others, and we choose material at the appropriate level for those children who need coaching. Every group includes some more able readers, however, and the membership in coaching groups changes regularly. Because coaching groups is just one of the formats we use to make our guided reading time multilevel and because we group children for all different kinds of reasons, these groups are not viewed by others or the children in them as "low" reading groups.

## *Summary*

Children differ on all possible dimensions. They begin at different points and move forward at different rates. Growth does not happen in equal increments. Spurts and plateaus occur in the development of any ability. The simple fact of individual differences is what makes teaching all children to read and write such a challenging task. In the past, many solutions were tried. Retention, tracking, and within-class groupings according to level were the most common attempts to provide instruction from which all children could benefit. None of these has any research to support its long-term effectiveness in accelerating the literacy development of struggling readers. Multilevel instruction contains multiple things to be learned and allows all students to feel successful. Motivation is directly related to the expectation of success.

This chapter has included a description of how self-selected reading and writing are inherently multilevel and how word activities can be stretched to become more multilevel. Guiding children's reading of text is the most difficult activity to make multilevel because the text is inevitably too hard for some and too easy for others. A variety of formats that teachers use to make guided reading lessons more multilevel were described. When children experience a balanced reading program that includes self-selected reading and writing as well as multilevel word and guided reading lessons, all children can experience success and progress at optimal rates for them.

# *Assessment*

Assessment is part of everything we do in life. Most of us make an assessment of the weather each morning to decide what to wear. We assess the food, service, and atmosphere as we dine at the new restaurant in town. We assess our new neighbors as we watch them interact with each other and move their furniture in. This chapter provides some examples of how you can make assessment an extension of your teaching, rather than just one more chore that has to be done.

# What Is Assessment?

Sometimes, it is easier to define something by beginning with what it is not. Assessment is *not* grading—although assessment can help you determine and support the grades you give. Assessment is *not* standardized test scores—although these scores can give you some general idea of what children have achieved so far. Assessment *is* collecting and analyzing data to make decisions about how children are performing and growing.

Caldwell (2002) describes four steps for assessment. First, we identify what we want to assess. Second, we collect evidence. Third, we analyze that evidence. Fourth and finally, we make a decision and act on that decision. Caldwell suggests three main purposes for reading assessment: to determine student reading level, to identify good reading behaviors, and to document student progress.

**RECOMMENDED resources**

This chapter only begins to discuss the complex topic of classroom assessment. We are indebted to JoAnne Caldwell for her wonderfully written, practical book, *Reading Assessment: A Primer for Teachers and Tutors* (2002). We learned a lot from reading this book and enjoyed all her lively examples and analogies. If assessment is one of the issues you struggle with, we highly recommend this book.

# Determining Student Reading Level

The previous chapter discussed the inevitability of children reading at different levels and how reading instruction can be multilevel. It also suggested that reading level is not a static entity. Rather, reading level is affected by individual factors within each child, such as prior knowledge and interest, as well as by instructional factors, such as type of pre-reading instruction, amount of support provided by the reading format, and whether a first reading or a rereading of a selection is being considered.

Despite the fact that reading level is not static, we still need to determine, to the extent we can, an approximate reading level for each child. Knowing the level at which a child is reading early in the school year serves as a benchmark against which to judge how well our instruction is helping that child raise his or her reading level. We need to know how to determine whether the books children are choosing for self-selected reading are too hard or too easy so we can help them make more appropriate choices. We need to have a general idea of each child's reading level so we can decide how much support each child needs to experience success during guided reading lessons with various texts. Finally, we need to determine reading levels because most schools and parents expect and require us to know the reading level of and document progress for each student.

To determine a child's reading level, you need to have the child read passages at different reading levels. Many reading series include graded passages with their reading textbooks. Teachers use these to determine the reading levels of their students. Some school districts and states have created graded passages or selected benchmark books that teachers use to assess reading levels. A number of published Informal Reading Inventories (IRIs) also include graded passages, such as the Basic Reading Inventory (Johns, 2001) and the Qualitative Reading Inventory (Leslie & Caldwell, 2001). These reading passages are graded in various ways. Traditionally, passages were specified as preprimer (early first grade), primer (middle first grade), first grade, early second grade, late second grade, third grade, fourth grade, and so on. Recently, books and passages have been divided into more levels. In the Reading Recovery system, for example, books are divided into many levels; levels 16–18 are considered end of first grade.

Regardless of the source or leveling system of your graded passages, you can use these passages to determine the approximate reading level of each student. Generally, you

A variety of systems have been developed for marking the oral reading of a child. Most systems work something like this:

> Once there was a farmer who lived with his wife and their ten children in a very small farmhouse. The farmer and his family were miserable. They were always bumping into each other and getting in each other's way. When the children stayed inside on rainy days, they fought all the time. The farmer's wife was always ~~shooing~~ *shooting* children out of the kitchen so she could cook. The farmer had no place to sit ~~quietly~~ *quickly* (SC) when he came in from *his* work. The farmer (finally) could stand it no longer. He said to his wife, "Today I am going ~~into~~ *to* the village to talk with a wise man about our crowded house. He will know what to do."

In reading this passage, the child read "shooting" for *shooing*; read "quickly" for *quietly* but then self-corrected (SC); inserted the extra word "his"; omitted the word *finally*; and read "to" for *into*.

have the child read aloud a passage, beginning with one you think he or she can handle. As the child reads, you mark the reading in some way that errors can be counted and analyzed. After the child reads the passage, you ask him or her to retell the passage or ask questions to determine how much he or she comprehends.

Once you have made a record of the child's oral reading and determined his or her comprehension from the retelling or the answers to questions, you decide what level of oral reading accuracy and comprehension is adequate. Many arguments and disagreements concern this decision. Most experts recommend that a child have an oral reading accuracy level of about 95 percent and demonstrate comprehension of 75 percent of the important ideas in the passage. The passage about the farmer and his wife has approximately 100 words. If you do not count the self-correction (which we would not because self-correcting is a good reading behavior that indicates the child is self-monitoring), the reader made four errors, giving him an accuracy rate of 96 percent. If the child's retelling indicates comprehension of most of the important ideas in this short passage, we will know that this reader can read text at this level quite adequately. We will not, however, know that this is the just right, or instructional, level for the child.

Instructional level is generally considered to be the highest level of text that a reader can read with about 95 percent word accuracy and 75 percent comprehension. To determine instructional level, we must continue to have the child read harder and harder passages until word identification falls below 95 percent or comprehension falls below

### Determining Reading Levels

1. Use passages or books that have been determined to get increasingly more difficult.
2. Have the child begin reading at the level you think he or she might be.
3. To get a measure of word reading accuracy, record oral reading errors as the child reads.
4. After the child reads, remove the text and ask the child to retell what was read or ask some comprehension questions.
5. If the child's word reading accuracy is approximately 95 percent and comprehension is approximately 75 percent, have that child read the next harder passage. If the child's word reading accuracy is below 95 percent or comprehension is below 75 percent, have that child read the next easier passage.
6. Continue to have the child read until you determine the highest level at which the child can read and still meet the 95 percent word accuracy and 75 percent comprehension criteria. This is the best general indicator of that child's just right, or instructional, reading level.

75 percent. Instructional level is generally considered to be the *highest* level of text for which the child can pass both the word and comprehension criteria.

Once you know the approximate reading levels of all your children, you can use this information to choose materials for guided reading and decide how much support your different readers will need with the various materials. Remember that prior knowledge and interest have a large influence on reading level. Remember that during guided reading lessons, you build both interest and prior knowledge (including meaning vocabulary) before children read. You then choose your format to provide enough support so that they can be successful at meeting the purpose for the lesson. Children can read text that is a little beyond their level if they are given the appropriate support before, during, and after reading.

### Why Not Use Standardized Tests to Determine Reading Levels?

In many schools, children take a variety of tests that yield a grade equivalent. Teachers get a printout that tells them that Billy reads at 2.5 and Carla reads at 5.5. Being trusting, logical people, they assume that this means Billy's instructional reading level is middle second grade and Carla's instructional reading level is middle fifth grade. Unfortunately, life is not that simple. If Billy and Carla are both in the second grade, most of the passages they read on the test are second-grade passages. Billy's score of 2.5 means that he did as well on the test as average second-graders reading second-grade text. Carla read the same passages and she did as well as the average fifth-grader reading second-grade passages would have done. We can certainly say that Carla is a good reader—certainly a better reader than Billy. But we cannot say that her instructional reading level is fifth grade because she did not read any fifth-grade passages!

Another reason that we cannot use standardized tests to determine individual reading level is that all tests have something called *standard error of measurement (SEM)*. Look in the manual of any test and it will tell you what the SEM is. If the SEM is 5 months, then the score a child achieves is probably within 5 months of the true score. Billy's score of 2.5 has a 68 percent chance (1 standard deviation) of actually being somewhere between 2.0 and 3.0. If we want to be 95 percent sure, we have to go out 2 standard deviations. Then we will know that Billy's score is almost surely somewhere between 1.5 and 3.5.

Across groups of children, these SEMs balance out. One child's score is higher than his actual ability, but another child's score is lower. If your class average score is 2.5, you can be pretty sure that your class reads about as well as the average class of second-graders on which the test was normed. Standardized scores give us information about groups of children but give us only limited information about the reading levels of individual children. To determine the reading level of a child, we must listen to that child read and retell and find the highest levels at which he or she can do both with approximately 95 percent word accuracy and 75 percent comprehension. Unfortunately, no shortcut will get us where we need to go.

Remember also that the size of the "leaps" children make has limits. If you determine that a child's reading level is late first grade, that child can usually be given enough support to feel successful with some second-grade-level material. However, material written at the fifth-grade level is probably not going to be accessible for that child.

Once you understand how to listen to a child read and retell to determine instructional level, you can use this knowledge during your weekly self-selected reading conferences. We do not do formal oral reading records during these conferences; neither do we want to take an "inquisition" stance as we discuss the text with the child. We do, however, listen to children read a part they have selected, and we do ask them to tell about the most interesting part of the book or what they have learned so far. As they read and tell us about their reading, our informal 95 percent/75 percent meters are running, and if we realize that a child is choosing books that are way too easy or way too hard, we can steer them toward some "just right" text.

## Identifying Good Literacy Behaviors and Documenting Progress

Determining reading levels is generally done early in the year, then at specific points during the year, and again at the end of the year. Day in and day out, however, we need to be assessing and monitoring how well students are reading and writing. To do this, we have to know what we are looking for. What are the good reading and writing behaviors? Throughout the chapters of this book, we have described instruction that develops good literacy behaviors. In this section, we suggest ways to assess these behaviors as children engage in literacy activities.

### Assessing Emergent Literacy

Chapter Three described many activities for building the foundation for literacy and concluded that there are seven signs of emergent literacy. These seven signs are the reading behaviors we look for as indicators that each child is moving successfully into reading and writing. These behaviors form the basis for our assessment of beginning readers. We assess these behaviors as children engage in their daily literacy activities.

Many teachers of young children keep a checklist such as the following example. Each day they put the checklists of two or three children on their clipboard and observe and talk with these children as they engage in self-selected reading and writing to determine how well they are developing critical behaviors. Teachers often use a simple system using a minus (–) to indicate the child does not have that behavior, a question mark (?) when the behavior is erratic or it is unclear that the child has it, and a plus (+) to indicate the child does seem to have developed that behavior. Three pluses on three different dates is a reliable indicator that that child has indeed developed that behavior.

## • Emergent Literacy Behaviors •

Name _____

**Dates Checked (– ? +)**

Pretend reads favorite books, poems, songs, and chants   — — — — — — —

"Writes" and can "read back" what was written   — — — — — — —

Tracks print   — — — — — — —
    Left page first
    Top to bottom
    Left to right
    Return sweep
    Points to each word

Knows reading jargon   — — — — — — —
    Identifies one letter, one word, and one sentence
    Identifies first word, first and last letter in a word

Reads and writes some concrete words   — — — — — — —
    Own name and names of friends, pets, family
    Favorite words from books, poems, and chants

Demonstrates phonemic awareness   — — — — — — —
    Counts words
    Claps syllables
    Stretches out words as attempts to spell
    Blends and segments words
    Identifies rhymes

Demonstrates alphabet awareness   — — — — — — —
    Names some letters
    Knows some words that begin with certain letters
    Knows some common letter sounds

## Assessing Word Strategies

As children move from the emergent literacy stage into the beginning reading and writing stages, we need to monitor and assess their development of sight words, decoding, and spelling strategies. Chapter Four contained many activities for developing these strategies. Our assessment, however, must take place while the children are actually reading and writing. The goal of word instruction is to teach children words and strategies they can actually use when they are reading and writing. What we want to know is *not* how children spell words during the daily word wall activity but how quickly they recognize these words when reading and how correctly they spell these words when they are writing.

There are many opportunities throughout the day to make these observations. During our weekly self-selected reading conferences with children, we ask them to read aloud to us a short part of what they have chosen to share with us. We don't do a formal oral

---

## • Sight Word, Decoding, • and Spelling Behaviors

Name _____     **Dates Checked (– ? +)**

Identifies word wall words automatically when reading     — — — — — — —

Spells word wall words correctly in first-draft writing     — — — — — — —

Uses letter patterns, picture and sentence cues to decode     — — — — — — —
  Beginning letters of word (*br, sh, f*)
  Rhyming pattern (*at, ight, ain*)
  Endings (*s, ed, ing*)
  Prefixes (*un, inter*), suffixes (*able, tion*) for big words
  Combines letter cues, picture cues, and sentence cues

Uses letter patterns to spell words     — — — — — — —
  Beginning letters of word (*br, sh, f*)
  Rhyming pattern (*at, ight, ain*)
  Endings (*s, ed, ing, er, est*)
  Prefixes (*un, inter*), suffixes (*able, tion*) for big words

Self-monitors     — — — — — — —
  Self-corrects when meaning is distorted
  Self-corrects when nonsense word is produced
  Rereads to correct phrasing
  Rereads for fluency

Reads fluently     — — — — — — —
  With phrasing
  Attending to punctuation
  With expression

Writes fluently     — — — — — — —
  Words are written quickly
  Handwriting is not slow and laborious
  Focuses on meaning

---

reading record at that time, but we do listen for how fluently they read; how automatically they identify the word wall words; and how they use patterns, context, and other cues to figure out unknown words. When using the partner reading format, we circulate to the different partnerships and ask them to read a page to us. Again, we can note how they use what we are teaching them about words as they actually read text.

Another opportunity to observe their sight word, word identification, and fluency behaviors is when we meet with small coaching groups. We observe their spelling behaviors by periodically looking at samples of their first-draft writing, by analyzing their spelling in writing samples we collect three times each year, and in our revising/editing/publishing conferences with individual children. As with emergent literacy behaviors, the − ? + system allows us to easily record what we observe on each child's word behavior checklist.

## Assessing Comprehension Strategies

Chapter Six described comprehension strategies and a variety of activities to use before and after reading that teach comprehension and foster thoughtful literacy.

As with emergent literacy behaviors and word strategies, we monitor and assess children's development of these behaviors as we interact with them during comprehension lessons and in our self-selected reading conferences. Because comprehension is so dependent on prior knowledge and interest, we are not so able to feel secure in our judgments that a

---

### • Comprehension Strategies—Story •

| Name _____ | Dates Checked (− ? +) |
|---|---|
| Names and describes main characters | — — — — — — — |
| Names and describes settings | — — — — — — — |
| Describes the goal or problem in the story | — — — — — — — |
| Describes major events that lead to resolution | — — — — — — — |
| Describes the resolution to the story | — — — — — — — |
| Makes inferences and predictions | — — — — — — — |
| Makes connections | — — — — — — — |
|     To self | |
|     To world | |
|     To other texts | |
| Expresses a personal reaction/opinion | — — — — — — — |
| Monitors comprehension and uses fix-up strategies | — — — — — — — |

---

## • Comprehension Strategies—Information •

Name _____    **Dates Checked (– ? +)**

Describes major ideas                                                    — — — — — — —

Summarizes important information                               — — — — — — —

Accurately recalls important facts/details                    — — — — — — —

Organizes ideas appropriately                                    — — — — — — —
    Sequence/chronology
    Topic/subtopic
    Comparisons
    Cause/effect
    Problem/solution

Makes inferences                                                        — — — — — — —

Makes connections                                                      — — — — — — —
    To prior knowledge and experience
    To information from other texts

Expresses a personal reaction/opinion                       — — — — — — —

Monitors comprehension and uses fix-up strategies    — — — — — — —

child can—or cannot—use a particular comprehension strategy. Often, children recall much information and respond to that information in a high-level way when the topic is familiar and of great interest but demonstrate little comprehension of less-familiar, uninteresting topics. We can use some checklists to indicate general use of comprehension strategies, but anecdotal records are also helpful because we can include comments about prior knowledge and interest as well as comprehension strategies. Many teachers find two checklists useful—one for story text and one for informational text.

Anecdotal records are the written records that teachers keep on individual children based on their ongoing observation of and interaction with them. We can make anecdotal records instead of or in addition to any of the checklists already discussed. Anecdotal records seem to be most important for noting comprehension behaviors. Comprehension is complex, and often checklists just do not seem to capture children's thinking as clearly as you could by making comments, perhaps even including some of your children's "exact words." Teachers can use any number of ways to efficiently record and update written observations about individual students. The one we have found to be the most practical uses file folder labels.

Any school supply or office supply store sells file folder labels by the sheet. The user types or writes on the sticky label, peels it off the sheet, and affixes it to the tab of the file folder being labeled. These sheets of file folder labels are also perfect for recording brief comments about children's understanding and engagement, success, or achievement with instructional activities.

The teacher places one or more sheets of file folder labels on a clipboard that he or she carries. When interacting with or observing students, the teacher notices a significant indicator of the child's comprehension (or lack thereof). It is quick, easy, and unobtrusive to record the child's initials, the date, and a brief comment on one of the file folder labels on the sheet in the clipboard. After school, the teacher takes a few minutes and affixes each label used that day to a page for that subject in the child's anecdotal records folder.

Many teachers analyze the anecdotal records for one child each day. At this pace, every student's anecdotal records can be analyzed every 4–6 weeks. The analysis of a child's anecdotal records consists of determining the degree of support in the folder for evaluative statements, which can be written as a narrative description of the child's learning or shared with a parent at a conference. Sometimes during this analysis, the teacher realizes that not enough observations have been recorded for assessing some important area of the literacy program. When this occurs, the teacher writes the child's initials on one of the file folder labels on the sheet in the clipboard along with a one- or two-word description of the observation needed for that child. While moving through the school day, the teacher then has several labels on the sheet that remind him or her to obtain particular observations of certain children. No more reliable or valid means of diagnosing or evaluating students' ongoing learning is possible than anecdotal records collected regularly and systematically and consisting of objective and specific descriptions of children's reading behaviors.

## Assessing Writing

As described in Chapter Seven, writing is perhaps the most complex act people engage in. The best way to determine how well students write is to observe them each day as they are writing, to look at first-draft writing samples, and to interact with them during writing conferences.

You can observe many aspects of writing as you move among the class. Do students struggle to identify topics for writing? Do students do some planning first when asked to write? Is handwriting easy for them? Are they using resources in the room and spelling patterns they know to spell words? Are they automatically using some of the mechanical and grammatical conventions they have been learning? Do students move confidently through a first draft? Do students revise and edit some as they write, or do they wait until they are publishing a piece? To record these observations, you may want to make a checklist similar to the previous examples but specific to the age and starting point of your students.

In addition to the observations you record, many teachers like to take a focused writing sample during the first week of school. They give the children a prompt to which they all can relate, such as "What Third Grade Is Like" or "My Most Favorite and Least Favorite Things." They then analyze the sample to determine where individual children are in their writing development and what the class as a whole needs to work on. They put this sample away and halfway through the year ask the children to write on the same prompt again. Once the children have written the second time, teachers return the first sample and let each child analyze the writing growth made. The teachers then analyze the second sample, comparing them to the first for each child and looking for indicators of things the class needs to work on. The same procedure can be repeated once more at the end of the year.

Writing is a very complex process. No matter how good we get, there is always room for growth. Because writing is complex, it is easy to see only the problems children still exhibit in their writing and not the growth they are making. Having three writing samples on the same topic across the school year provides tangible evidence of growth to both teacher and student.

## Assessing Attitudes and Interests

It is hard to overemphasize the importance of children's attitudes toward and interests in reading and writing. If developing avid readers and writers is one of your major goals, you need to collect and analyze some data so that you can identify needs and document progress.

Early in the year, it is important to determine what your students like to read and how they feel about reading. Many teachers start the school year with the following homework assignment: "Next Monday, bring to school the three best books you read all summer." They encourage students to go back to the library to check out a book previously read. If children can no longer find the book, the teachers ask them to tell why they thought it was such a good book. Young children are encouraged to bring favorite books they like to have read to them.

When the children bring their books, we let each child tell why he or she likes the books. Some teachers do this book sharing in small groups. As the children share, we note the titles of the books they bring and their reasons for liking them. This tells us a lot about their current reading interests and also suggests selections for read-aloud books to try to broaden interests.

Some children do not bring three books, or they bring books but have nothing to say about them and may not have liked or even read the books. This tells you a lot about the current interests, attitudes, and home environment of these children. It also lets you know that all the efforts you plan to make to encourage and support reading are truly important and needed.

You might want to follow up this "best-books" assignment with another homework assignment to bring in magazines and parts of the newspaper they have read. Again, follow up this assignment with group sharing and make notes about what each child brings (or does not bring). Record your results on a "Beginning Interests and Attitudes Summary," such as that shown here. In addition to noting what each child shares, summarize the interests of the class by noting which topics and types of books are shared most. You have now assessed your students' entering interests and attitudes and can plan how much and what kinds of motivational activities to do.

Just as with any kind of assessment, your assessment of reading interests and attitudes should be ongoing. By linking your assessment directly to your instruction, you ensure

| Children's Names | Books Shared | Magazines/ Newspapers | Current Interest (none, little) some, much) |
|---|---|---|---|
| Carol | Ramona the Pest Charlotte's Web | none | some |
| Sheryll | 3 Bobbsey Twins mysteries | none | some |
| Sue Ann | Whales Dinosaurs Runaway Horse | U.S.A Today | much |
| Travis | none | Sports page | little |
| Ray | none | Fishing | little |
| David | 3 Star Trek books | Sports Illustrated | some |
| Jason | Cannonball Death at High Noon Dirty Dozen | Time | some |

**Topics of interest to many children:**

Sports, fantasy

**Types of books read:**

| ✔Realistic fiction | ✔Science fiction | Historical fiction |
|---|---|---|
| ✔Mystery | Myths/legends | Folk/fairy tales |
| Fantasy | Biography | Autobiography |
| ✔Informational | Other _____ | |

---

**• Literacy Attitudes •**

Name _____ **Dates Checked (– ? +)**

Seemed happy when engaged in reading       — — — — — — —

Seemed happy when engaged in writing       — — — — — — —

Talked about reading at home       — — — — — — —

Talked about writing at home       — — — — — — —

Showed enthusiasm when sharing a book with peers       — — — — — — —

Showed enthusiasm when sharing a piece of writing       — — — — — — —

Showed enthusiasm during self-selected reading conference       — — — — — — —

Showed enthusiasm during writing conference       — — — — — — —

Chose to read rather than engage in another activity       — — — — — — —

Chose to write rather than engage in another activity       — — — — — — —

---

that your assessment is valid. By assessing interests and attitudes on a regular schedule, you get a more reliable indicator than if you assess only once or twice a year. Also, as in any assessment, you can use a variety of methods to assess interests and attitudes. One of the best methods of assessing is to observe what your students actually do. Many teachers fill out checklists for everyone early in the year and then fill them out again for one-sixth of their class each week. If you do this all year, you should have six or seven indicators of reading attitude throughout the year and should be able to document which students have better attitudes at the end of the year than they did at the beginning.

## *Summary*

Assessment is a part of everything we do. To make any kind of decision, we collect and analyze evidence and then act on that evidence. Literacy assessment includes determining reading levels for children, assessing and monitoring their reading and writing strategies and behaviors, and documenting their progress. The systematic use of checklists and anecdotal records gives you the most valid and reliable results. You can then use these records to document the progress of each child and report that progress to parents and other stakeholders. Assessment in real life is a natural and productive activity. We hope that the practical ideas presented in this chapter help make assessment a natural and productive part of your literacy instruction.

# *Extra Support*
## *for Students Who Need It Most*

We wrote this book to provide classrooms teachers with the most effective tools for moving *all* children forward in their reading and writing. Throughout the book, we have included multilevel activities that include all children. In every classroom, however, there is a child or two who needs "above and beyond" support. This chapter suggests ways that you can provide extra support for your students who need it most.

# *Form an After-Lunch Bunch*

An after-lunch bunch is a small group that gets together for 10–15 minutes after lunch (or at another time—just choose another name for it!) and reads easy books "just for fun." For example, in one first-grade classroom in January, the teacher was observing the children as they were partner reading. They could all read with a partner's help. The teacher knew from observing the partners, however, that four of the first-graders were missing many words and were not really at instructional level in these books.

The teacher decided that these children needed some additional reading with easy materials. Thus, the after-lunch bunch was formed. Membership in the after-lunch bunch changed daily, but the teacher made sure that the four children whose needs had instigated the formation of this group were in the group often but not every day. Every child was included in the after-lunch bunch every week, but the best readers were only included once each week. Thus the membership changed daily, but the group always included a majority of children who needed some easier reading and other children who were good reading models. No child ever suspected that this was "a low group" (and in fact, it wasn't!).

Each day when the children returned from lunch, they would check the list posted at the back table to see whether they were in the after-lunch bunch that day. The six children who found their names gathered eagerly at the back table "to read some fun books with the teacher." The children read for 10–15 minutes, often reading through several easy stories. During this after-lunch bunch, no comprehension strategies were taught, as they are during guided reading. The teacher did, however, coach them on how to figure out words, and meaning was always emphasized.

The after-lunch bunch idea can be used at different grade levels and with a variety of materials. Teachers find it most useful for guided reading when they have just a few children who are not at instructional level with the materials the class is using. If children share books, you can do an after-lunch bunch with only three or four copies of the easy material you have selected. It is critical for the children to view the after-lunch bunch as a chance to "just read and enjoy" some fun material and to see that the membership varies. No child is in the same group every day, and some good reading models are always present.

### Scheduling Easy Reading Time

After-lunch reading can also be after-school reading (or even before-school reading, if school opens later). We have seen programs similar to the one described above that involved teachers, parents, and children after school. In some cases, the reading and special education resource teachers work on "flex-time" and begin their school day a bit later than other teachers to be available to organize the after-school reading for this extended day program, at no additional cost. In one of these schools, each teacher schedules a single child to stay after school each day (except Friday) to work with individually for 15–20 minutes. The child then joins the after-school children for some fun, easy reading with a small group.

# Schedule 30 Minutes of Open-Center Time into Your Day

We know what you are thinking. You are thinking that you cannot get it all done now, much less with 30 minutes less time! We are going to try to convince you that you can get back your 30 minutes in increased productivity during the rest of the day, that students need time to pursue their own interests, and that freeing you up to work with individuals and small groups on the most pressing needs is a valuable use of your time.

First, let us consider what *open centers* are—and what they are not. Open centers contain things kids like to work with and opportunities to pursue their own interests. Open centers usually do not change very much, although a new center is often added that connects to a current theme or unit. Open centers often contain the following items:

Legos or other building materials

Puzzles

Board games

Computer with games, drawing, and publishing software

Computer linked to the Internet

Math manipulatives

Math games

Science manipulatives

Play-Doh or other sculpting material

Chalk, paint, or other drawing material

Markers, paper, stamps, and other writing/drawing materials

Children's magazines

Children's encyclopedia and other reference books

VCR and monitor showing a Reading Rainbow book or other video

From this list, you should get the idea that open centers contain open-ended materials, things children can enjoy and learn from on their own not unlike the way they might play at home, if they lived in this kind of enriching environment. Open centers do not contain worksheets or assignments. Although students do "produce" things in some centers, these are things they choose to make. Students are not required to complete things and turn them in, and nothing is graded or checked on.

To get open centers to work, you must have rules and routines and spend whatever time is required making sure everyone understands and follows them. Decide on a way of determining who goes to which center. Because children follow their interests, it is not necessary or even desirable that every child go to every center. In many classrooms, children are designated as days of the week and do a variety of things on their days. On Mondays, the Monday children share in the Author's Chair, conference with the teacher during self-selected reading time, and so on. Use this or some other system to let children choose centers. On Monday, the Monday children choose first and then the Tuesday, Wednesday, Thursday, and Friday children choose. But on Tuesday, the Monday children are the last to choose because the order is Tuesday, Wednesday, Thursday, Friday, Monday. The number of children allowed at each center is determined, and once children choose a center, they stay in that center for the remainder of the 30 minutes. Appoint one child in charge of each center for a week. Choose a child who often chooses that center, and let center leaders go to their centers and get materials ready a minute before others go to the centers. At the end of center time, the center leader sees that all of the center materials are stored and ready for the next day.

Before beginning center time, use 30 minutes to have some class members role-play what should happen in each center, how center materials are treated, and the quiet voices required if everyone is to work in centers. Stop the role-plays regularly and ask the children who are watching what is being done right and what needs to be done differently. Do not begin centers until all children understand, even if they do not perfectly carry out, what must happen in the centers. When you begin open-center time, spend whatever part of the 30 minutes is required getting kids to the centers, making sure they know what they are allowed to do there, reminding them not to migrate to other centers, and making sure centers are tidy and ready for the next day. If children are not used to caring for materials and working independently, it may take several weeks of your persistent reminders to teach all your children what is expected. Do not hesitate to close a center—sending the members back to their desks—if the whole group at the center is not following procedures. If an individual child is not cooperating, sharing, using a quiet voice, and so on, send that child back to his or her seat. Some teachers require that the children sent back to their seats use this seat time to write an explanation of what they were doing and what they should have been doing. They are not allowed to choose a center the next day until a satisfactorily written explanation is produced.

Eventually, if you are determined and persistent, your centers will work almost without you. Leaders will care for materials, and children will know which days they get to choose first. The occasional child who must be removed will, after sulking for a few minutes, write the required explanation so that he or she can go to centers the next day. Once this happens, you can begin to reap the benefits of this time. Explain to the children that on some days, you need to use some of their center time to work with them individually or in small groups. Explain further that because you are taking some of their time today, they get first choice of the centers tomorrow, regardless of which day of the week they are. Now you have some uninterrupted time to do any number of things: to tutor individuals, to work with small after-lunch bunch groups, to do individual running records, to catch a

. . . . . . . . . . . . . . . . . . . . . . . . . . . . . . . . . . . . . . . . . . . . . . . . . . . . . . . . . . . . . . . . . . . . . . . . . . . . . . . . . . . . . . . . . . . . . . . . . . . . . . . . . . . . . . . . . . . . .

**219**

child up who has been absent for a week, or to chat with a child who needs some attitude adjustment as well as some of your undivided attention.

The notion of balance in classrooms is a critical issue. We must balance the instructional approaches we use because children learn in different ways. We must allocate time to different subject areas because many important things need to be learned. One way in which many classrooms are out of balance is addressed by the concept of open centers. Children who are exploring through manipulating, drawing, playing games, and so on are learning, but they are pursuing their own interests and learning in a way for which they are best suited. If you consider Gardner's (1993) important concept of *multiple intelligences* and you look at what happens across an entire school day, you often do not see many learning opportunities for children whose intelligence is more visual/spatial, musical, or rhythmic. Because centers contain a variety of activities and because children choose their centers, the learning possibilities are greatly expanded.

Open centers also create a more balanced classroom day by freeing up the teacher to do whatever is most needed on that day for particular groups or individuals. When every minute of every day is allocated to a particular subject and the teacher has just that time to teach that subject to everyone, individual needs go unmet. One of the great frustrations of teaching is seeing something that desperately needs to be done and in many cases even knowing what to do about it but not being able to find the few minutes it would take to do it. Classrooms with smooth-running open-center time provide teachers opportunities to do the little things that add up to big differences in a particular child's learning.

Now, if you are convinced that you need some open-center time, where will it come from? In most classrooms, a lot of time is wasted in transitions. Teachers who are looking for 30 minutes should clock how long it takes to settle down after lunch and how much time they spend waiting for everyone to get ready. In some classrooms, 15 minutes is spent taking attendance each day, and children spend 15 minutes getting ready to go home! To find that 30 minutes, try carving 3–5 minutes off transitions, attendance taking, getting ready to go home, and so forth and see whether it cannot be done. If your school day ends at 3:15, imagine it was ending at 2:45. You do not want to leave any subject out, but could you "tighten it up a bit" and find 30 minutes? Most school days contain 30 minutes of slack, and this 30 minutes could provide you and your students with a more balanced, less frustrating day.

# Find and Train a Tutor for Your Most Needy Child

In many classrooms, teachers are overwhelmed by the scope of the literacy problems our children have and by how much needs to be done. If we have lots of struggling readers, we may realize that we cannot do everything, so we end up doing nothing. Think now about the one child you have who is most behind in reading and writing and is not receiving any individual help. Perhaps this child is just learning to speak English or has not attended school regularly. For whatever reason, this child's reading and writing level is well below that of the other children.

Most children who are far behind in reading and writing can make considerable progress if they have a strong classroom program and some one-on-one tutoring. Before thinking about where you might find this tutor, you must decide what you would train the tutor to do. The most important component of any successful tutoring program is the repeated readings of materials at the child's instructional level. So your first task is to find some materials that are just right. As described previously, disagreement exists about what exactly constitutes instructional level, but materials in which the child misses no more than 5 words per 100 and that are interesting to the student are ideal. Fortunately, you have a wealth of easy materials to choose from. The best list of easy-to-read books can be found in Marianne Lanino Pilla's *The Best High/Low Books for Reluctant Readers* (1990). In this book, she describes 374 books that she has found to be accessible and appealing to reluctant readers. Of course, new books are being published at a phenomenal rate, so you should be constantly on the lookout for easy books that appeal to your students.

In addition to high/low series of books, many other books have a particular appeal to struggling readers. Many teachers find that their students like to read books that relate to movies and TV shows, such as the *Star Wars* books and *Voyager* books. Many struggling readers enjoy books about real things, such as David Macaulay's books *Pyramids* and *Cathedral* or the Time-Life *How Things Work, Ripley's Believe It or Not,* and *The Baseball Encyclopedia.* Cartoon characters such as Garfield and Heathcliff are enormously popular with some intermediate-aged children. Comic books have long been a mainstay of preteen reading and actually require sophisticated reading skills to follow what is happening.

So your first task is to find some books that will interest your student and that the student will be able to read with some help from the tutor. If your student is a "nonreader" or such a beginning reader that you cannot find anything, you will have to create the materials. This is not as hard as it sounds. Simply sit down with your struggling reader and write an introductory paragraph of five or six sentences about him.

> Carlton is 9 years old. He goes to Washington School. He is in the fourth grade. Mrs. Cunningham is his teacher. He likes Washington School. He likes Mrs. Cunningham, too.

This paragraph will become the reading material he reads with the tutor for the next several days until he can read it fluently and knows most of the words in it. When he

## RECOMMENDED resources

### Easy but Interesting Books

Any list of high/low books is out of date before it is published, but the following list is a sampling to give you some idea of the variety available and to entice you to find some books that will appeal to your kids:

*Eek: Stories to Make You Shriek!* (Grosset and Dunlap). Easy-reader chapter books in which children experience scary, spooky—but not violent—adventures.

*Eye Witness Books* (Dorling Kindersly). Science and social studies topics—rocks, birds, machines, and so forth in an attractive, highly visual format.

*Bridgestone Early Reader Science* (Capstone). Reading levels 1–3. Our favorite is the transportation set, featuring bulldozers, fire trucks, freight trains, and tractors.

*Capstone High–Low Nonfiction* (Capstone). Dozens of theme sets on reading levels 3–4. Our favorites are the set on lizards and the one on racing, which includes hot rods and stock cars.

*The Reading Scene* (Continental Press). Each book contains four (7-page) stories. Mysteries, biographies (including those of Bruce Springsteen and Bill Cosby), and young adolescent problems are the major topics covered.

*Galaxy 5* (Fearon, David S. Lake Publishers). This science fiction series of six books (60 pages each) follows the adventures of the crew of the spaceship *Voyager* as it establishes a colony of humans on a far-off planet.

*Laura Brewster Books* (Fearon, David S. Lake Publishers). This mystery series of six books (60 pages each) finds a jeans-clad Laura Brewster roaming the world and solving mysteries for her insurance company employer.

*Sportellers* (Fearon, David S. Lake Publishers). This series of eight (60-page) books gives a fictionalized account of how stars in various sports train and grow.

*Tom and Ricky Mystery* Series (High Noon Books). This series of 10 (45-page) books, and several other series also published by High Noon, have reading levels of first and second grade and are particularly helpful in providing easy reading material to very poor readers for whom English is a second language.

*Great Lives* (Scholastic). This is one of several themed collections available. The series focuses on biographies of famous Americans and offers links to social studies topics.

*Concept Science* (Modern Curriculum Press). This series includes 44 titles, such as *Earthworms Are Animals* and *Our Changing Earth.* The books are available in Spanish.

*World of Dinosaurs* (Steck-Vaughn-Raintree). This series includes 10 books and offers short, easy-reading opportunities about a most popular topic.

demonstrates to you that he can do this, ask him what else he would like the book to tell about him and have him watch while you write the second page:

> Carlton has six brothers and sisters. Their names are Robert, David, Manuel, Thomas, Patrice, and Jackie. They live on Willow Road. His father works at the Ford place. His mother works at Ken's Quik-Mart. His cousin, Travis, lives with them, too.

The procedure continues with the teacher creating the pages of Carlton's book and the tutor reading and rereading them with Carlton until he can fluently read each page and most of the words. Future pages tell about any pets Carlton has, places he has gone, friends and what they do together, foods he likes to eat, jobs he does at home, things he does not like, and so forth. Once Carlton can fluently read this beginning book, he will have a good bank of known high-frequency words and should begin being tutored in one of the easiest high/low books.

Once the material has been chosen or created for the child to read, tutoring procedures follow a predictable pattern.

1. The child rereads pages for several days. After reading each page, the child puts checkmarks on index cards next to previously missed words that he or she was able to read correctly today. Words with three checks are "retired."

2. The tutor and child preview a new book or several new pages of a book, naming things, talking about what is happening in the pictures, and reading any headings or labels.

3. The child reads one page without help from the tutor, figuring out words in whatever way he or she can.

4. The tutor points out good strategies the reader used: sounding out an unfamiliar word, using picture clues, going back and correcting at the end of a sentence, and so on.

5. The tutor then points out any words that the child did not read correctly and helps him or her figure them out by showing how the picture, the letters in the word, and the sense of the sentence help with that word.

6. The tutor writes the missed words on index cards along with the page number on which they were missed.

7. The same procedure is repeated with each page. Pictures, headings, and labels are discussed. The page is read by the child unaided. The tutor points out good strategies the reader used and then gives help with missed words. The missed words are written on index cards with the page numbers.

8. When several pages have been read and three to six missed words are written on cards, the tutor and child return to the first page read that day. The missed words are displayed in front of the child, but they are not pronounced by the tutor or the child. When the child has finished the page, he puts a check next to any word correctly read in the text this time. The tutor and the child talk about words that were not correctly read and how they can be figured out. The child continues to reread pages with the index-card words for that page visible as he reads, checking those correctly read when the page is finished and getting help with those incorrectly read.

9. The word cards are put in an envelope and clipped to the book and are ready for the next day's reading.

10. Together, the tutor and the child write in a notebook a sentence or two summarizing what was read today. The child and the tutor first agree on what to write. Then the child writes, getting help from the tutor with spelling as needed. The tutor and child decide on one word each day to add to the child's portable word wall folder. This folder has the alphabet letters and spaces for words needed. By having the folder open while writing, the child can quickly find a word he or she remembers deciding that he or she needs to learn to spell.

| A | B | C | D | E | F |
|---|---|---|---|---|---|
| are also about | before | can't could | don't | enough | first favorite |
| G getting | H have | I I'm into | J | K know knew | L let's |
| M myself | N new | O one our | P people | Q | R really |
| S said school | T then there threw to | U until | V very | W want was wear whether | X | YZ your you're |

For Carlton's book, this procedure should be varied somewhat. Because Carlton knows almost no words, each sentence should be written on a sentence strip, read, and then cut into words. Carlton should reassemble the words to match each sentence in the paragraph. Eventually, he should make the whole paragraph by matching and assembling the cut-apart words. Carlton should write a sentence at the end of each day, perhaps choosing his favorite sentence from the paragraph and then trying to write it without looking with spelling help from the tutor. He and the tutor decide on a word each day to add to his word wall folder, and Carlton learns to find and use these words to help him write his sentence each day.

As you can tell, the trickiest part of this tutoring is finding the right book. If you find a book in which the child is missing a word every 20 words or so, the reading is fluent enough so that the child can figure out words and self-correct. The number of missed words you write on index cards is small enough so that the child is able to learn these words and accumulate the three checks necessary to retire them. Once you have the tutoring set up, you need to monitor the progress of the child. When children are accumulating few index-card words, it is time to move them to slightly harder books. Now how can you find this tutor? Consider these possibilities:

1. Do you know a parent who drops off or picks up at school every day and could stay 30 minutes or come 30 minutes early? Many parents are on a tight schedule, but most schools have some parents with the flexibility to spend 30 minutes tutoring a child if they know they are needed and have a specific, workable tutoring system, such as that just described.

2. Does a capable lunchroom worker or bus driver have 30 minutes a day to spare? Some part-time workers would love to have the opportunity to make a difference in the life of a child. Some schools even have money to pay this person a little extra each week for the extra hours worked.

3. Does a high school nearby begin or end earlier or later than your school? Many high schools encourage (or even require!) volunteer service by their students. Perhaps a future teacher would love to have the experience tutoring your child could offer.

4. Does your school have older students, one of whom might be your tutor? Ask a teacher friend who teaches older children if some student could afford the half-hour it would take each day to tutor your child. The schedule could be staggered so that the tutor did not miss the same thing each day, or the tutor could come when other students are going to band, chorus, and so forth.

5. Do you have a student who could be the tutor? If you are an intermediate teacher and you have a sophisticated, nurturing, budding teacher in your classroom, you may already have the help you need. Most intermediate-aged children are not sophisticated or dedicated enough to do this, but there is often one in every class.

(6) If you cannot get one person to come for 30 minutes every day, could you get four people to come for 2 hours 1 day each week? One school found four retired people willing to give up one afternoon each week to tutor children. Two teachers worked together to find and train these tutors. On their day each week, each tutor worked individually with four children, two from each class. Each tutor knew the procedures and each wrote a note in the child's notebook for the next day's tutor, telling how far they had gotten and pointing out any "good things" the child had done that day. On Friday, the classroom teachers took turns meeting with each child being tutored while the other teacher read to both classes. During this Friday time, they monitored the progress of each child and decided when to move each child to higher-level books. They also wrote a note in the child's notebook letting the tutors know how much progress each child was making and how appreciative they were of the help.

**A Model for Volunteer Tutors**

The University of Virginia sponsors a volunteer tutoring program. The program is organized by reading specialists and graduate students. Their job is to determine reading levels for children and take running records on books read. They put critical words on cards in pockets in the back of books. When a child has read that book and learned the words, these word cards are added to the child's shoebox word bank. The tutor makes a duplicate set of word cards to replace those in the pocket. Each child's shoebox word bank has an alphabet strip and sound boxes taped on the outside. For more details, see Invernezzi, Juel, and Rosemay (1997).

## Partner Older Struggling Readers to Tutor Younger Struggling Readers

This idea is based on a tutoring program set up at Webster Magnet School in Minnesota (Taylor, Hansen, Swanson, & Watts, 1998). Fourth-graders who were reading at beginning third-grade level tutored second-graders, most of whom were reading at primer level. The second-graders were all participating in an early-intervention program in their classroom in which they read books on their level. The fourth-graders spent 45 minutes on Monday and Tuesday with the reading coordinator or with their classroom teacher preparing for their 25-minute tutoring session on Wednesday and Thursday. On Monday, the fourth-graders selected a picture book to read to their second-grader and practiced reading the book. They also practiced word recognition prompts that they would use when their second-grader read to them. On Tuesday, they practiced again and developed extension activities to develop comprehension strategies, including story maps and character sketches. They came up with several good discussion questions based on the picture book they were planning to read.

On Wednesday and Thursday, the fourth-graders met with their tutees. During this session, they listened to their second-grader read the book currently being read in their classroom's early intervention program. While listening, they helped their second-graders identify words by giving them hints: "Look at the picture" "It starts with *pr*"; "Sound in and out in chunks—what would this part be (covering all but the first syllable)?" Next they read from the picture book they had chosen, built meaning vocabulary from the book, led a discussion based on their discussion questions, and did the comprehension extension activity.

On Friday, the fourth-graders had debriefing sessions with their teacher in which they discussed how their tutees reacted to the book, how well their word recognition prompts were working, the success of their discussion and comprehension activities, as well as problems encountered and progress noticed. They also wrote a letter to project coordinators detailing the successes and problems of that week. They received a response to their letter on Monday.

Data reported on this project show that both the second- and fourth-grade struggling readers made measurable progress. This is not surprising because this program combines all the elements essential for reading growth. Second-graders were getting daily guided reading instruction in materials at their level in their classrooms. In addition, during the tutoring session, they were reading material at their level to someone who knew how to help them with word recognition. They were also increasing their knowledge stores and comprehension strategies as they listened to their fourth-grade tutor read the picture book to them and as they engaged in the discussion and comprehension activities. Fourth-graders got lots of practice using the material at their instructional level, reading the picture book, and learning word recognition and comprehension strategies, as they prepared and carried out the tutoring with their second-graders.

Getting this to work would take some organization, and if you have a reading coordinator/specialist at your school, it would be good to get him or her involved. Given the results reported and the "just plain sensible" nature of the cross-age tutoring program, you are almost guaranteed to "get your money's worth" out of the time required to set up such a program.

## *Coordinate with Remedial Reading and Resource Room Teachers*

Many struggling readers participate in remedial or resource room instruction in addition to classroom reading instruction. Such programs can provide much-needed support for the children, but they can also result in a confusing and unhelpful conglomeration of reading lessons and activities. Special programs are most effective when they provide supportive instruction that is designed to ease the difficulties that participating children are having in their classrooms.

To accomplish this, however, means that remedial and special education teachers must be familiar with the classroom reading program. Federal regulations for remedial and special education programs promote cooperative planning of instruction between class-

chapter 10 / Extra Support for Students Who Need It Most

room teachers and specialist teachers. In addition, the support instruction must be designed to improve classroom performance. The goal of these regulations is to accelerate children's reading development to move them back into the classroom with no further need for assistance.

Struggling readers who participate in remedial or resource room instructional support programs are the very children who need the kind of reading instruction that is coherently planned and richly integrated. We have seen a variety of ways in which classroom teachers work with support teachers to develop such programs.

In one school, the support teachers come into the classrooms to work with participating children. They support the children's progress through both the basal and trade books that are used in the core-reading/

**RECOMMENDED resources**

*Early Success* is a small-group intervention program for grades 1 and 2 based on Barbara Taylor's Early Intervention in Reading model, which many classroom teachers have found very useful and usable. For older students, *Soar to Success* provides programs for grades 3–8. *Soar to Success* uses real books and a reciprocal teaching framework for instruction. Both programs have a solid research base. (*Early Success* and *Soar to Success* are both published by Houghton Mifflin.) Information about these programs can be found on their website, **www.hmco.com**.

language arts program. The special teachers may have the children reread a story and work on fluency and self-monitoring behaviors. At times, they reteach a strategy lesson from the basal or model summary writing for a *Weekly Reader* article. These teachers work with both small groups and individuals, depending on the classroom and the students. With support teachers in the room working at supporting progress through the core curriculum, less time is needed to meet and plan instructional roles.

In another school, the support teachers work in the classroom occasionally but more often work on extending classroom reading lessons in another room. In this case, the coordination is achieved through the use of a traveling notebook that the teachers have children carry back and forth each day. Both teachers jot down comments about what they are working on and the problems or successes the children had that day. The notebook allows the support program teacher to monitor core-curriculum lessons and to develop lessons that extend or support this learning.

In another school, the support teachers work only with the trade books that children are reading in the classrooms. The support teachers focus on extending comprehension of the texts being read in the classroom by working with children to develop scripts from books and stories and to develop performances of these. Another example of classroom/special teacher coordination is found in one school where the sixth-graders who attend the remedial program read trade books linked to their social studies curriculum. With the support of the specialist, these struggling readers read historical fiction and biographies; this adds greatly to their background knowledge and allows them to be active participants in social studies class discussions. A similar link could also be made between reading and science.

What is common among the very best remedial and special education programs is that children spend most of their time actually reading and writing in a way that supports classroom success. The support children receive from the specialist teacher provides immediate returns in improved reading and writing during classroom instruction.

## *Use the Latest Technology*

We have to be careful about "plugging" our children who struggle into the computer and hoping "the computer will do it." Many computer programs are just high-tech worksheets and do not teach children anything they can actually use as they read and write. Also, all children need the high-quality, responsive instruction that only a teacher can provide. There are, however, some computer programs that allow children with a variety of disabilities to read and write much better than they could "the old-fashioned way."

Mainstreamed into most classrooms today are children with a variety of physical limitations that make writing difficult or impossible. Children with limited vision often

### Computer-Assistive Devices and Software

- *Co: Writer* (Don Johnston). This is a talking word prediction program. Based on what the child has written and the first few letters of the next word, it predicts what the whole word will be. When the child clicks on the word, it becomes part of the text. This software also contains Flexspell, which translates phonetic spelling.

- *Write: Outloud* (Don Johnston). This is a talking word processor that gives immediate speech feedback as the student types words, sentences, and paragraphs. Its spelling check includes a homonym checker, which recognizes homonyms and offers definitions so that the child can choose the correct word. Text also can be read back to the child. This program is particularly helpful for children with visual impairments.

- *Draft Builder* (Don Johnston). This program helps children organize ideas through a variety of visual maps. Speech feedback is included.

- *IntelliTalk II* (Intellitools). This talking word processor combines graphics, text, and speech. A variety of templates and overlays are included to produce different kinds of text.

- *Kidspiration* (Inspiration). This program is based on Inspiration but easier to use. It integrates pictures and writing to help children develop visual maps to connect and expand ideas. These maps, along with audio support, help children write organized text.

- *Special keyboards and other devices*. For children who cannot use a regular keyboard, there are special keyboards, switches, and eye gaze pointers that allow children with limited mobility to word process and create text.

cannot write with paper and pencil. Children with speech difficulties often find writing and sharing their writing arduous. Children with cerebral palsy and various other physical problems may not be able to write with pencil and paper or even with a normal computer keyboard. Special computer devices and programs are absolutely necessary to allow these children to learn to write. It is even more critical that these children learn to write because many lack fluent speech, and being able to write gives them a way to express themselves and participate in classroom life.

There are word prediction programs, which use what the child has written and the first few letters of the next word to predict what the whole word will be. There are talking word processors, which give immediate speech feedback as the student types words, sentences, and paragraphs. Many of these talking word processors include graphic organizers, clip art, talking dictionaries, and frames to help children organize their thoughts prior to writing.

No teacher can be expected to know the specifics of all the devices available. What you do need to know is that if you have a child with a physical disability that makes writing in the normal way impossible, devices are available that will allow this child to write. Also, by federal law, the child is entitled to have access to these devices, regardless of the cost. If you need help to make writing a reality for a physically disabled student, contact your administrator or special education coordinator. If you need support to get what you need, contact the child's parents and let them know what is available and that their child is entitled to have it.

## Increase the Support You Are Providing Your English Language Learners

According to the 2000 U.S. Census, almost 20 percent of children in elementary schools spoke a language other than English as their home language. By now, that percentage is probably closer to 25 percent. That means that one out of every four or five children in our classrooms must learn to *speak* English as they learn how to read and write English. English language learners (ELLs) can be found in almost every school and classroom. What kind of special support can we provide for ELLs who face the difficult task of becoming literate in a new language as they adjust to a new culture?

As we were revising this book, the presence of English language learners in all our classrooms was always at the front of our minds. We included in all the chapters of this book teaching strategies and activities designed to teach all children—including ELLs—to become the very best readers and writers they can. The next several sections describe the ways the activities in the different chapters will help all children, including ELLs, along with a few specific adaptations for ELLs.

## Teacher Read-Aloud

The benefits of teacher read-aloud are particularly important for children learning English. In a supportive, nonthreatening environment, children can hear the language and become familiar with English sentence patterns and language structures. Teacher read-aloud is one of the main sources of meaning vocabulary development for all children. Meaning vocabulary development is particularly crucial for children learning a new language. If you teach the Three Read-Aloud Words activity suggested in Chapter Five, you will increase the probability that your children learning English will add words to their meaning vocabularies through your daily read-aloud. Chapter Two suggested reading aloud all kinds of books—including easy books and informational books. This is particularly important for your English language learners. Easy (everyone) books often have limited vocabulary and lots of picture support. Informational books are often rich with pictures and build prior knowledge and vocabulary for a whole variety of topics. If you have several English language learners in your classroom, be sure to include lots of predictable books in both your read-aloud and shared reading. As children listen to books with repeated sentence patterns, they quickly learn those patterns. Consider the language-building possibilities of repeated sentences such as:

> Run. Run as fast as you can. You can't catch me. I'm the gingerbread man!
> "Who will help me plant this wheat?" said the Little Red Hen.
> Brown bear, brown bear, what do you see? I see a red bird looking at me.

When you read a predictable book to your children, make an audiotape of that reading. Then put that audiotape along with the book in a listening center, and let your ELLs listen as many times as they like. This extends the teacher read-aloud time and increases the probability children will learn both language patterns and vocabulary from the read-aloud book.

Chapter Two also suggested including multicultural books in your read-aloud. If you make an extra effort to include books that reflect the home cultures of your ELLs, you will find their motivation to read will increase as they see themselves and their families in books. This is also a very easy and tangible way to demonstrate your respect for the cultures children come from. If you have many children whose first language is Spanish, you can take advantage of the many books that are published in both English and Spanish. Read both books to your students, or ask a volunteer or older child to read the Spanish version, if you are monolingual.

## Self-Selected Reading

Along with teacher read-aloud, time for independent reading should be provided daily in every elementary classroom. Chapter Two described the importance of obtaining the widest possible variety of materials for students to choose from and of holding weekly conferences with all children about their reading. All children grow in their reading fluency, motivation, and vocabulary as they engage in independent reading, but children who are learning English probably benefit the most. Imagine the anxiety you would feel if you were in a new culture, learning a new language and constantly being assessed on how rapidly you were progressing. Assessment is important, but children also need time to read with no standards, tests, or assignments. Many children whose first language is not English don't have English language books or magazines in their homes, so your classroom is probably their only source for English reading materials.

When scheduling your weekly conferences with children, spread out your struggling readers across the days and make one of these children the first person on your daily conference schedule. English language learners deserve some of those first spots and will benefit greatly from your help in selecting books they can read and will enjoy. If your ELLs can read in their home languages, encourage them to do some of their independent reading in those languages. When given the opportunity, children learning English often delight in reading the same text in their two different languages and then sharing their dual-language abilities with a teacher who "oohs" and "aahs" about how smart they are to be able to read in two languages!

## Building the Foundation

Chapter Three focused on activities to help all children build the foundation necessary to become successful readers and writers. This foundation includes knowing why we read and write, background knowledge and vocabulary, print concepts, phonemic awareness, concrete words, letter names and sounds, and the desire to learn to read and write. All the activities in that chapter will help children learning English get off to a successful start in literacy.

If you teach older children and just skimmed Chapter Three, thinking not much of it applied to you, or if you have some older children who are just becoming literate in English, you may want to look again at that chapter. Regardless of age, all children need to develop this foundation, and the activities described in Chapter Three can be adapted for children of any age.

## Decoding and Spelling

Along with vocabulary and prior knowledge, learning the patterns needed to decode and spell English words presents special challenges for English language learners. Participating in word wall activities, as described in Chapter Four, can help ELLs learn to decode and spell the most common words and words with common spelling patterns. Activities such as Guess the Covered Word, Making Words, Using Words You Know, and Reading–Writing Rhymes teach all children how to use patterns to decode and spell words. Because these activities are designed to be multilevel, all children—even those just beginning to learn

RECOMMENDED
## resources

If you need to know more about the similarities and differences between English and Spanish and how to adapt your instruction to accommodate them, you may want to read Lori Helman's "Building on the Sound System of Spanish: Insights from the Alphabetic Spellings of English Language Learners," in *The Reading Teacher* (February 2004, pp. 452–460).

English—can experience success with them and learn whatever patterns they are currently ready for.

If your ELLs come from Spanish-speaking homes, you will need to be alert to some confusion these children may have, given the different sounds some letters represent in Spanish versus English. Spanish-speaking children often experience great difficulty with vowels because the vowel system in Spanish is much simpler than that in English. Spanish does not have the vowel sounds represented by the *a* in *man*, the *e* in *pen*, the *i* in *is*, the *u* in *up*, the *er* in *her*, the *ou* in *could*, the *a* in *along*, or the *au* in *caught*. Furthermore, some sounds that both English and Spanish share are spelled differently in Spanish. The *a* sound in *cake*, for example, is spelled with an *e* in Spanish. The *e* sound in *bee* is spelled with an *i*. The *i* sound in *like* is spelled with an *ai*. The *o* sound in *on* is spelled with an *a*. When teaching phonics to children whose first language is Spanish, it is probably best to start with the letters that have the same sounds. The consonant letters *p, b, t, k, m, n, f, s, w,* and *y* have almost the same sounds in both languages and provide a good place to begin. As children develop some confidence in their decoding ability, the sounds that do not exist in Spanish and the letters that have different sounds in Spanish and English can be introduced.

Some words are similar in English and Spanish. Words derived from the same base or root word are called *cognates.* Here are some Spanish–English cognates:

| | |
|---|---|
| piloto | pilot |
| exactamente | exactly |
| clima | climate |
| curioso | curious |
| familia | family |
| decidir | decide |
| hospital | hospital |

Instruction in Spanish–English cognates should follow the suggestions given for teaching morphemes described in Chapter Four. Students need to become sensitive to the meaningful parts of words and get in the habit of deciding if two similar-looking words share meaning as well.

## Vocabulary

Far and away, building English vocabulary is the greatest challenge for English language learners. The first suggestion given in Chapter Five for developing vivid, vital, and valuable vocabularies was to provide as much real experience as possible. Bringing real objects into the classroom, "mining" the school environment for real objects about which to build vocabulary, and taking advantage of visuals and dramatizations will help English language learners build their English vocabularies. When using real objects, visuals, and dramatizations, get in the habit of asking your children who speak two languages how they say these words in their home languages. If possible, ask the questions in their home languages. Even those of us who are limited to one language can learn to ask:

¿Cómo se dice "table" en español?
Comment dit-on "table" en français?

Remember that as young children are learning to speak English, they are constantly pointing to objects and asking "What's that?" You want your English language learners to be equally eager to add new English words to their vocabularies. They will be more eager to learn words in your language if you regularly display an eagerness to learn some words in their languages.

Taking "picture walks" and reading alphabet books were recommended as excellent vocabulary-building activities in Chapter Five. Imagine how much more important they are for your children who are learning English. Focusing on Three Read-Aloud Words will help your ELLs learn words and, more importantly, will help them learn how everyone can increase his or her meaning vocabulary by paying attention to new words while reading. When everyone is given a sticky note one day a week on which to write a wonderful new word he or she finds while reading, ELLs will be eager to identify new words (instead of pretending they just know them all!). In fact, you may want to let your ELLs have sticky notes all the time to "flag" new words whenever they are reading. After reading, allow them to show their sticky-note words to a friend, and let that friend play "teacher" and explain the new words.

If you have a big vocabulary push in your classroom and include many of the activities described in Chapter Five in your daily schedule, adding wonderful words to your vocabulary will become "standard operating procedure." All the children will be on the lookout for new words and proud of their burgeoning vocabularies, and your English language learners will not feel signaled as needing "vocabulary fixing!"

## Comprehension

Look again at the comprehension-building activities described in Chapters Six and Eight. Imagine the amount of talking that is going to go on as children engage in these activities in pairs, small groups, and with the whole class. When two children are reading a selection together to get ready to do the Beach Ball activity or help complete a graphic organizer, they not only read together but they also talk to each other. Think about the language that will be developed as children engage in literate conversations, including "Oprah Winfrey" and Questioning The Author. When you do think-alouds with your students, you are modeling the "conversation in your head" that is generated by what you are reading. When children share the "conversations in their own heads," they are using all their language resources to connect to the text. All the doing the book activities involve talk, as groups work to make books come alive.

Engaging your ELLs in conversations in which they use their developing English skills is crucial to their becoming literate. The comprehension activities described in Chapters Six and Eight will help your children learn to think about text and to talk about text.

## Writing

Look again at Chapter Seven, and consider the activities discussed there from the vantage point of an English language learner. The teacher begins each writing time with a mini-lesson in which he or she models, demonstrates, and talks about what and how he or she is writing. Next, the children write and, early in the year, the teacher circulates, encouraging the children in their topics and helping them stretch out words and use resources in the room for spelling. The children soon learn that the teacher cares more about what they are *telling* than how perfectly they are *spelling*. Each day during the writing and sharing time, all children—including English language learners—see that their ideas and what is important to them are valued.

As the writing instruction continues and children learn to edit, publish, and revise, they are supported in these efforts by the teacher and by working with peers to "fix" their writing and make it "even better." Before publishing, children have conferences with the teacher, in which the teacher fixes whatever needs fixing and provides correct spellings. For any child whose writing is "uneditable," the teacher listens to what he or she wanted to tell and then produces a well-written version of it that the child can illustrate and publish. The children who are just learning English are often the children with "uneditable" pieces who need this extra support and scaffolding from the teacher.

As anyone who has ever tried to learn a second language knows, listening and reading are easier than speaking a new language and writing is hardest of all. Writer's Workshop, with the all the supports described in Chapter Seven, allows all children, including ELLs, to learn to write and provides them with another avenue for learning the English language.

## Extra Support for English Language Learners

Finally, consider the suggestions in this chapter as they apply to your English language learners. Can you find a tutor to work one on one with some of your ELLs? If you have some open-center time at the end of each day, can you spend some of that time reading and rereading easy, predictable text with your ELL students? Would using Co-Writer or some other software that scaffolds reading and writing allow your English language learners to read and write more fluently and add to their vocabularies? Do your English language learners get help outside your classroom that would benefit them more if you coordinated your instruction with that of their special teachers?

## *Summary*

There are two levels of struggling readers in most classrooms. Some children have a literacy level that is close to grade level but need to become more thoughtful readers and writers and often need more experience with the informational texts found in science and social studies and with the big words that comprise these texts. Most of these struggling readers can achieve a basic and even proficient level of reading and writing if their elementary years are rich in the type of instruction described in the previous chapters of this book.

This chapter has described a variety of ways teachers can organize and "mobilize" to meet the needs of children whose literacy level is way below grade level. Teachers who have several children for whom the material used for comprehension lessons is not at instructional level can hold short after-lunch-bunch type easy reading sessions, in which everyone is included on some days but the children who really need this extra reading are asked to join the group more often. Teachers might find the time for meeting with this easy reading group, as well as for meeting other individual needs, by scheduling 30 minutes of open-center time during the day. In addition to freeing up the teacher to meet whatever needs are most pressing that day, the open-center time allows children to pursue their own interests in a variety of ways.

Children who find learning to read particularly difficult often benefit from regular tutoring in addition to all the classroom instruction. If carefully structured, tutoring can be provided by a variety of people, including older struggling readers. The most effective teachers know what is happening to their children when they are with special teachers and work with those teachers to provide a nonfragmented, noncontradictory instructional program.

Technology now exists that allows all children to participate in thoughtful literacy activities. Children who need this technology are entitled by law to have it, but they need teachers who know it exists and who will become their advocates in obtaining it. Finally, many English language learners need additional support in learning to read and write. Specific ways of adapting the strategies and activities in previous chapters for English language learners were described in this chapter.

# A Day in a Building Blocks
# *Kindergarten Classroom*

Many children have had 1,000 or more hours of "informal" literacy encounters before coming to school. From these encounters, they develop critical understanding about the nature of reading and writing and "I can" attitudes toward their inevitable inclusion into the literate community.

1. They know that when you read or write, you are trying to understand or communicate some information or story.

2. They know reading and writing are two important things that everyone who is bigger than them can do and that they too must learn to do because they want to be big.

3. They know from the overwhelming adult approval and pleasure at their fledgling attempts at pretend reading, at reading some signs and labels, and at writing that they are succeeding at mastering this mysterious code.

Our major literacy goal in kindergarten should be to simulate the reading and writing encounters many children have had that led them to develop these critical understandings and attitudes. It is important to think of at-risk kindergartners primarily as children who have had few experiences with print, stories, and books. Thinking of these children as "inexperienced" creates a different view of their instructional needs than thinking of them as "developmentally delayed," "language impaired," "slow," "unready," or any of the other labels commonly given to children who enter school inexperienced in literacy activities. The critical nature of providing these children with a print-rich, story-rich, book-rich classroom becomes clear when we take this view.

The rest of this chapter is devoted to how one day might look in a Building Blocks kindergarten. For more information about Building Blocks, see *The Teacher's Guide to Building Blocks* (Hall & Williams, 2000) or go to www.wfu.edu/fourblocks.

## 8:00–8:45 Choice Centers

The children arrive at different times, depending on buses, rides, and so forth. They come to the classroom immediately and, once in the classroom, come to one of the many centers in the room. During this time, they can choose to go to any center as long as there is space at that center. Each center has a limited number of tickets that are laminated and strung with yarn. The children choose a ticket, put the ticket on, and then go to that center. They can stay at each center as long as they like but must return that center's ticket and get another one before moving to another center.

The teacher spent a lot of time and effort at the beginning of the year helping the children learn what they could and could not do at each center, how to clean up the center before they left, and so on. This initial effort paid off; now there are seldom problems with behavior and routines during center time.

During center time, the teacher circulates throughout the room, greeting children and helping them get the day off to a good start. As always, she has her file folder labels on a clipboard, and when she notices accomplishments, problems, or other things that she wants to remember, she records them by putting the child's initials, date, and the comment she wants to make on one of the labels. At the end of the day, she peels off these labels and attaches them to each child's anecdotal record folder. Today she jots down notes about the child "reading" a little book in the library corner to a stuffed animal, noting that his voice sounds like a reading voice and that he is doing a good job of telling a story that matches the pictures. She also notes that another child is drawing at the writing table and "reads" her drawing when asked by the teacher. Also at the table is a child who has created strings of letters in rows and "reads" her "writing." The notes describe the different levels of conceptual development that each child exhibits about writing.

The teacher tries to talk to each child during the morning center time and spends a few extra minutes with the children she has identified as being most needy. For her children whose English is limited, either because English is not their first language or because they have had few real conversations with adults, she makes sure to engage them in some conversation about what they are doing at the center. She points to things in the pictures they have painted or to their block construction and fosters their talk with her by asking what they are doing. She asks them about the little books that they are "reading" and about the writing they produce. Because these conversations are one-on-one and are related to something they actually are doing, the children are more willing to talk than they are in a small-group or whole-class setting. She also notices that the children talk with each other more during center time. In fact, knowing that listening and speaking are major goals of kindergarten, she encourages this child-to-child talk as she visits the various centers and engages the children in conversations in which she gets them to talk to one another about what they are doing.

## 8:45–9:15 Opening, Calendar, Morning Message

When the teacher goes to the rocking chair and sits down, the children realize that center time is over. They quickly clean up what they have been working on and come sit on the floor in front of her. The teacher begins the big-group activities with the usual questions: What day is it today? What was yesterday? What day will tomorrow be? What is the date? What is the weather? How many days have we been in school? The children answer each question and then find the word cards (Thursday, Wednesday, Friday, March 24, windy) to finish the sentences on the sentence strips in the pocket chart. They count the 12 bundles of "tens" and the 8 "ones" and talk about what they will do today in kindergarten.

Now the teacher picks up a black marker and gets ready to write on a large piece of lined chartpaper. She writes the morning message on the chartpaper as all her children watch. She does not talk (as she did at the beginning of the year) but instead writes quietly as the students read quietly her daily greeting—"Dear Class." She begins her message by asking what day it is. The children respond, "Today is Thursday." She asks the children how to spell *today,* and they quickly answer, "*t-o-d-a-y.*" They also know how to spell *is* and *Thursday.* Those children who are not sure look on the sentence strips in the pocket chart nearby to help spell *Thursday.* The teacher writes three more sentences: *March is a windy month. Today is a windy day! Can we fly a kite outside?*

After she finishes the morning message by writing *Love* and her name at the end, she lowers the chartpaper and asks, "Who can count the words in these sentences?" The teacher calls on a student who could not count when school began and praises him for correctly counting the words in each sentence. Next, she asks, "What do you notice?" The children notice many things—the words they know, the capital letter at the beginning of each sentence, the periods, exclamation point, and question mark at the end of the sentences, and so forth. To end this big-group session, the teacher leads the children in some of their favorite marching and moving songs and closes with some fingerplays using familiar rhymes; she knows that a few children still need this practice to strengthen their phonemic awareness.

## 9:15–9:45 Shared Reading

The teacher takes out the big book *Brown Bear, Brown Bear, What Do You See?* by Bill Martin. It is clear from the children's response that they have read this book before. First, the teacher points to the name of the book on the cover. She reads "Brown Bear" with the children. Next, she points to the author's name, Bill Martin, as she reads that with the children.

Before reading the teacher begins the lesson by reviewing the colors and animals in this book. First, she holds up a brown circle and asks, "What color is this?" Then she asks, "What animal in the book is brown?" She encourages the students to remember what animal is coming next and what color it is. At first this is easy, but after several animals the children become confused. She continues putting the red, yellow, blue, gray, purple, green, pink, white, black, and orange circles in a row in the pocket chart and talks about which animal is that color. "Now, let's read this story together and see whether we put the colors in the right order and remembered all the animals in this book."

The children join in and share the reading of this "big book" with the teacher. She points to the words as the children read in chorus with her:

"Brown bear, brown bear, what do you see?"

Before turning the page, she asks the children whether they remember what animal is next. The children know the red bird is next. She turns the page, and the children are delighted to see that they are correct. Led by the teacher, who continues to point to words, they all read:

"I see a red bird looking at me."
"Red bird, red bird, What do you see?"

The teacher and the children continue in this manner until they have completed the book. After the book has been read and enjoyed one more time, the teacher reviews the sequence of this book by talking about the colors in the pocket chart and the animals they read about. Did they put them in the right order? Yes!

The teacher gets the "wiggles" out by having the children move like the animals in the book. She then passes out color circles to the children, although fewer colors are passed out than are in the book. The teacher then puts on a tape recording of their favorite color song by Hap Palmer. The children stand up, sit down, and march around the room as they sing along with the tape and follow the directions for whatever color circle they are holding.

## 9:45–10:15  Writing

After this brief but essential break, the children settle back down while the teacher picks up a marker and gets ready to write. She thinks aloud about what she might write. She models different levels of writing on different days. Sometimes she "drites," both drawing and writing on a blank page. Other times she writes a few sentences. Still other days she adds to some sentences written previously and writes a complete paragraph. As she writes, she models invent-spelling some words for the children. She says the word aloud very slowly and writes down some letters to represent the sounds she hears. In this way she demonstrates for the children many different levels of writing and shows them that all these ways of writing are acceptable.

On this day she writes two sentences:

> Mr. Hinkle will vizit us after lunch.
> He will bring his pet turtl.

She does not read the words aloud as she writes them, except when she models invented spelling for the children by saying a word very slowly. The children watch closely and try to read what she is writing. Many of them recognize the words *Mr., lunch,* and *pet.* She then draws a simple picture to illustrate the sentence and labels the drawings of Mr. Hinkle and the turtle. Even though (or perhaps because) she is not artistic, the children love to watch her draw. Once her drawing is complete, she reads what she has written, pointing to each word as she does. The children are amazed to hear that Mr. Hinkle, who teaches fourth grade, has a pet turtle. They also point to her stick figure drawing of him and re-mark that they cannot wait for Mr. Hinkle to see his picture! The teacher promises to hide it before he arrives!

The teacher asks the children what they are going to write about today. As each child tells the teacher what he or she is going to write about, they stand up and go back to their tables where their writing journals are waiting for them. As the children write, the teacher circulates around the room, encouraging or coaching children as needed.

## 10:15–10:45  Recess/Snack

As the children line up to go outside, the teacher picks a child and asks the child what let-ter she or he wants the children to be as they go outside. The child thinks and decides that they should all be M's today. The teacher lets that child lead the line, and all the children march to the playground because *march* is the action they have learned for the letter *m*. (Earlier in the year, they learned an action for each consonant letter. Now, they review this every day by performing the correct action on the way to the playground. On days when they have to stay inside during recess, they play games in which they review all their letter actions.)

When they return to the classroom, they find some peanuts on each of their desks. They look up at the food board and notice that the teacher has attached a picture from the peanut jar to the space under the letter *p*. As they munch on their peanuts and whatever else they might have brought for snack time, they review the other foods on their food board. So far, only five letters have food pictures attached to them:

*b*—bananas, *d*—donuts, *m*—milk, *j*—juice, *p*—peanuts

The children are curious about what foods might go with the other letters. They make the sounds of the letters and try to predict what they might find for a snack one day. One child says he hopes there are hamburgers for *h,* but another child protests, "She won't bring us hamburgers for snacks!" The teacher picks up on their conversation and helps them think about possibilities for the various letters. She suggests that as they eat lunch today and when they eat meals and snacks at home, they should look at the packages and think about what letters begin the names of these foods.

## 10:45–11:45  Assigned Centers

During this time, the children go to centers once more. But unlike the morning hour, when they choose centers and activities, now they are assigned to centers, and the children all rotate through all the activities. Today, the teacher has set up four centers, and children are to spend 15 minutes in each. Before they go to the centers, she directs their attention to each center and makes sure they know what they are going to do.

In the math center today, she has put a pile of the laminated words used in yesterday's Being the Words activity for *Brown Bear* and has labeled each of eight baskets with a number from 1 to 8. The children's job in the math center today is to take the words from *Brown Bear,* count the letters in each word, and put them in the appropriate basket. She points out the baskets designated 1–8 and helps the children see that some words only have one letter and that the longest words have eight letters. She reminds the children that at the math center, they work with their partner and take turns counting and then checking each other. She has a math partnership come up to demonstrate how one child picks up a word, counts the letters, and points to the basket that the word goes in. The partner's job is to play "teacher" and respond with encouragement, "Right!" or to give help, "Let's count those letters again." After each word is counted, the partners switch roles. The one who counted first becomes teacher for the second word, and so on.

The children have been working with partners in the math center, alternating the teacher/student roles for several weeks now. They understand the procedures, and even though they have not counted letters in words before, they have counted all kinds of concrete objects. She reminds the children that they will spend 15 minutes in the math center and will not have time to count the letters in all the words: "Just count and sort until your math center time is up," she encourages them.

The activity at the next center takes little explanation. The children are making their own take-home books patterned on the *Brown Bear* book. Their book is about the animals you might see in a zoo. Each day they make a page by tracing the printed sentence at the bottom and drawing a picture to illustrate that page. On one side of today's page, they trace:

I see a yellow lion looking at me.

Printed on the back is the sentence:

Yellow lion, yellow lion, what do you see?

The teacher picks up one of these duplicated sheets and reads it to the children. She also points to several books that are opened to display various lions and reminds the children that their lion should be yellow but that it can be as big or as scary or as cuddly as they like. "People who draw the illustrations in books use their imaginations to make their illustrations different from anyone else's," she says.

The third center that the children visit today is the listening center. Here they listen to a tape of two books about real animals. The teacher picks up the books and quickly shows the children some pictures, reminding them that they have been studying animals and reading books about how real animals live and what they do and have also been reading silly books about imaginary animals. Today, they listen to two books about real animals and perhaps learn some facts to add to the animal chart this afternoon. As she says this, their eyes turn to a data chart made by stringing yarn along a bulletin board. Going down the chart are the names and pictures of some animals that are being studied. The columns across are labeled with words such as *eat, move, live, body covering,* and so forth. The teacher reminds them that the chart is not yet finished; where there are spaces, they need to add information for the animals that are listed as well as add five more animals. The teacher reminds them that because there is only one book, the group leader of the day gets to turn the pages and must try to hold the book so that everyone can see.

Finally, the teacher points to the writing center. The writing center has a variety of things to write and draw on and with. Besides paper, index cards, labels, postcards, and old stationery are available. The teacher reminds the children that she wants them to write something in addition to drawing something and that scribble writing and one-letter writing are fine, as long as they know what they are writing.

For the next hour, the children rotate in 15-minute blocks through each of the four centers. The children are assigned to groups, each of which contains the whole range of children—from those most experienced with print to those least experienced and from the most agreeable to the most difficult. Each group has a leader for the day. This child is "in charge" at the center and sees to it that materials are put away and are ready for the next group as they leave each center. As the children work, the teacher circulates with a clipboard and file folder labels in hand. She stops for a few minutes at each center and makes observations and/or coaches as needed.

While observing in the math center, she notices one child counting the letters in a word, from right to left. She stops and explains to this child that we always have to start the other way when we read words and that it is important to always go a certain way when we look at the letters in a word. She then helps the child count some letters correctly and notes this directional confusion on a label that she will attach to his folder. Having seen one child do this, she is alerted to this problem, which other children might have. As the group rotates into the math center, she notices that several children are counting the letters from right to left. She notes this on labels and makes a note to herself to pull these children together soon and work on left-to-right directionality with them.

As she observes the children in the listening center, she notices that two children are very inattentive to the tape. One child has a very limited use of English. The other is a very "antsy" child. She worries about their inattentiveness and decides to think about ways to alleviate it; she makes these notes on the labels.

The children doing the yellow lion page of their take-home book are busy tracing and drawing. Again, she notices some children tracing the letters from right to left. She explains that they must go the other way when they read and that they should trace this way to get in the habit. She helps them get reoriented and again jots a note to herself to pull together the children who lack this print orientation. She begins compiling a list of these children. She asks several children to read their page to her and to touch the words as they read; she notes their success on labels, which she will attach to their folders later.

As she stops in the writing center, she is once more reminded that all children can write, if whatever writing they do is accepted. She picks up a paper that is clearly a list in scribble writing and says, "Read what you wrote to me." The child proceeds to point to each scribble and tells her that these are foods he likes to eat, and he then reads his scribbles about the foods. The teacher notes on the child's label that he can read his own scribbles, seems to have top–bottom and left–right orientation, but has not written specific letters yet. Another child has made a drawing of himself and his pet and has labeled the drawing with his name and his pet's name. One child is writing sentences that have many correctly spelled words in them and other words that are clearly readable from his invented spelling. Another child is listing animals, copying the words from the newspaper animal board, from the list of animals on the side of the data chart, and from a book on animals he has picked up from the bookshelf next to the writing center.

*A Day in a Building Blocks Kindergarten Classroom*

The teacher reminds herself that children have various levels of experience. Some children arrived at school understanding that writing is talk written down, but many did not. Some had been writing at home for a long while. Others did not hold their first pencil until starting school. Knowing this and knowing the importance of providing many experiences with written language, she has all the children write every day. She encourages children to write words in any way they can, but some children will not write them unless they know they are writing them correctly! She realizes that by providing acceptance for a variety of writing levels and by providing words available in the room support for children who have to do it right, she allows children to write in whatever ways they can.

## 11:45–12:15 Lunch

Just before the children line up, the teacher reads the lunch menu. Usually, she just reads it to them, but capitalizing on their interest in the letters that begin the names of favorite foods, she generates some little riddles to give them clues about the foods on the menu and the beginning letters of the food words.

> "Today, you are having another food that begins with a *p*. The one you are going to have just has cheese on it. I like it with cheese and with another *p* word—*pepperoni!*"

The children make happy sounds as they realize their favorite food—*pizza*—is on the menu.

> "With your pizza, you will have something that is very nutritious and contains lots of vitamins. It has lettuce and other vegetables and begins with an *s*."

Most children guess *salad*.

> "For dessert, you will have something that comes in different flavors and colors. Sometimes it is yellow, sometimes brown, sometimes white. Today it is white with chocolate frosting and begins with the letter *c*."

The children guess *cake* and have no trouble guessing that their beverage is the *m* food from their food board—*milk*.

## 12:15–12:45 Reading to Children and Independent Reading

When the children arrive back from lunch, some go to their tables; others go to a corner of the room that contains all the predictable "big books" that they have read this year; others go to the reading corner that has puppets and stuffed animals in addition to books.

An observer would have trouble figuring out which children were supposed to go where, but the children know exactly where to go. Each child has one day to read in the reading corner, another day to read big books, and three other days to read at their seats. This procedure has been in place for two weeks now and is working quite well. Having all the children spread out in the room created problems because not enough good "spreading-out places" were available. This new arrangement seems to have just the right balance of freedom and structure so that the children spend most of their time actually reading (or pretend reading, if that is what they are doing!).

Reading at their tables, the children find trays of books there. The trays contain a variety of books and are rotated so each table gets a different tray each day. One tray is filled with animal books—the topic they are studying in a combined science/social studies unit. Included in the tray are the two books children listened to at the listening center this morning. Many of these books are too hard for most of the children to read, but they love talking about the pictures and do find some animal names they recognize.

A second tray contains books gathered up for the last topic studied—weather. The children enjoy looking at these books, most of which have been read to them. Many children can read the predictable books, such as *What Makes the Weather?* and *Our Friend, the Sun.* Another tray of books contains "oldies but goodies," which the children request to have read again and again. All children can make some attempt at reading favorites such as *Go Dog Go, Clifford the Big Red Dog,* and *The Three Little Pigs.*

A fourth tray contains class books. The books written during shared writing and illustrated by the children are perennial favorites. The first class book contains a photo and a few sentences about each child in the class. This is still one of the most popular books and is reread almost every day by someone. Currently, they are writing and illustrating a class book about animals that will be added to this tray when it is finished.

Two trays of library books also are available. One tray contains books checked out from the public library, and the other contains books checked out from the school library. The teacher has arranged with both libraries to check out 20–30 books to keep in the classroom for a month. She chooses two or three children to go with her on a special trip to the public library every month to return the old books and pick out new ones for the public library tray. By the end of the year, all children will have made this special after-school trip. For many children, it is their first trip to the public library, and some of them (and their parents!) are amazed that you can get books to take home "for free." At the end of the year, the whole class makes a trip to this library again, and most of the children get library cards. The monthly trips with two or three children to the public library and the library card field trip takes extra time and effort, but the teacher feels that introducing these children to a free, unlimited source of reading material early on makes the time and effort worthwhile.

Each day, when the children return from lunch, they read books. They can read by themselves or, if they use quiet voices, with a friend who sits near them. The children who go to the book corner often read to the puppets and stuffed animals that reside there.

When the children have read their own books for about 10–15 minutes, the teacher chooses several books or parts of books to read to the class. She chooses from a variety of books, often reading a few pages from an informational book, an old favorite (that the children never tire of having reread to them), and a new book. As she reads aloud, the teacher talks about print and artwork, allowing children to "see" how a good reader thinks while reading. She turns the book to face the children and shows them features of the book.

Today they have a guest reader, Mr. Hinkle. He sits in the rocking chair and shows his turtle to the children gathered at his feet. He talks to the children about the turtle and then reads them a book about turtles. When Mr. Hinkle finishes the book, the teacher reminds the children of the three ways children in kindergarten can read books: (1) They can read the words; (2) they can retell the story; or (3) they can read the pictures. The teacher tells the children that most kindergartners cannot read all the words in the book about turtles. She asks the children how they could read this book if they picked it up from one of the trays. The children quickly tell her they could "read" the pictures.

## 12:45–1:15  Math

This half-hour is devoted to math. Today children graph their favorite colors and then their favorite animals from *Brown Bear*. Each child is given a bag with buttons inside to graph by color on a laminated mat the teacher passes out. When they finish, they may quietly help the other children at their table.

## 1:15–1:45  Shared Writing—Predictable Chart

The teacher talks about what a windy month March has been. They talk about the kites they made in the art center last week and about the time the wind caught a kite they took out at recess and how the kite soared high into the sky. Then the teacher shows the predictable chart she wrote with their help on Monday and finished on Tuesday. Looking at a piece of lined chartpaper, the teacher and the class read the title and the first line together:

"If I Were a Kite!"
"I would fly to"

She reminds the children that the first response is from Justin, who would fly to New York. She reminds them how she repeated his sentence saying the words and writing them. Each child repeated the predictable phrase "I would fly to" and finished it the way he or she wanted. On Wednesday they all "touch read" the sentences they dictated to the teacher.

Today, they will build these sentences. The teacher has chosen Raheem's sentence. After writing it on a sentence strip, she cuts the words apart. She gives one word each to five children and hands Raheem his name. Sentence Builders is a favorite activity; children love "being the words" and building sentences in front of their classmates. *I* knows his place at the beginning of the sentence. A little girl has the word *would* and matches it to "would" on the chart and gets in the second spot. The next word is *fly,* and the child with that word counts to three and becomes the third word in the sentence. "*To*" excitedly says, "I know this word. I can read *to!*" She gets in the fourth spot in the sentence. The last word in this sentence is *Kentucky.* One rather large kindergarten boy says, "I am the longest word. I go next. I am *Kentucky.*" Raheem quickly gets in his spot at the end. He knows that the names always go at the end! Once the words are in place, the children who are not being the words for this sentence read the sentence as the teacher moves behind each child holding a word card. The teacher praises the students for doing such a good job. The teacher writes and cuts apart two more sentences, and different children get their turns being the words and building the sentences.

Next, the teacher shows the children how she takes her cut-up sentence and pastes the words in the right order at the bottom of a piece of paper. She explains how she is going to illustrate her sentence at the top of this paper. The teacher gives each child in the class their cut-up sentence and a large piece of paper on which they will paste the words in the correct order, then illustrate. Each child makes a page for the class book *If I Were a Kite.*

*In March, this class studied about, made, and flew kites. Here is the predictable chart on which the teacher recorded where the children would choose to fly if they were a kite.*

## 1:45–2:15  P.E.

As the children march to P.E. class, the teacher leads them in a whisper version of a favorite song or rhyme. Today they are marching along to one of the raps recorded by African American poet Lindamichellebaron (*The Sun Is On,* book and tape available from Harlin Jacques Publishers, 507 Panache Suite, 200 Fulton Ave., Hempstead, NY 11550). This use of rhythm and rhyme serves the children because it is fun and helps them develop their phonemic awareness.

## 2:15–2:45

On three afternoons, the children have this half-hour once again to choose activities in the various centers. One day each week, they go to the computer lab. On another day, today, their "big buddies" from the fifth grade arrive to read and write with the children. Each fifth-grader is assigned one kindergarten buddy. They bring a book that they have practiced reading and read it "lap style" to their kindergartner. They then let the kindergartner choose a book to read to them. (It took some explaining, but the fifth-graders have learned that pretend reading is a critical beginning reading step, and they now accept whatever kind of reading their kindergartner does.) Next, they write whatever their kindergartner would like them to write in that child's "All About Me" book. They have learned to talk with the child about "the interesting things that have happened since I came last week" and to record some of these things in simple sentences. These weekly journals are records of lost teeth, new jackets, birthdays, family moves, births, and deaths. The children love to have someone record what has happened in their lives, and once today's record is made, they pester their big buddies to "read all about me from the beginning of the year."

## 2:45  Daily Summary/
## School–Home Connection

The children prepare to go home. They talk about what they have done today and what they will do tomorrow. They look forward to finishing their pages for the class book on kites. They also are ready to do another page in the take-home zoo animals book they are making.

The teacher lets each of them choose a little book, an index card, and a pencil to put in a reclosable bag. Each night, their "homework" is to read the book to someone or have someone read it to them and to write or have someone write something for them on the card. Today, given their interest in how foods are spelled, they are to try to copy some names of foods they like from the boxes and cans that they find at home.

Once the children are gone, the teacher peels the file folder labels off the backing and attaches them to the appropriate children's folders. She thinks about how each child is developing in his or her literacy and looks again at the list of literacy goals she has for them:

1. They pretend read favorite books and poems/songs/chants.

2. They write in whatever way they can and can read what they write even if no one else can.

3. They "track print," that is, show you what to read and point to the words using left–right/top–bottom conventions.

4. They know critical jargon, can point to just one word, the first word in the sentence, just one letter, the first letter in the word, the longest word, and so on.

5. They recognize and can write some concrete words—their names, names of other children, and favorite words from books, poems, and chants.

6. They are developing phonemic awareness—including the ability to clap syllables, recognize when words rhyme, make up rhymes, and stretch out words.

7. They can name many letters and tell you words that begin with the common initial sounds.

8. They are learning more about the world they live in and are more able to talk about what they know.

9. They can listen to stories and informational books and can retell the most important information.

10. They see themselves as readers and writers and as new members of the "literacy club."

The teacher feels that even though they are at very different places, all her kindergartners are making progress toward achieving these critical understandings. Even though some children arrived without print, story, and book experience, her classroom is organized to immerse these children in literacy experiences. These experiences with print, stories, and books form the base for her instructional planning. She thinks about whole-class, small-group, and individual activities she can do tomorrow to further children's development.

# A Day in a Four Blocks Primary Classroom

The activities described in the previous chapter are equally appropriate in first grade, particularly at the beginning of the year. Some children spend the summer in print-rich home environments, but others have few such experiences from the day they leave kindergarten. Reimmersing all children in print-rich classrooms goes a long way in fostering easy and early reactivation of the concepts and strategies they developed last year. Print-rich classrooms, shared reading and writing, opportunities for every child to read and write daily, rhymes and chants to develop phonemic awareness, and opportunities to expand knowledge through science and social studies units are the cornerstones of successful literacy programs for at-risk first-graders. The 10 goals listed at the end of the previous chapter are the goals that first-grade teachers must evaluate and work toward as they begin the year.

As children demonstrate that they have the emergent literacy knowings under varying degrees of control, first-grade teachers must provide activities that further the development of reading and writing. We organize important primary-grade activities within a framework we call Four Blocks. These blocks—Guided Reading, Self-Selected Reading, Writing, and Working with Words—provide numerous and varied opportunities for all children to learn to read and write. For more information about Four Blocks, see *The Teacher's Guide to the Four Blocks* (Cunningham, Hall, & Sigmon, 1999) or go to www.wfu.edu/fourblocks. The rest of this chapter is devoted to what one day in a Four Blocks primary classroom might look like.

## 8:30–8:50 Opening

The children enter and prepare for the day. When they have their gear stowed, they gather around the teacher. They share things that have happened to them over the weekend, do some calendar activities, and talk about the events planned for the day. Next, the teacher reads a new informational book with lots of pictures of seeds and the plants that grow from them. She tells the children that they will learn much more about seeds and plants as they begin their new science unit. As she finishes reading the book, she places it in the tray labeled Seeds and Plants, which has many other books in it. As she picks up three or four of the other books and shows a few pages of each, she reminds the children that each time they start a new science or social studies unit, she gathers up books from both the school and the public library and puts them in a special tray. The children are all anxious to look at the books, but it is time to get on with other things. They know, however, that this tray of books will be waiting for them during self-selected reading time. Finally, the teacher shows them a seed catalog that she has brought from home, quickly flipping through it and pausing briefly to show a page or two of the illustrations. She then puts the catalog on the tray also.

## 8:50–9:20 The Working with Words Block

The 2 hours and 15 minutes designated for reading/language arts in this class are divided into four blocks of 30–40 minutes each. The first block this teacher does is the Words block. Activities in this block are designed to help children achieve two critical goals. To read and write independently, children must learn to automatically recognize and spell high-frequency words, which occur in almost everything we read and write. They must also learn to look for patterns in words so that they can decode and spell the less frequent words they have not been taught. To accomplish these two goals, the teacher depends on a daily word wall activity and a second activity designed to help the children become better decoders and spellers.

The children are seated at their desks, and because today is Monday, they are eager to see what five new words will be added to the wall today. The teacher looks at Roberto, who just arrived in her classroom last Wednesday, and realizes that he does not really know what the word wall is for. She decides to use this opportunity to remind the children about the importance of the words selected for the word wall.

The teacher begins by directing the children's attention to the bulletin board word wall. She asks the children how many words they think are currently on the word wall and gets some wild guesses. She decides that this is a good math opportunity and leads the children to count the words. There are 95 words. She then asks someone to explain to Roberto how many words are added each Monday and how she decides what words to add.

The children explain that five words are added each week and these are the most important words. When asked what "most important" means, the children explain:

"You use them all the time."

"You can't read and write without them."

"A lot of these words aren't spelled the way they should be, so when you want to write one of the word wall words, you look up there to remember how to spell it instead of trying to figure it out."

"Why are the words arranged according to their first letter?" the teacher asks.

"To make it easier to find them. When you need the word, you just think how it begins and then you can find it faster."

"Why are the words different colors?" she asks.

"To make the word wall pretty," one child explains.

"Well, it does make the word wall pretty to have the different colors, but does it help us in any other way?"

"It helps you remember the words that look almost alike, which word is which—*they* is pink and *them* is green, and I can find *them* quicker if I look for the green one under the *t.*"

Satisfied that the children understand why learning to read and write these words is so important and how to find them when they need them in writing, she goes on to show the children the five new words that she will add today. She reminds the children of the selections they had read last week during the guided reading time and that she had introduced them to many new words as they read these selections.

"It was hard to choose only five words, but I chose the ones that you see most often in books and that I think you all need when you write. I also chose one word that occurs fairly often but that also begins with a letter for which we don't have any words yet. Some of you have been complaining about not having any words that begin with *q* or *z,* and I have told you that not many words begin with those two letters. But I have been on the lookout for a *q* or *z* word in one of our selections, which you might see in books and need in your writing. Last week, as you were reading, I spotted one."

As she says this, she puts the word *question,* written with a black permanent marker on yellow construction paper, on the word wall next to the *q.* "Remember that everyone kept telling the boy not to ask so many *questions* in the story you read. *Question* will be our word wall *q* word." She then writes *question* on the overhead as the children write it on their handwriting paper. She reminds the children of the proper letter formation as she writes each letter. They seem pleased to have a *q* word on the word wall and are amazed that it is such a big word. The teacher leads them to count the letters in *question* and points out that many of the words we read and write most often are pretty short words.

Taking less time, she adds the other high-frequency words to the wall that were introduced last week during guided reading—*about, where, many, this*—and demonstrates correct letter formation. She has the children write the words on their half-sheet of handwriting paper. Once they have written them on the front, with the teacher's direction for handwriting, the children turn their paper over to the back, and the teacher gives clues to the five words that were just added to the word wall. "The first word I want you to practice is our new *th* word. Who can remember what it is?" The children respond, "*this.*" The teacher then points to *this* and has them clap rhythmically and chant the letters three times—"*t-h-i-s, t-h-i-s, t-h-i-s—this!*"

After clapping and chanting the word, they write it on the back of their handwriting paper. The teacher does not demonstrate how to write *this* this time, but she does remind them to make the letters just as they did on the front. She continues to ask them to identify, clap, and chant in this manner, and to write the other four new words that were just added to the word wall. After they have written all five, she demonstrates how to write them once again, and the children check their own papers.

She finishes the word wall activity by reminding the children that on Monday, when five new words were added, they practiced only those five new words. "From now on this week, I will pick different words from the wall to practice." (On days when old words are being practiced, the procedure is for the teacher to call out any five words, and the children clap and then write them. Next, they check the words for correct letters and handwriting by tracing around the word as the teacher traces around the same word on the board or overhead.)

One child points out that if they had 95 before they added today's words, they must have 100 now. Several children look skeptical about this, so the teacher lets them count the words once more; sure enough, they have reached the magic number—100! The children seem very pleased to have 100 "important" words on their wall and to finally have a word for *q.* The teacher promises to be on the lookout for a *z* word in one of the selections they read so that every letter will have at least one word!

Next, the children go to the second activity in the Words block; today they are making words. (On other days, the activity might be Guess the Covered Word, Using Words You Know, or an activity with lots of rhyming words.) The Monday children at each table (who, of course, are the people in charge on Monday!) pick up the letter tray that is on their table and distribute the needed letters to each child. For this particular lesson, each child has five consonants, *c, r, r, s, t,* and two vowels, *a* and *o.* In the pocket chart at the front of the room, the teacher has large cards with the same seven letters. Her cards, like the small letter cards used by the children, have the uppercase letter on one side and the lowercase letter on the other side. The consonant letters are written in black and the two vowels in red.

The teacher begins by making sure that each child has all the letters that are needed. "What two vowels will we use to make words today?" she asks. The children hold up their red *a* and *o* and respond appropriately. The children then name the consonants they have and are surprised to notice that they have two *r*'s. The teacher tells them that sometimes you need two of the same letter to make certain words and that they will need both *r*'s to spell the secret word that ends the lesson.

The teacher then writes the numeral *2* on the board and says, "The two-letter word I want you to make today is a word that you already know—*at.* She watches as the children quickly put together the letters *a-t* and she checks to see that Roberto is able to follow along. She sends someone who has correctly spelled *at* to the pocket chart to make *at* with the big letters and to put an index card that has the word *at* written on it along the chalk ledge.

Next, she erases the *2* and writes a *3* on the board. "Add just one letter to *at* to make the three-letter word *sat,*" she instructs. She chooses a child who has arranged his letters correctly at his desk to make *sat* with the big pocket chart letters. The lesson continues with children making words with their individual letter cards, a child going to the pocket chart to make the word, and the teacher putting a card with that word along the chalk ledge. (The teacher does not wait for everyone to make the word before sending someone to the pocket chart, and some children are still making their word as the word is being made with the pocket chart letters. Before starting to make another word, the teacher reminds the children to fix their word to match the one made with the big letters.) Directed by the teacher, the children change *sat* to *rat, rat* to *rot, rot* to *cot,* and *cot* to *cat.* "Now, we are going to work some magic on the word *cat,*" the teacher explains, "Don't take any letters out and don't add any either. Just change the places of the letters and you can turn your *cat* into *act.* After we read stories, we like to *act* them out." The teacher has the children say the word *act* slowly, stretching out the sounds to figure out where to move the letters to transform *cat* into *act.*

The teacher erases the *3,* writes a *4* on the board, and asks the children to make *Rosa.* "We read a story earlier this year about a girl named Rosa who was unhappy about always being too little. Make the name *Rosa.*" She observes them saying "Rosa" very slowly, emphasizing each sound, and then finding their letters. She is pleased to notice that almost everyone turns the *R* card to display the capital *R.* She had been including at least one name in almost every Making Words lesson, and the children were getting very good at remembering that names need capital letters. Next, they make *coat* and then *oats.*

The teacher erases the *4* and writes a *5* and tells them that if they add just one letter to *oats,* they can turn *oats* into *coats.* She then has them, without adding any letters or taking any out, transform their *coats* into *coast* by changing the order of the letters. She helps them say the words *coats* and *coast* slowly and to listen for how these words sound. Most children are able to move the *s* and the *t* around to make this change; she notes their growing phonemic awareness. "Now make one more five-letter word by changing just one letter and turn your *coast* into a *roast.*"

As a child is making *roast* at the pocket chart, many of the other children are manipulating all their letters, trying to come up with a word. They know that each lesson ends with a word that uses all their letters, and they always like to figure it out. The teacher walks around looking for someone with the secret word, and just as she is about to declare that no one can figure out the secret word, so she will, she notices a child who has made the word and sends that child to the pocket chart where he makes the word *carrots.*

After making the words, it is time to sort for patterns and to use those patterns to read and spell a few new words. The teacher has the children read all the words they have made, now displayed in the pocket chart:

| at  | sat  | rat  | rot   | cot   | cat   | act     |
|-----|------|------|-------|-------|-------|---------|
| Rosa | coat | oats | coats | coast | roast | carrots |

She picks up *at* and says, "Who can come and hand me three words that rhyme with *at?*" A child hands her the words *sat, rat,* and *cat.* She then has someone find the word that rhymes with *rot—cot,* the word that rhymes with *oats—coats,* and the word that rhymes with *coast—roast.* The children spell the rhyming words and decide that these words all have the same letters from the vowel *on.* The teacher reminds the children that words that have the same spelling pattern usually rhyme and that knowing this is one way many good readers and writers read and spell words.

She shows them an index card on which the word *lot* is written. "What if you were reading and came to this word and didn't know it? Don't say this word even if you know it, but who can go and put this word with the rhyming words that help you figure it out?" A child places *lot* under *rot* and *cot* and all the children pronounce all three words and notice that they have the same spelling pattern and rhyme. The same procedure is followed with another rhyming word, *flat.*

"Thinking of words that rhyme helps you when you are trying to spell a word too. If I were writing and wanted to write *boats,* which of the rhyming words that we made today would help me?" The children decide that *boats* rhymes with *oats* and *coats* and will probably be spelled *b-o-a-t-s.* "If I were writing about foods I liked and I wanted to spell *toast,* what rhyming words would help me?" The children decide that *toast* rhymes with *roast* and *coast* and will probably be spelled *t-o-a-s-t.*

A Day in a Four Blocks Primary Classroom

**Take-Home Sheet for Making Words**

| a | o | c | r | r | s | t |
|---|---|---|---|---|---|---|
|   |   |   |   |   |   |   |
|   |   |   |   |   |   |   |
|   |   |   |   |   |   |   |
|   |   |   |   |   |   |   |

The letters you need to "make words" tonight are at the top of the page. Write capitals on the back. Then, cut the letters apart and see how many words you can make. Write the words in the blanks.

Finally, she shows them their take-home Making Words homework sheet. The letters *a, o, c, r, r, s, t* are in boxes along the top and beneath are larger boxes for children to write words. "When you show this to someone at your house, do you think they will figure out the secret word or will you have to tell them?" she asks. Most children think that this will be a "toughie." They always enjoy their Making Words homework sheet. They cut the letters apart, write the capitals on the back, and fill the boxes with the words they can make—including some made in class and others they think of. Parents and older siblings often get involved and because the letters formed the secret word made in class that day, the children are always smarter than anyone else and enjoy stumping their often competitive families!

## 9:20–10:00 Guided Reading

In this classroom, the Words block is followed by the Guided Reading block. On some days, they do a shared reading in a "big book." The teacher reads the book first and the children join in on subsequent rereadings. On other days, the teacher guides the children's reading in selections from basal readers, literature collections, or trade books, of which they have multiple copies. For today's lesson, the teacher has chosen *The Carrot Seed* (Krauss, 1945). As often as possible, the teacher tries to find reading material that ties in with the children's science or social studies unit. *The Carrot Seed* is perfect for their current seeds and plants unit.

The teacher picks up *The Carrot Seed* and points to the title. She asks, "What word do we see here that we made with an *s* added in our Making Words lesson?" The children quickly identify the word *carrot*. The teacher then points to the word *seed* and asks the children to look at the picture on the cover of the book. She asks them to think about what the boy is doing and what word the letters *s-e-e-d* might spell. The children realize that the boy is planting something; using the picture clue and what they know about letters and sounds, they are able to figure out the word *seed* and read the title of the book, *The Carrot Seed.*

Next, the teacher directs the children to look at all the pictures in the story and to think about what is happening. "You know that we can read lots of words we haven't seen before if we look at the pictures, think about what is happening, and then think about what words we might read to tell what is happening." She leads the children on a picture walk in which they use the pictures to make predictions and develop some vocabulary. First, they look at the pictures and identify the characters—a little boy, his mother, his father, and his big brother. The children all know the word *mother;* she writes it on the board and underneath it writes *brother.* She underlines the *other* in both *mother* and *brother* and asks the children what they know about words that have the same spelling pattern. The children respond that the words usually rhyme, and the teacher leads them to figure out the new word *brother* from their known word *mother.* The teacher follows the same procedure to help them decode the new word *weed* based on the rhyming word *seed.*

Next, the teacher leads them to decide what the boy is doing on certain pages. On the first page, they decide that the boy looks like he is planting the seed. The teacher asks them to say the word *planted* slowly and decide which letters they would use if they were making the word *planted.* The children decide that they hear a *p-l* at the beginning and that it ends in *e-d.* "Look on this page and find a word that might be *planted.* Put your finger on it when you find it." The children quickly find and say the word *planted.*

The children look at other pages and decide that the boy is pulling up weeds and sprinkling the plant with a watering can. The teacher has them say the words and think about which letters they would use to make the words *pull* and *sprinkle.* Now they search the text for these words. Throughout this phase of the lesson, the teacher develops useful strategies for children to use as they read. This lesson, using pictures to predict specific text content and attending to sounds in spoken words, represents an attempt to support children's development of the integrated strategy, using both the meaning and sounds of words in combination with one another.

Having guided them to look at the pictures, to talk about what was happening, and to use that knowledge to figure out some unfamiliar words, the teacher then asks them to make some predictions about what they will find out as they read the story with a partner. Finally, she tells them what they will do when they gather back together after reading the story. She shows them six index cards on which she has written the words:

| | | |
|---|---|---|
| carrot seed | mother | little boy |
| carrot | father | big brother |

*A Day in a Four Blocks Primary Classroom*

She also shows them that she has written the word *everyone* on 17 other index cards. The children read the words with her, and she tells them that after reading she will shuffle and distribute the cards, and they will get to play a part in acting out the story. Everyone will get a part, even if their part is to be part of the "everyone." Because they do not know which card they will get, they should read the story and think about what they would do for each part, no matter which card they get.

The children go to read the story with their partners. The teacher has partnered up struggling readers with better readers. The children have learned to take turns reading pages and to help each other when help is needed. The teacher reminds the children to examine the pictures before beginning to read and to help figure out, but not tell each other, an unknown word. She then reminds them of the steps they have learned for figuring out words that they do not recognize immediately:

1. Put your finger on the unknown word and say all the letters.
2. Use the letters and the picture clues.
3. Try to pronounce the word by seeing whether it has a spelling pattern or rhyme you know.
4. Keep your finger on the word and read the other words in the sentence to see whether it makes sense.
5. If it does not make sense, go back to the word and think what would have these letters and would make sense.

She also reminds the children that when their partner is reading a page, they are to play "teacher," and if their partner is having trouble with a word, they should go through the steps, instead of just telling what the word is.

The partners go to designated places and read the story. The teacher circulates, with clipboard and labels in hand, and makes notes on how fluently the children are reading. She praises the partners who are helping other children use the steps to figure out unfamiliar words by telling them that they could "soon have her job" and that "they are great little teachers!"

It takes only about seven minutes for the partners to finish reading. When she notices they have finished, she hands each of them an index card indicating what part they will play in the story reenactment. She then gathers the children around her again and has them retell the story, with emphasis on what the main characters do. The child who got the seed card will be put on the floor and lie there, motionless. The carrot will be pulled from the ground and wheeled away by the little boy. The mother, the father, the big brother, and everyone will shake their heads and say, "It won't come up!" The little boy will plant, sprinkle, pull weeds, and finally wheel the carrot away proudly.

· · · · · · · · · · · · · · · · · · · · · · · · · · · · · · · · · · · · · · · · · · · · · · · · · · · · · · · · · · · · · · · · · · · ·

**259**

Space is cleared in the center to make room for a stage, and *The Carrot Seed* is acted out. This low-budget, off-off Broadway production lacks props, costumes, and rehearsal, but no one seems to care. The children take their places, and the story is retold with the events happening in the correct sequence. The only complaint comes from the children who are part of the "everyone" and who want starring roles instead! The teacher assures them that tomorrow they will reread the story and act it out again, and more people will get the "big parts"!

## 10:00–10:15  Break/Snack

The children and the teacher go outside and take one brisk walk around the school, singing a favorite marching rhyme on their way. Once inside, they all have juice and crackers. Many children in this school do not eat nutritious meals, and the ones who need it most either brought no snack at all or brought junk food. The teacher has prevailed on those parents who could send something to send large cans of juice and boxes of crackers or to donate money so that she could buy juice and crackers at the local warehouse. Many parents donated willingly because they did not have to send something each day, and when everyone had juice and crackers for a snack, their children could not pester them to bring junk! Arranging for the juice and cracker morning snack took some time and preparation, but the teacher knew that some children needed this healthy snack; she also could not stand to watch some of them eat while others sat there hungry. During this break, the teacher talks with the children about the kinds of seeds and plants that produce much of the food they are eating. She even thought to bring in some raw carrot slices for everyone to munch on and a whole raw carrot for all to examine.

## 10:15–11:15  Math and Science
## or Social Studies Unit

During this hour each morning, the class does math and activities related to their science or social studies unit. On some days, it is impossible to integrate the two so they do one or the other or divide the hour between the two. Today, she integrates a math lesson with the new science unit on seeds and plants. She passes out containers filled with various kinds of seeds. She then leads the children in a variety of counting, sorting, predicting, classifying, and weighing activities with the seeds. The children work in groups at their tables, sorting the seeds by putting the ones that are alike together, estimating, counting to see how many of each type of seed they have, and graphing to show which seeds they have more and less of. The teacher gives out simple balance scales and has the children predict which seeds weigh the most and the least. They then weigh the different seeds and determine that it would take "more than they have" of the tiniest seeds to weigh as much as one of the largest seeds. The children are particularly amazed by how tiny carrot seeds are.

When the hour allotted for this hands-on math/science activity is almost over, the teacher shows the children some pages from the seeds and plants book that she read to start the day. She helps the children identify the seeds and the plants that grew from them. The children are amazed to realize that hickory nuts, acorns, and white beans were once all seeds. They remember seeing seeds like the little ones they had when eating cucumbers and apples. The children then regretfully dump all their seeds back into the containers, and the teacher promises that they will do more exploring and computing using the seeds tomorrow.

## 11:15–11:50  Writer's Workshop

Each day after math/science, the children have their Writing block. This block always begins with a minilesson in which the teacher writes something on the overhead as the children watch. As she writes, she thinks aloud, modeling the way she thinks about writing. This think-aloud writing supports children as they develop into readers and writers. She writes about a variety of topics and in a variety of formats. Today, she decides to capitalize on the children's interest in the new seed and plant unit by writing about some of the things they found while exploring with the seeds.

She sits down at her overhead, pen in hand. The children settle down on the floor in front of her, eager to see what she will write about today. They watch and listen as she thinks aloud about what to write.

> "I always have so many things I want to write about on Mondays. I could write about going shopping this weekend and finding my car with a flat tire when I came out of the store! I could write about the funny movie I watched on TV. I could write a list of the different seeds I ordered from the seed catalog this weekend. But I think I will write about what we did with the seeds this morning because you all seemed to have so much fun with them."

The teacher writes a description of some of the activities the children have just done. As she writes, she models for them how she might invent-spell a few words. (Early in the year, she told the children that she used to love to write when she was their age and that she would write all kinds of things. She wrote stories and kept a diary and was always making lists. She pretended that she was a great writer and wrote wonderful books for children to read. She explained that, of course, when she was their age, she could not spell all the words she needed, so she just put in all the letters she could hear so she could read it back. She told them that she used to invent-spell the big words and would show them how she used to do this at the beginning of each Writer's Workshop.) As she writes, she stops and says a word aloud slowly and writes down the letters she can hear. She also looks up at the word wall a few times and says, "I can spell *many* because we just put it on our word wall" and "I will look at *some* on our word wall because *some* is not spelled the way you think it should be." When she is ready to write the last sentence, she picks up the book and says, "I can use this book to help me spell the names of some of the seeds we had." She also omits one ending punctuation mark and fails to capitalize one word.

When she is finished writing, she says, "Now, I will read it to make sure that it makes sense and that it says what I wanted it to say." She reads aloud as the children watch. As soon as she finishes, the children's hands are raised, volunteering to be editors. She gives one boy a different color marker to go to the overhead and lead the class in helping her edit her writing. Each editing convention the children have learned so far is covered, and the class checks her draft for these. When they find something that needs fixing, the editor fixes it. Possible misspelled words are circled, and capitals and punctuation marks are added. The boy who is editing makes changes and insertions like a pro! So far, they have learned five things to look for. They read the short paragraph and put a check on the bottom as they check each of the four things:

1. Every sentence makes sense.
2. Every sentence begins with a capital and ends with a punctuation mark.
3. People and place names have capital letters.
4. Words that might be misspelled are circled.

The writing minilesson takes approximately 10 minutes, including the editing. The children are then dismissed from the big group to do their own writing. The children are at various stages of the writing process. Five children are at the art table, happily illustrating their books. When asked why they get to make books, they proudly explain that you have to write three pieces first. Then you pick the best of the three and get a friend to be your editor—"just like we do for the teacher at the overhead." Then you get to go to the editing table, and the teacher helps you edit. Then you copy it in one of these books (holding up a premade half-sheet construction paper book that is covered and stapled). One child who is illustrating a book about her best friend proudly turns to a blank last page in her book and says, "That's where she's going to write about me." When asked what the teacher might write, the author responds, "She's gonna say, Nikita is 7 years old. She has three brothers and four sisters, and this is her fourth book!—something like that!"

Four children are at the editing table with the teacher. She is helping them do a final edit of their pieces in preparation for copying them into books. A pair of children are helping each other edit before proceeding to the editing table. The other children are working away at their desks, in various stages of producing their three pieces so that they too can get to the art table. Children write about whatever they choose to. Some days, they continue writing on something they started the day before. Other days, they start a new piece. This morning, some children write about seeds and about what they did with the seeds. Another child pages through the seed catalog and writes a list of all the seeds that they want to order. Other children write about things they did over the weekend. The teacher's minilesson and her pondering about what to write each morning always gets the children thinking about what to write. The children often write about what the teacher writes about, although the teacher neither encourages nor discourages them from choosing the same topic. Many children can be seen glancing up at the word wall when they realize that the word they are trying to spell is up there. Some children have a book open to use as a reference for ideas and spelling.

The classroom is a busy working place for about 15 minutes. Then, with a signal from the teacher, the children once again gather on the floor and the Monday children line up behind the Author's Chair! (All the children are designated by a day of the week; on their day, they get to share!) The first child reads just two sentences of a piece that was started today. He calls on various children who tell him that they like the topic (dinosaurs) and give him ideas he might like to include. One child suggests a good dinosaur book for him to read. The second child reads a completed piece. She calls on children who tell her they like the way she stays on the topic (her new baby sister) and ask questions ("What's her name?" "Does she cry all night?" "Is this the only sister you've got?"). The third and fourth children read some unfinished pieces and receive praise and suggestions. Nikita is the final Monday child. She reads her book and shows her illustrations and then hands it to the teacher, reminding her to "write about me on this page!" The sharing takes approximately 9 minutes, for a total of 34 minutes of Writer's Workshop.

## 11:50–12:30  Lunch/Recess

Each day, as the children are lining up, the teacher reads the lunch menu to them. Today, she tells them that one of the foods they are going to have for lunch is made mostly from seeds. She then reads the menu. No one can figure out that peanut butter is the food made mostly from seeds. Many children seem quite astonished! The teacher decides that a peanut butter cooking activity would be a great tie-in to the unit.

## 12:30–1:45  P.E./Library/Art/Music/
## Open Centers/Coaching Groups

During this time each day, the class is scheduled for their time with the specialists. They do not have specialists for the whole time each day; they also use this time to go outside or to the gym or library or to do music or art. On some days, they have open-center time for part of this time. The teacher also uses this time to meet with small coaching groups and teach them how to be word coaches.

## 1:45–2:15  Self-Selected Reading

Each day, the teacher begins this block by reading aloud to the children for 10–15 minutes. After reading to them, she dismisses them to their tables for their own reading time. The teacher has arranged books into several plastic crates and has put one crate on each of the five tables. The crates contain a variety of books, including some related to the science unit—seeds and plants; some old favorites, such as *Are You My Mother?, One Fish, Two Fish,* and *Robert the Rose Horse;* some class books; and some books the children have written. The trays are rotated each day so that all the children have lots of books to choose from without leaving their seats but do not see the same old books every day.

The children eagerly read the books. As they read, the teacher conferences with the Monday children. Each child brings the teacher a book that he or she has selected and reads a few pages from that book. The teacher makes anecdotal notes about what the Monday children are reading and about how well they are reading. She notes their use of picture clues, their attempts to figure out unknown words, fluency, self-correction, and other reading behaviors. She also asks them what they like about the book they are reading and sometimes suggests another book they might like to read.

## 2:15–2:30  Daily Summary/
## School–Home Connection

During this time, the children prepare to go home and the teacher helps them talk about what they have learned today and what they could talk about at home. Because so many of these children come from homes in which English is not the spoken language, she feels that promoting as much home/school talk as possible is important. She help them recall the seeds they learned about in the book and what they did with the seeds. She reminds them that they ate peanut butter—made mostly from seeds—at lunch. She makes sure they have their song sheets from music class and asks them whether they think someone at home would enjoy learning the song. She reminds them of *The Carrot Seed* and has them think about their part in the reenactment. She distributes the Making Words homework sheets and reminds them to bring them back tomorrow so she can see what other words can be made from these letters that she had not been smart enough to think of!

Next, she gives them their take-home word wall and has them find and highlight the five new words with their yellow crayon. "Be sure to show your family that we finally have a *q* word—*question*—on our word wall and that we are looking for a useful, important word that begins with the letter *z.*" She also reminds them to tell about what they wrote about during Writer's Workshop and what they were reading during self-selected reading. She reminds the Tuesday children that tomorrow is their day to do everything special and that they should decide which book they want to share with her during their conference tomorrow. Finally, she gives them a science homework assignment:

> "Look around your house and street and try to find three different kinds of seeds. You might find these seeds in your kitchen. Sometimes, the seeds might be part of a food. Some seeds can be found outdoors. Bring in these seeds, if you can. If not, write down their names so you can remember them when we share what you have found first thing tomorrow morning."

After the children leave, the teacher attaches the labels on which she has written anecdotal comments to each of their folders. She then puts a clean sheet of labels on her clipboard. She writes the initials of each Tuesday child on several labels so that she will remember to take note of their progress and problems tomorrow. She also writes the initials of several other children and a few questions on several other labels to remind her to observe the problem areas she was concerned about for particular children tomorrow: Solves math problems? Using self-correction strategies? Using strategies taught for figuring out unknown words? Really reading during self-selected reading? Then she begins to organize the materials for tomorrow's science lesson—planting beans in cups and watching them sprout. Of course, the children will observe, sketch, and write descriptions of the growth of the bean plants over the next 2 weeks.

# chapter 13

# A Week in a Big Blocks Intermediate Classroom

Throughout the chapters of this book, we have tried to convey to you that when working with children who find learning to read difficult, the earlier we start teaching them to read, the better. Children who receive the kind of instruction provided in Building Blocks kindergartens and Four Blocks primary classes are usually reading and writing when they reach the intermediate grades. They do still need good instruction but have achieved some basic literacy skills and, perhaps more importantly, view themselves as readers and writers. They have—in the current lingo—the right attitude!

Unfortunately, children who have experienced many years of frustration and failure have developed, justifiably perhaps, the wrong attitude! They say with their eyes, their bodies, and, sometimes, boldly with their mouths:

"I won't do it!"

"You can't make me!"

"Reading and writing are dumb and stupid and sissy!"

"I don't care!"

"Who needs it?"

What most of them really mean is

"I can't do it!"

Throughout this book, when describing activities for intermediate-aged, still-struggling children, we have tried to describe activities that involve real reading and writing and that provide for success on a variety of levels. Six principles are behind the activities we have described:

1. All children can learn to read and write—and all of them really want to.
2. Success precedes motivation, and once children see that they can be successful, they will participate; thus, teachers must engineer success!
3. Real reading and writing are intrinsically motivating.
4. Traditional seatwork is a waste of time.
5. Children learn from each other.
6. The mastery model is wrong; teachers must teach for and look for improvement, growth, and approximation—not perfection.

Given all they must accomplish, intermediate teachers cannot usually do everything every day in the same way that primary teachers can. In addition, intermediate-aged children need larger blocks of time to pursue reading, writing, and research. We call our intermediate-grades literacy framework Big Blocks because we schedule larger blocks of time and integrate at least one subject area with our reading and writing instruction. For more information about Big Blocks, see *The Teacher's Guide to Big Blocks* (Arens, Loman, Cunningham, & Hall, 2005) or go to www.wfu.edu/fourblocks.

In the remainder of this chapter, we describe a week of instruction in an intermediate Big Blocks classroom. We assume a 5½-hour instructional day (330 minutes, not including recess and lunch). We assume that 40 minutes of each day is given over to specials—

music, art, computers, P.E., foreign language, and so on—and that another 50 minutes is allocated to math. We further assume that, as in most states, 120 minutes should be allocated to the language arts daily, 50 minutes to science, 50 minutes to social studies, and 20 minutes to health. In our classroom, however, the teacher alternates between teaching a social studies unit and a science unit each week. Health is combined with science, when possible, and thus a combined science/health unit might merit 2 weeks. If the curriculum demands it, a week-long health unit is taught. Most 9-week grading periods contain four week-long social studies units, four week-long science units, and one week-long health unit.

Thus, each day, we have 240 minutes available to teach language arts and one topic from science, health, or social studies. This allows us to meet the guidelines for content subject teaching in most states while reducing the fragmentation found in classrooms that schedule each subject every day. We make every effort to foster reading and writing development, even during content topic time. Students develop strategies for comprehending informational text and for writing factual reports as they learn the content of their science, social studies, and health subjects. Of course, schedules differ from school to school and from teacher to teacher within a school. For our example, we assume the following daily schedule:

| | |
|---|---|
| 8:15–8:30 | Arriving and Settling In (children arrive at different times, depending on buses, breakfast, and so on; attendance taken, routines, and so on) (noninstructional time) |
| 8:30–9:10 | Language Arts—Self-Selected Reading (40 minutes) |
| 9:10–9:40 | Language Arts—Working with Words (30 minutes) |
| 9:40–10:30 | Math (50 minutes) |
| 10:30–10:50 | Break/Recess (noninstructional time) |
| 10:50–11:50 | Language Arts/Science or Social Studies Unit Time (60 minutes) |
| 11:50–12:20 | Lunch (noninstructional time) |
| 12:20–1:40 | Language Arts/ Science or Social Studies Unit (80 minutes) |
| 1:40–2:20 | Special Subject (40 minutes) |
| 2:20–2:50 | Language Arts/ Science or Social Studies Unit (30 minutes) |

Once we know the time frame we are working with, we can decide what happens. Not all components can be included every day, but all the important ones should be

A Week in a Big Blocks Intermediate Classroom

implemented on a regular basis. A successful teacher of struggling readers might follow these time allocation guidelines:

### Every Day (No Matter What!)
- Teacher reads to the class from a book.
- Teacher reads something to the class from a newspaper, magazine, riddle book, joke book, book of poetry, or other "real-world" source.
- Children read something they choose from a large and varied selection.
- Children learn more about the topic they are studying.
- Children do a word wall activity with high-frequency, commonly misspelled words and/or with topic-related big words.

### Two or Three Times a Week
- Children participate in guided reading activity.
- Children participate in a focused writing lesson.
- Teacher models topic selection and writing a short piece.
- Children write on a topic of their own choice.
- Children work with words—looking for patterns, learning how to chunk and decode big words, and so forth.

### Once a Week
- All children share something they have written.
- All children share something they have read.
- One-third of the class revises, edits, and publishes a piece of writing.
- Children read to their little buddies.
- Children do research related to a topic.

This is what one week of instruction might look like using the allocated 250 minutes and making sure that all the activities in which we want children to engage happen as often as we have decided.

## 8:30–9:10 Self-Selected Reading

Many important things must be done each day in an intermediate classroom. Every activity wants more time than it can be allotted. Interruptions and schedule changes sometimes force activities to be "scrapped" or postponed until tomorrow. The teacher in this class has decided that the most crucial goal for her students is that they all become readers—people who choose to read even when they are not forced. All her students can read some, although many do not read at grade level (and a few read above grade level). She knows that the major determinant of how well they will read by the end of the year is how much they read. She also knows that many of her students do not read on their own at home and view reading as "something you have to do in school." The teacher knows that she can provide two activities that have the greatest potential of getting her kids "hooked on reading"—reading to them and giving them consistent and ample time to read materials of their own choosing. To make sure that reading to the class and giving them time to read does not get crowded out as the day goes on, she schedules it first thing every morning.

Each morning she reads two pieces to the class. The first piece she reads is a "quick-read," and she tries to make it as current and "in sync" with the interests of her students as she can. On Monday mornings, the teacher usually brings in a newspaper and shares some of the more interesting tidbits with the children. Children are encouraged to bring in interesting things from the weekend paper too. Pieces shared are added to the collage-style newspaper board. Other mornings, the teacher reads from informational books, magazines, joke and riddle books, pamphlets, and so on. The message that the children begin with each day is that reading is an essential part of their real world.

The second piece she reads each day is a book—or a chapter of a book. She chooses books of high interest to readers at this age but of varying genres so the children are exposed to a variety of literature. She tries to include equal numbers of fiction and non-fiction titles and is always on the lookout for good multicultural books. This week, she is reading *Get On Out of Here, Philip Hall* (B. Greene, 1981). When she finishes each book, many children always want to read it for themselves. Those who want the book write their names on little slips of paper. She pulls one slip (without looking) and hands the book to that lucky winner. The other slips are also pulled and used to make a waiting list in the order they were pulled, just like they do at the library.

This procedure is perceived as fair by the children, and the chapter books that the teacher reads aloud always have waiting lists. Even children who could not read the book by themselves the first time can often read and enjoy it once they have listened to it read aloud. Whenever possible, the teacher tries to read a book aloud by an author who has written similar books or by one who has several books in a series. Children who are on the waiting list for the book are often delighted to get a similar book to read in the meantime. The class does not know that the teacher has hidden away a copy of Greene's *Philip Hall Likes Me, I Reckon Maybe*.

Next comes the students' time to read. Many children have a book at their desk that they are in the middle of reading. Other children choose a book from the trays of books that rotate to different tables each week. Each tray is filled with a wide variety of books, including some high-interest, easy vocabulary books and some informational books with lots of pictures. Children are grouped by days of the week, a fifth of the class for each day. On Day 1, the Day 1 people can read anywhere and anything in the room, including newspapers, magazines, joke books, the newspaper board, and so on. On the other days, they stay at their seats and read books. In this way, everyone gets a chance to "spread out" and read anything 1 day each week, but most of the class is seated quietly at their desks reading books.

While her students read, the teacher holds quick conferences with one-fifth of her students each day. The students have been taught how to prepare for the conference; they come to the conference with the pages they want to read and talk about marked with a bookmark. When making the schedule for the daily conferences, the teacher spreads out her most struggling students across the 5 days—beginning each day with a conference with one of her struggling readers and giving that reader a few additional minutes. The teacher views these weekly conferences as "conversations" rather than "interrogations," and all her students look forward to their weekly one-on-one time with her.

## 9:10–9:40 Working with Words

This half-hour each day is devoted to words. The goals are that children (1) learn to spell the high-frequency words that they need in their writing; (2) learn to read, spell, and develop meanings for big words that are part of the science, health, or social studies topic they are studying; and (3) learn to decode and spell unfamiliar words—particularly polysyllabic words.

Monday is usually the day on which a new unit of study begins, so the teacher adds 10–12 unit-related big words to a Big Word Board. These words are related to the unit topic for the week. As the teacher puts the words on the board, she helps the children associate meanings for the words. This week's unit is on pollution. Twelve words are added to the Big Word Board:

| | | |
|---|---|---|
| pollution | environment | recycle |
| pollutants | environmental | conservation |
| resources | chemicals | fertilizers |
| pesticides | combustion | renewable |

Each week, the teacher tries to include some words that have the same root— *pollution/pollutants, environment/environmental.* As she introduces the words to the children, she helps them distinguish the different forms of the words from one another. She helps them understand that *pollution* is the word we use to describe the whole problem and that *pollutants,* including *fertilizers, chemicals,* and *pesticides,* are *some of the things* that cause pollution. Although the word *pollute* is not included on the board (the number of words must be limited if children are really going to focus on them and make them part of their listening/speaking/reading/writing vocabularies), she writes it on the chalkboard. She reminds the children that an *e* at the end is often dropped when endings such as *tion* and *ant* are added and helps them see that "*pollute* is what you do that causes the problem of *pollution.*" In a similar way, she helps them understand that the *environment* is the surroundings in which we live, and *environmental* is the word we use as a describing word. "We can say that pollution is a problem for our environment or that pollution is an environmental problem." She has the children contribute several sentences describing how pollution is a problem and using the words *environment* and *environmental* to help them develop a sense in their listening vocabulary of when each word is used.

The other words get introduced and the teacher alerts the children to similar morphemes and meanings. *Recycle, renewable,* and *resources* all begin with the prefix *re* and have related meanings. "When you *recycle* something, you use it again. *Renewable* resources, such as trees, will grow again." The teacher also writes the word *nonrenewable* on the board and helps the children think about what the addition of *non* does to *renewable* and to think of some *nonrenewable* resources.

The words *pollution, combustion,* and *conservation* are discussed. Then the teacher writes the words *pollute, combust,* and *conserve* on the board, drawing their attention to how the word changes as it is used differently in both speaking and writing. Throughout this introduction phase, the teacher talks about the words, defines them, uses them in sentences, and focuses on word structure and other cues.

Once all the words have been introduced and attention has been devoted to their meaning and to similar chunks, the teacher leads them in a clapping/chanting activity similar to the cheering you would hear at a basketball game. The children say each word, clap and chant its spelling, and then say the word again. The teacher leads them to spell the word in a rhythmic way, pausing briefly between the syllables—"*pollution— p-o-l___l-u___t-i-o-n—pollution, pollutant—p-o-l___l-u___t-a-n-t—pollutant.*" The lesson ends with each student writing the 12 words in a vocabulary notebook. One of their regular Monday night homework assignments is to write a sentence and/or draw a picture giving a personal example for each word.

In addition to helping intermediate children develop a store of big words, many struggling readers still misspell (or do not know how to spell) common words that are needed in their writing. This classroom has a word wall of frequently misspelled words. The teacher began the word wall at the beginning of the year with words she knew many of the children would misspell. Five words were first added to the wall:

they    were    friend    from    said

The next week, she added five more frequently written but often misspelled words:

are    what    because    could    once

A Week in a Big Blocks Intermediate Classroom

As the year went on, she became alerted to words many children were misspelling in their first-draft writing and added words the children evidently needed. She also added homophones, putting a picture or word clue next to all but one of the words:

to     two     too     there     their     they're     buy     by     write     right

Now the word wall contained the contractions that the students used a great deal:

can't     didn't     won't     wasn't     we're     let's

Five high-frequency words were added to the word wall each Tuesday. After adding the five new words, the teacher calls out the five new words for the week and five review words. The children clap, chant, and write these 10 words. The teacher is adding five new words this week:

new     knew     doesn't     terrible     until

Each Wednesday, Thursday, and Friday, the children write big words and word wall words in a variety of ways. On some days, the teacher simply calls out five words from the Big Word Board and five from the word wall of frequently misspelled words and has the children clap, chant, and write them. On other days, she gives clues to the words and the children have to guess them. She also dictates short sentences that can be made by combining words from the Big Word Board and the word wall. Regardless of what activity she uses to review these words, she always involves the children in some chanting and writing because these activities focus their attention on all the letters in the words. In addition, when children are writing, she encourages them to use invented spellings or whatever resources they have for spelling words. The teacher insists, however, that the words from the Big Word Board and the word wall be spelled correctly because they are so readily accessible. Students' eyes can be seen going to the board or the wall when they are writing.

On Monday and Tuesday, most of the 30 minutes devoted to working with words is consumed with introducing, adding, and reviewing words on the board and the wall. On the other 3 days, however, a quick review activity takes only 5–10 minutes; the remaining time is devoted to activities designed to help them see patterns in words. Generally, the teacher does a Making Big Words activity on Wednesday, an activity designed to teach particular prefixes or suffixes on Thursday, and everyone's favorite—"The Wheel"—on Friday.

**9:40–10:30   Math**

**10:30–10:50   Break/Recess**

**10:50–11:50   Unit Time**

This time is usually devoted to learning about the topic, expanding both world and word knowledge. Whenever possible, the teacher uses real experiences—experiments and demonstrations during science, simulations, and imagined journeys during social studies. At least one day each week includes a guided reading activity, and another day includes a focused writing lesson. The students are taught strategies for reading and writing informational text and study strategies, including note-taking and summarizing. Sometimes, the focused writing lesson is a follow-up to the guided reading activity, and sometimes the two are topic related but not related to each other. On Fridays, the student usually brainstorm questions they would still like to know the answers to and go to the library to find answers to the questions. Students work in pairs to find answers.

This week, the topic being studied is pollution. On Monday, they watch a video that shows some of the most serious sources of pollution and begin to fill in some information on the accompanying data chart graphic organizer. The video described some general pollution problems but was not specific to the geographic area in which the school is located. The teacher finishes the lesson by asking students to write down the three pollutants that they think are most problematic where they live. For homework, they are to interview two adults about pollution in the local area and determine what these adults think the most significant problems are.

| Environmental Pollution | | | |
|---|---|---|---|
| **Where** | **Causes** | **Possible Solutions** | **Our Area** |
| Air | | | |
| Water | | | |
| Soil | | | |
| Land | | | |

Tuesday's lesson begins with the students sharing what they found out in their interviews with the two adults. Most had talked with someone about the problem and were

A Week in a Big Blocks Intermediate Classroom

surprised to learn how high the level of concern was. The teacher shares some newspaper articles from local sources that she has been saving until this unit. More information, particularly in the last column, Our Area, is added to the data chart.

On Wednesday, the teacher leads the students in a guided reading activity in which they read about what can be accomplished with recycling. She uses a KWL to help them organize and connect what they knew before and after reading. Their homework assignment for Wednesday night is to find out what they can recycle from their homes and where to take the recyclables.

Thursday begins with a discussion of their home recycling efforts. The teacher then describes some recycling efforts that are being made by various businesses. She explains that on her recent plane flight, the flight attendants were collecting cans and other recyclables separately. The school secretary comes in and explains how copying and computer paper are being recycled. Next, the teacher gives out a list of local businesses. Included on the list are stores and fast-food restaurants that the children visit on a regular basis. She does a focused writing lesson in which she demonstrates for the children how to write a list of questions they can ask to find out what, if anything, a business is doing about recycling. As the children watch, she writes a list of questions to ask her brother, who works at a car dealership.

After watching her write her questions, she lets each child decide who or what business they will interview and has each child make a list of questions to ask. She helps the children see that some of their questions might be just like hers:

> Do you have a place to collect recyclable aluminum cans?
> Do you have bins in all the offices for recyclable paper?

Other questions were particular to a car dealership:

> What happens to the old oil when you do an oil change?
> What happens to old tires and worn-out car parts?

She gives the children the option of doing the interview by themselves or with a classmate, assuming that the pair can get together over the weekend to do the interview. The children who are going to interview together pair up to make the list of questions. The others do theirs by themselves. The teacher circulates and helps each child make a readable list.

Normally, on Fridays, the class goes to the library to do research designed to answer the unanswered questions they have about a topic. This Friday, however, the teacher decides to have them do some "field research." She gets the class together and asks them to predict what kind of litter and how many pieces of it they might find in the area surrounding the school and where that litter might have come from. Once they have made their predictions, she divides them into teams, arms each team with a trash bag, and gives them 20 minutes to see how much litter they can pick up in the designated area.

Dividing the children into teams is a problem in some classes. The children fuss about who they are with and who gets to do what. In this classroom, however, the teacher has a system for forming teams and distributing responsibilities. She uses this system quite often, and it is perceived as fair by all the students. She uses a deck of playing cards, taking out as many numbers as she has children present today. She has 27 children present and decides to form six groups of four and one group of three. Thus, she takes out all four suits of the cards numbered 1–6 and three of the 7s. The cards are dealt and children form teams based on the number they get! Sometimes, she uses the suits to designate who will do what. Today, she writes these responsibilities on the board:

- *Spade*—Carrier—Carry trash bag.
- *Club*—Leader—Lead the team in whatever direction this person chooses; team must "follow the leader."
- *Diamond*—Tallier—Tally the trash collected into different categories as team counts it.
- *Heart*—Reporter—Report team's results to the rest of the class.

As she writes these responsibilities, the different class members cheer and grumble as they get responsibilities they like and others they eschew. As in real life, everyone wants to lead and no wants to "carry the load," but the children accept what they get because they have seen the cards shuffled and dealt. They know that it was "the luck of the draw" and not teacher favoritism that determined their "fate." (The team that has only three members is lacking a tallier, and the teacher tells them that the reporter will have to double up and also be the tallier for their group.)

The class goes out and collects the litter. As they collect each item, they count and tally their "treasure" and then add up the results for the reporter to report to the class. As each group reports, the children tally the results reported by the groups. Finally, they compare what they actually found to what they had predicted. They decide that much too much litter is around, that most of it came from students, and that some of it can be recycled. They sort out the recyclables, decide who can take it where, and take the rest out to the big dumpster.

This unit, like some others, extends into the following Monday. The class has done a good job of interviewing local business owners and employees, and many children are encouraged by what they have found. Others discover that there is still much to be done that is not being done. After discussing their results on Monday, the teacher leads them in another focused writing activity. This time, they watch as she writes a letter to her interviewee (her brother), thanking him for taking time to be interviewed, praising him for the good things the car dealership is doing, and suggesting that someone needs to find out what is being done with all those old tires that are just being hauled away.

The students use her model to write their own letters. The teacher uses some of the time to help them revise and edit their letters as needed. Then they copy the letters to make them as "readable" as possible and deliver them to their interviewees (including one to the school principal with suggestions for increasing recycling at the school).

## 11:50–12:20 Lunch

## 12:20–1:40 Guided Reading or Writer's Workshop

Each day this time is used for guided reading lessons and for children to write, revise, and edit on topics of their own choosing. It varies according to what they need to do. Most weeks, the teacher does guided reading lessons on Mondays and Tuesdays and Writer's Workshop on Wednesdays and Thursdays. On Friday, the children often have a choice of whether they want to read or write or do some combination of both during this hour.

The teacher uses a variety of materials and a variety of formats for guiding their reading. The children in this class read on many different levels, and the teacher tries to make sure that over the week, children read something at their instructional level or easier during this time. Sometimes, she finds two or three pieces, similar in genre, topic, or theme, that different students can read. Whenever possible, she finds something related to the topic being studied, but often the reading done at this time is unrelated to the topic.

This week, they are going to read two stories. The stories are not about pollution (one is about a current-day family that survives a fire and the other is set in the old West), but the teacher sees possibilities for tying in what they have been learning about pollution to both stories. The story about the family that survives the fire is from a grade-level basal and is too hard for many of the students to read by themselves. The other story is from another series that features stories of interest to intermediate-aged children, have more vocabulary control, and are much easier to read.

She decides to have them read the fire story on Monday. Because this story will be difficult for many of her students, she reads the first three pages of the story to them. Before reading, she begins a character web on the board. The class has done character webs many times before and knows that they need to decide on a couple of adjectives that best describe the main character in the story. They know that they will fill in details next to the adjectives the teacher has chosen and then try to come up with other adjectives that they think "sum up" the main character.

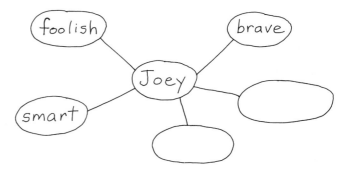

The teacher reads the first three pages of the story and the children listen so that they can tell her what to fill in as evidence that Joey was brave, smart, or foolish. They are also thinking of adjectives they would use to describe Joey.

When the teacher finishes the three pages, the children are eager to offer support for all three adjectives and to suggest others. The teacher writes some of their supporting statements out next to the adjectives and adds the other adjectives that they suggest. She then tells them to finish the story with their partners and to come back ready to add more adjectives and more support for the other adjectives. She reminds them as they read that they should "think" just as they did when she was reading to them: "Think about Joey and his role in the fire, and decide what word you think best sums him up and why you think so."

The children then go to read with their partners. Each struggling reader in the class is paired up with a better reader. The teacher had to change the partnerships several times but finally paired up most of the children with someone they liked and who would help them without making it too obvious. Most of the partnerships alternate between periods of oral and silent reading, with partners first reading a page to themselves and then alternating the lead role in discussing, summarizing, or asking the other partner questions. They may reread sections aloud to clarify a point or to emphasize a major point. At times, they take turns reading pages to each other. The teacher encourages them to "help with words they don't know" by focusing on the use of appropriate strategies. Generally, better readers do not interrupt to correct or supply a word to their partners. Instead, they respond as their teacher does, by saying, "That didn't sound right," or "I didn't get that."

As the partners read, the teacher circulates with her clipboard in hand. She has attached file folder labels to the clipboard and written the initials of six children whose reading she wants to monitor today. (These six children are six of her average readers. Tomorrow, when they read the selection from the easier basal, she will monitor six of her struggling readers.) She stops and asks each child to read aloud very softly and then asks the child which adjective he or she thinks is best and why. She makes notes on the children's labels about their reading fluency and their ability to think about characters. She spends about 2 minutes with each child she is monitoring and notes that each child is able to read the story fluently and could think about and justify character traits.

After about 12 minutes, the teacher notices that many of the partners have finished reading the story. She tells them to start a list of adjectives and justifications while the others finish. After another 4 minutes, she signals the class to join her and help complete the web. (One pair has still not finished reading the story; she tells them to continue and join the group as soon as they finish.)

The class joins her and suggests many more adjectives and justifications for each. She adds the adjectives and writes in a few words of justification next to each. She ends the lesson by letting each child vote on the one adjective that they think best describes Joey. She tallies the votes next to each and reminds the class that the story did not tell them directly what kind of person Joey was. "We had to figure out what kind of person he was the same way that we figure out people we meet in real life. Just as we do not always agree about people we meet in real life, we also do not always agree on characters we read about in books. What matters when you read is that you think about the characters and decide what *you* think!"

Finally, she tells them, "The story wasn't about pollution, but did it have anything to do with pollution?" The class talks about it and decides that if the newspapers had been recycled and if the old paint had been disposed of, the fire probably would not have happened. They also talk about the air pollution caused by the smoke from the fire.

On Tuesday, they read a story about a family homesteading in Iowa. Before reading, the teacher begins a Then and Now Chart and has the children brainstorm some of the differences they thought would exist in their lives if they were transported back to the prairieland of the 1800s. Once again, the partners read the story together. Today, the teacher has put the names of some of the struggling readers on the labels. She makes notes about their reading fluency and their comprehension of this material, which is closer to their instructional level. When the partners finish reading, they reconvene and complete the chart. The teacher then has them vote on whether they would have rather lived then or now. (*Now* won hands down!) Finally, she asks them whether the homesteaders had to worry about pollution. A lively discussion ensues as the children realize for the first time that pollution is a relatively new problem for society to contend with.

On Wednesdays and Thursdays, this time is used for Writer's Workshop. Each day, the teacher models how to think of topics and writes a short piece on the overhead. She tries to write a variety of pieces so the children see that writing can take many forms. She has told the children that she used to write a lot when she was their age—most of her writing was for herself and she did not let anyone else see it. They know that she used to keep a diary and write in it every night. Sometimes, she writes in her diary still, the way she did when she was their age. They think it is hilarious when she writes as an intermediate-aged child. She does not read aloud what she is writing, except when she is inventing the spelling of a word. During invented spelling, she says the word slowly, exaggerating the sounds. The children are always eager to see "what she will write today."

On Monday, she decides to write an imaginary diary entry. The children always recognize when she is doing this because she writes the date and "Dear Diary":

> February 14, 1967
>
> Dear Diary,
>
> Today was valintin's day. I was so exsited! I sent my best valintin to YOU KNOW WHO! He sent me one too but it wasn't a speshul one he sent a speshul one to ANITA! YUK! I got 23 valentins in all. My Dad bought me some a big box of candy and it was very exspensiv. It cost $1.59!

The children were all reading along as she wrote. They laughed when she sounded out how to spell *valentine, excited, special,* and *expensive.* They could not imagine that you could ever buy a big box of Valentine's candy for just $1.59. When she finishes writing, she says, "Now, I will read it all to make sure it makes sense and that it says what I wanted it to say." She reads it aloud as the children watch. As soon as she finishes, the children's hands are raised, volunteering to be editors.

She reminds the children that a diary entry probably would never be edited because it is personal writing and is certainly not meant to be public. But to provide practice (and because it was not a true entry!), she lets them edit it. She then hands a girl a different color marker, and the girl goes to the overhead and leads the class in helping the teacher edit her writing. They use a class-created editing checklist that has seven things to check for:

1. Every sentence makes sense.
2. Every sentence begins with a capital and ends with a punctuation mark.
3. People and place names have capital letters.
4. Words that might be misspelled are circled.
5. The writing stays on the topic.
6. Things people say have commas and quotes (She shouted, "Help!").

Each editing convention the children have learned so far is read; the class then checks for these features and volunteers what they think needs fixing. Possible misspelled words are circled; capitals and punctuation marks are added. They decide that a diary entry does not need a title but that it does need a date and a "Dear Diary," both of which this entry has. Some children think that only the first letter of *Anita* should be capitalized, but others argue that it was all in caps for emphasis and that, if it were your diary, you could write it that way!

After this writing minilesson, the teacher takes the children who are publishing a piece this week to the back table with her while the other two-thirds of the class pursue their own writing. Some children begin new pieces. Others continue writing an already begun piece. Some children look in books to help them get ideas and for words they want to spell. Children also look at the word wall and Big Word Board when they need spelling help. They can be heard saying words very slowly and listening for the sounds they want to represent as they invent-spell some words, just as their teacher did.

The third of the class that the teacher takes with her is composed of a whole range of students. She divides the nine children into three trios and has them read their stories to each other. The children have learned how to help each other revise and edit and know that on the first day they focus only on revising for meaning. When one person reads his or her piece to the other two, the listeners cannot see the writing. They are listening for something they like about it and for something they can suggest to make the piece clearer or

*A Week in a Big Blocks Intermediate Classroom*

more interesting. It takes about 5 minutes for each member of a trio to read the piece and listen to the praise and suggestions. While they are doing this, the teacher circulates and adds her own praise and suggestions.

Once the children have all read and listened, they return to their seats and make whatever additions or changes they choose to. They do the adding and changing right on the page because they have learned to write all first drafts on every other line in their writing notebooks, leaving space for revisions. The teacher circulates, giving encouragement and suggestions to the revisers and those working on first drafts.

On Thursday, they have their second Writer's Workshop of the week. Once again, the teacher writes, but today she claims to be in a poetry mood, so she writes the following cinquain about pollution:

**Pollution**

Pollution
Scary, Disgusting
Trash, Chemicals, Pesticides.
They threaten our environment.
Recycle!

As she writes today, she makes it obvious that she is getting the spellings of many of the big words from the Big Word Board. After writing, she reads it aloud and then chooses a boy to be the editor. Once again, the editor and the class read through the checklist and help her edit the piece.

The children who are publishing this week bring the piece they revised for meaning yesterday to the back table. The teacher then pairs eight of the children up with partners of similar writing ability. These partners help each other edit using the editing checklist and the procedures used each day when a student edits the teacher's writing. The teacher takes for her partner the child who is having the most difficulty communicating through writing. (When dividing the class into thirds for revising and editing, the teacher makes sure to put the three children having the most difficulty writing in three different groups.) This child needs more help from the teacher, but the teacher is able to use the blank lines to write in words and to help the child produce a piece that he can copy over or type on the computer and can illustrate and be proud of.

As the partners finish helping each other, they bring their pieces to the teacher who reads them and helps fill in needed words, punctuation marks, and so on. Misspelled words are corrected and other obvious problems are fixed. Once the piece has been through a "teacher edit," the children publish it in some form, depending on the piece and how it will be displayed or shared. Some children type their piece into the computer and then print it out. Other children copy their piece on some special paper and illustrate it. Still other children make a book from their piece.

On Friday, during this hour, children are engaged in a variety of activities. This Friday, like most Fridays, the children whose week it is to publish are copying, typing, or illustrating their finished pieces. This is also a time during the week when children can do more reading and research on their expert topic. Each child has been designated class expert on a topic of that child's choice. Every 3 weeks they take a portion of this Friday time to share new information they have learned about their topic. Today is not an Expert Share Friday, but children who are not publishing can choose to spend this time in the room or in the library finding out more about their expert topic. Several children spend this time "just reading"—a Friday afternoon activity encouraged by the teacher. Several children who know that next week is their week to revise, edit, and publish a piece are busy finishing up the piece they have decided to work with. The rules for this afternoon time are simple. It is a time for reading and/or writing, and children can do whatever they choose to as long as what they are doing involves reading or writing.

## 1:40–2:20  Special Subject
## 2:20–2:50

The last minutes of any school day are difficult to structure and, in many classrooms, are just "waiting-to-leave" time. When teaching struggling readers, however, we have no time to waste. In this classroom, the teacher has a different activity each day. Children look forward to it, and it also helps her accomplish some of her weekly goals.

*Monday*   On Mondays, the children get ready for Tuesday's reading to the kindergarten children. Every Monday after lunch, some kindergartners bring favorite books from the kindergarten. On a sticky note attached to each book is the name of the kindergarten child who would like to have that book read to him or her tomorrow. (The teacher and the kindergarten children have chosen a book for each child.) The books are quickly distributed to the big buddies, who then practice reading that book in preparation for tomorrow's reading. Some children tape record their reading to check how they sound. The teacher reminds her big kids of the steps in reading the book to their little buddies:

1. Read the book title and author's name, and ask your little buddy what she or he thinks the book will be about.

2. Look through the book, talking about the things you see in the pictures before reading.

3. Read the book and help your little buddy talk about it. Ask questions that get your little buddy involved with the book:

> What do you think will happen next?
> Would you like to do that?

A Week in a Big Blocks Intermediate Classroom

4. When you finish reading, ask your little buddy to find his or her favorite page and tell why it was the favorite.

5. Go through the book again and let your little buddy tell you what is happening or help read it to you if some parts are very easy.

The children eagerly read the books, which include such classics as *Robert the Rose Horse, The Little Red Hen,* and *Caps for Sale.* The teacher sits with one boy who is a very hesitant reader and who needs her help to read this book successfully tomorrow. She leads him to look through the pictures and to predict what will happen, in the same way that she wants him to do with his little buddy tomorrow. As they look at the pictures, she supplies words and phrases needed so he can successfully read the book. She then reads and enjoys it with him. She praises him for his reading and asks him to read it with her once more as soon as he arrives at school tomorrow so that he will be able to read it with expression and enthusiasm.

*Tuesday*   The kindergartners arrive and the big buddies read to their little buddies. The intermediate-grade teacher and the kindergarten teacher circulate, stopping to listen to children read and helping them engage their young listeners with good "reader involvement" questions. The kindergartners come with all their gear, prepared to go home from here. Many of the big kids walk out with their little buddies in tow.

*Wednesday*   On Wednesdays, the children are divided into groups of four (using the deck of playing cards again), and each child has 5 minutes to read about or tell about something he or she has read this week. The cards are passed out and the children get together wherever the teacher has put that number. (The teacher places big number cards around the room—1 at the back table, 2 at her desk, 3 in the corner, and so on.) They share in alphabetical order of the suit they get—clubs, diamonds, hearts, spades. The teacher sets her timer for 5 minutes; the children have become good at preparing for this 5 minutes. Most know right where to find the scary, funny, silly, or fascinating part of the book that they want to read. Some children have riddle and joke books with the best riddles and jokes ready to share. The teacher circulates, making notes on her clipboard labels about books children choose and whether the accuracy and fluency exhibited while reading suggest that the book was an appropriate choice. When the timer sounds, she says, "Diamonds," and the second person in each group gets her or his 5 minutes. If a few minutes remain after all four people have had their turns, the teacher asks different children to share something particularly interesting with the whole class.

*Thursday*   On Thursdays, the same procedure is used to have children share writing that was used on Wednesday to share books. Cards are dealt. Children go wherever the teacher has put their number and have 5 minutes to share something they have written or that they are in the process of writing. Usually, but not always, the children who are revising that week share their piece. Other children read a piece they have decided to revise next week. Still other children read a piece they have just begun and tell what else they intend to write. If the child finishes reading before the 5 minutes are up, the reader can call on the listeners to tell "things they liked." The teacher makes notes on her clipboard labels indicating what different children have written about and have chosen to share.

*Friday*   Once again, Friday varies. Usually, the teacher takes a few minutes to have the children who have just published something show it to the class. On this Friday, the teacher is nearly finished with a chapter book, and the children are eager to see how it ends, so the teacher devotes the entire last 35 minutes to finishing reading the book aloud to the class, letting them respond to it, and drawing slips to see who gets the book and to form the order of the waiting list.

Each day, when the children leave, the teacher removes the labels from the clipboard and puts them on the outside of each child's folder. (Inside this folder are samples of writing, reading responses, and other work.) As she puts on new labels with new comments, she looks at the previous labels and considers how each child is growing. Sometimes, as she reflects on the different children whose reading and writing she has focused on that day, she thinks of other questions she has about that child's literacy development. She then puts this child's initials, tomorrow's date, and a few words to remind her of what to look for on the label and spends some time focusing on the same child again tomorrow. Although she focuses on some children more often than others, she tries to focus on each child at least once a week. The combination of weekly anecdotal records and samples of writing and reading responses kept in the folder gives the teacher a basis for deciding how well children are progressing toward becoming more literate, as well as information that guides her whole-class, small-group, and individual instruction.

# *Beyond the Classroom:*
## *Ten Things Worth Fighting For*

We wrote this book to help classroom teachers provide the highest-quality literacy instruction for all children. As much as possible, we have confined ourselves to discussing changes, adaptations, and additions that, as classroom teachers, are within your power. You can decide that real reading and writing will take precedence in your classrooms and commit to providing the necessary time, materials, models, and motivation. You can decide to involve all children in comprehension and writing activities on a daily or weekly basis. You can decide that all children should learn to read and spell high-frequency words automatically and that they should develop effective strategies that help them figure out how to read and spell unfamiliar words. You can make sure that you include effective vocabulary instruction and expand your children's world knowledge.

To some extent, you have control of grouping and scheduling. You can create larger blocks of time by integrating reading and writing with the content subjects. You can help your children learn to work cooperatively with one another and can use a variety of partner, trio, and team groupings. You can pair up with another like-minded teacher and have big buddy–little buddy arrangements. You can coordinate with specialists and/or enlist the help of tutors so that your most needy students receive additional instruction.

The premise of this book is that you, as a classroom teacher who has control of almost 1,000 hours of learning time, can make and carry out decisions that result in greatly increased literacy levels for your children. Research and experience tells us that what the classroom teacher does, day in and day out and minute by minute, has the greatest effect on what children learn. For most children who "beat the odds," a teacher made that difference.

We know that other factors accelerate the achievement of struggling readers, but they are not within the power of classroom teachers. These changes, additions, and adaptations usually require a total school effort, an administrative decision, or some form of community action. Some require political action in legislative arenas. For more specifics on these beyond-the-classroom solutions, see our book *Schools That Work: Where All Children Read and Write* (Allington & Cunningham, 2007). Whereas the major efforts of a classroom teacher are rightfully expended within one classroom, we feel that you should know which beyond-the-classroom suggestions are worth whatever crusading efforts you are able to make. The remainder of this chapter is devoted to elaborating our list of "things worth fighting for."

## 1. Smaller Class Size

Smaller class size, by itself, does not necessarily make a significant difference in children's learning, but smaller class size combined with the best instruction does. Recently, many large states have moved to reduce class size, particularly in the primary grades, but with increasing school enrollment, class size is creeping back up in many schools. McGill-Franzen and Allington (1991) noted that schools spend substantial sums of money on things that they know do not work—that is, retention in grade and transitional-grade programs, to name but two. If the money allocated to support these practices were redirected, class sizes could be reduced substantially in many schools.

The research available shows that having smaller classes does facilitate better teaching and more personalized instruction (Achilles, 1999). The key to enhancing the quality of instruction lies in increasing teachers' expertise in effective reading instruction and in helping teachers act appropriately on that knowledge. With smaller classes, the latter is easier to accomplish but not assured.

## 2. Early Intervention

A variety of studies have demonstrated the effectiveness of early intervention programs (K–2) compared to interventions begun later (Pikulski, 1994). The best early intervention programs are targeted to the needs of children rather than designed for "one size fits all." All schools need effective early intervention programs in place but especially schools that serve large numbers of children who arrive with few experiences with books, stories, and print. Early intervention efforts must be designed to provide each child with access to sufficiently intensive expert reading instruction. The available research indicates that an effective early intervention plan is comprised of three components: effective classroom reading instruction, targeted small-group support, and one-to-one tutoring (Allington, 2002).

Even if every classroom offered the effective classroom reading instruction we have described in this book, some students would still need additional instructional support. The evidence indicates that a trained reading teacher can conduct small-group (two or three students) support lessons that often foster accelerated reading development. Larger-group remedial support does not work very well, nor does small-group instruction offered by paraprofessionals (Allington & Cunningham, 2007). The most effective small-group support is well coordinated with the classroom lessons and provides added opportunities for reading and writing and more expert and more personalized teaching.

Some children need very intensive one-to-one support if they are to become readers and writers. Tutoring those children can produce dramatically improved reading achievement (Shanahan, 1988). The Reading Recovery program is often criticized for being expensive, but it has the best track record for bringing struggling readers up to the average reading level of their classmates in a limited number of one-on-one tutoring sessions (Clay, 1993).

## 3. Better School Libraries and Better Access to Books

Perhaps it is not surprising that schools with large numbers of poor children often have wholly inadequate school libraries and nonexistent classroom libraries. We must provide all children with access to books. Currently, children in schools that are located in low-economic neighborhoods have about 50 percent fewer books in their schools than children going to schools located in wealthy communities (McQuillan, 1998). These poor schools serve the very children who are least likely to live in literate home environments and least likely to have access to public library facilities. These are the schools that should have (and must strive to have) the very best school libraries with the largest selection of informational texts, picture books, and multicultural literature. The classroom libraries in these schools need to include several hundred books.

These schools need to have the most liberal library policies for loaning books to students and their families. The school library needs to be open before and after school so children without books at home can have access to the resources at school. This library needs to invite children to drop in at virtually any time to browse, read, search for, study, and select books. These school libraries need multiple subscriptions to magazines so that they too can be loaned out. They even need to be open during the summer vacation period.

Upgrading the quality and quantity of library resources in schools with large numbers of disadvantaged children is worth fighting for. Enhancing access to the school library is also important. Expanding classroom library collections is necessary. Having wonderful books is of little use if access is limited!

## 4. *Responsive Special Programs*

Millions of dollars of federal, state, and local money are spent each year on children who fall in specific "categories." In many cases, the special education programs and remedial programs have simply established scores and levels that determine whether a child can receive any special help. Some children qualify for many programs and may be seen by several different special teachers each day. These different specialists (e.g., speech teacher, reading teacher, counseling psychologist) rarely coordinate what they do with each other. Some of these children receive minimal classroom instruction because they are seldom in the classroom. Despite this, their assigned classroom teacher is usually held accountable for their progress! Other children "fall through the cracks," often because they just miss the cutoff point on whatever test or tests have been selected to determine eligibility.

We hope to soon see more "responsive" programs and fewer children labeled and categorized. Responsive programs respond to children's needs as soon as they are evident, not after they finally test eligible for some available categorical program. We hope to see interventions that provide children with access to extra-instructional efforts on the day they first need them. For instance, if Maria misses four days of school because of illness, a school program should provide her with extra assistance on the day she returns and until she catches up with her classmates.

We hope to soon see schools design intervention programs that provide children with sufficient extra instruction to return them to the classroom at a level with their peers in a very short time. Too often today, at-risk children receive what is available, not what they need. Too often, special help comes too late—a year or more after it becomes apparent that a child is in trouble. A whole year may be spent waiting for the child to become eligible for some categorical program. By not providing immediate extrainstructional support, the problem is intensified and becomes more difficult to resolve.

The present system of categorizing children and specifying what kind of support various children can or must get is not meeting the needs of most struggling readers. Classroom teachers should work with administrators, parent groups, and others to develop ways to meet children's needs that do not require rigid entry standards and inflexible categories.

## 5. *Extending the School Day or Year*

We are not in favor of the mandatory, for-everyone, more-is-better time extensions that many reformers are calling for. However, we would like to see optional extensions for children who want it or need it most. We believe after-school and summer school programs are needed to provide added expert instructional support for children who need it. We do not have enough hours in the present school day or year to provide every struggling learner with all the mind- and body-enriching experiences needed to effect optimal learning. In too many poor neighborhoods, as well as some not-so-poor neighborhoods, too many latchkey children are going home to empty houses and mindless hours in front of the TV. We would like these children to be able to stay at school and participate in extended-day activities that strive to increase their world knowledge and their motivation to learn. In addition, too many children in these and other neighborhoods spend all summer with little or nothing to read. The net result is a summer "reading loss" of several months, a loss that could be ameliorated if these children had access to the books and magazines locked away all summer in the neighborhood elementary school.

Many elementary schools could manage to provide extended school days with few additional personnel and with little additional funding. For instance, schools could schedule special teachers (art, music, computer, guidance, P.E., remedial reading, resource room, ESL, etc.) to begin their working day at 10:30 and end at 5:30. Some of their special classes would be scheduled between 11:30 and 3:30, but these classes would also be scheduled during the after-school programs. Thus, some children would receive their small-group remedial reading in the after-school program and perhaps afterward go to an after-school computer class to work on a related reading/writing activity. On other days those students might participate in an after-school art activity related to their reading or writing work in the after-school program. In addition to providing both intensive and enriching after-school activities, this arrangement would result in all classroom teachers having totally uninterrupted teaching time from 8:30–11:30 each day!

Several high-poverty schools in New Mexico have added an additional 40 days to the kindergarten schedule. Kindergartners have an extra month of instruction at the end of school and return a month early. Preliminary results show that most kindergartners who have participated in this Kindergarten Plus program are reading when they enter first grade and demonstrate better reading comprehension and social maturity.

## 6. *An End to Retention and Tracking*

An abundance of evidence reveals that many traditional "solutions" to the problems of underachievement actually contribute to the problems struggling learners face. For instance, in over 100 years of research, study after study has shown that retaining struggling learners (usually struggling readers) has no positive effect on their achievement and increases the likelihood that retained students will drop out of school (Shepard & Smith, 1989). In addition, retention is typically the most expensive school response to underachievement. The cost of an additional year of schooling far exceeds the cost of more effective interventions, including small-group remediation, tutoring, and summer school (Allington & McGill-Franzen, 1995).

Likewise, a long history of research has shown the negative effects of tracking children by achievement levels (Wheelock, 1992). Filling a classroom with all the low-achieving students (or all the high-achieving ones) fails to have a positive effect on learning for many reasons, but even more important, tracked schools do not resemble the real world. Not all the people we know, work with, go to church with, or interact with were high-achieving students, nor were they all low-achieving students. One important goal of schools is to prepare students to participate in our society, which means learning to work productively with many different folks, all different from us. Additionally, creating classrooms with 20–25 children who have similar achievement levels across the range of subjects taught is almost impossible. Some kids may be low achieving in reading but above average in math (and vice versa). Some may be good at recognizing words but not so good at understanding what they read, but they end up with the same reading level on an achievement test as the child who comprehends well but has problems with word recognition. In short, although tracking may narrow the achievement range a bit, tracking does not create classrooms in which one-size-fits-all instruction works to meet the needs of all students.

## 7. *Head Start/Even Start*

Head Start and Even Start are programs for economically disadvantaged 4-year-olds. Head Start has been around since the sixties and has been fairly successful in improving the school readiness of participating children. Even Start is a family literacy program that includes preschool children and their parents. Both children and parents go to school. Parents work to complete their high school education or receive adult literacy instruction. Children participate in a preschool program.

We know that children from high-literacy homes enter school with over 1,000 hours of informal reading and writing encounters, from which they develop an understanding about print that is essential to success in beginning reading. The literate home simulation kindergartens described in this book are designed to make up for some of the experiences many children have missed out on. Children who participate in Head Start or Even Start programs can be provided with many of the critical early literacy experiences, especially if the programs are modeled after the opportunities available in the literate home environment. When preschool programs immerse children in a print-rich and story-rich environment, the children acquire the same kind of knowledge about reading and writing as more advantaged children. When these programs also include effective parent support, we can begin to close the gap that now exists between children from different communities.

## 8. *Family and Community Involvement*

Schools that have unusually high success rates with struggling readers are usually schools with high levels of family and community involvement. These schools make superhuman efforts to reach out to the parents and surrogate parents—aunts, cousins, grandmothers—and involve them in the school. Getting the parents of at-risk children to come to school is often not an easy task. Many of the parents did not succeed in school themselves, and their memories of school are not pleasant. Many of the parents have very limited literacy levels, and many are not proficient in English.

But all parents want the best for their children and, when they do feel welcome and included, can become a powerful source of support for teachers. Schools that want parental support provide a variety of school-based programs and services. They have monthly parent meetings in which the children "star" in a variety of productions. They send home weekly parent-friendly newsletters that have lots of pictures and announcements showing their children excelling! Administrators and home–school coordinators visit homes and bring along games, books, tape recorders, computers, and other activities that parents can borrow and use with their children. Catherine Snow and her colleagues (Snow, Barnes, Chandler, Goodman, & Hemphill, 1991) found that urban teachers who rated their parents as interested and involved were teachers who made 10–15 teacher-initiated parent contacts for every 1 contact made by teachers who reported uninterested parents. Parents of struggling readers often do not initiate contact with schools and teachers. However, they can be enticed to involve themselves in the school and their child's schooling. But the enticing of the involvement seems critical.

Many parents would like to help and know they should but do not know how. Patricia Edwards (1991), of Michigan State University, found that many less well educated parents simply did not know how to read *to their children,* even if they could read themselves (some could not). If parents never experienced lap reading themselves, how would they learn how to do it? In the case of the parents that Edwards worked with, they learned from a series of videos she prepared (available from Children's Press) that showed parents reading to and with their children and that explained what the parents were doing. These videos can be shown at parent meetings or loaned out to parents to review at home. Edwards demonstrated that just telling parents to read to their children or to help their children with school work is often insufficient.

Researchers at the Center for Disadvantaged Students, at Johns Hopkins University (Slavin, Karweit, & Wasik, 1993), delivered this same message after their work developing homework packets for parents. They found that low-income parents were very willing to work with their children, but they often needed more guidance than schools made available. These researchers worked with teachers to target key skills and strategies that parents could work on with their children and then organized homework packets with easy-to-follow directions. Not only were they surprised at the overwhelmingly positive response from parents but also at the increase in student achievement that followed.

## 9. *Fairness in Funding*

Jonathan Kozol (1991), in *Savage Inequalities,* candidly described the steady movement in this nation toward a two-tiered educational system—one system that serves our suburbs and the other our urban and rural areas. The former is substantially better funded than the latter. Why would we create an educational system in which schools with large numbers of poor children routinely receive 50 percent less funding per child than schools with virtually no disadvantaged children? Why would we have a system in which poor parents pay a substantially larger proportion of their paychecks to support schools but still cannot match the wealth generated in communities serving wealthier families? Why would we support a system in which New York City schools receive 50 percent less money than those in suburban Scarsdale, a system whereby some public schools spend three to four times as much per pupil as others in the same state? Why should we tolerate a system in which some children have carpeting and air conditioning whereas others have sewage and rats in the hallways?

Educating children costs money. Educating some children will inevitably cost more then educating others. Currently, our system is more likely to provide more funding to schools with few needy children than to schools with many. If we are serious about all children learning to read and write, we must seriously work to alter existing funding patterns and to provide some sort of modicum of fairness in funding. It is not that money will cure everything, but a good education does cost more than offering a bare minimum.

## 10. Teacher Input on the Business of Running Schools

In many schools today, teacher committees have a say in how the money is spent, how special subjects are scheduled, and who their administrators are. This power has been entrusted to teachers not because of any new high regard for "regular" teachers but because it is becoming increasingly clear that the top-down bureaucratic procedures of the past have not resulted in better schooling. In many schools, classroom teachers have the opportunity to effect changes beyond their classroom; they should seize the moment! The kind of decisions they make can determine whether they continue to have any power.

Whereas individual schools must set their own priorities, some general considerations apply to all schools. Teachers who want children to engage in lots of real reading and writing should see to it that a good chunk of whatever money is available for materials gets spent on books and magazines, both for the school library and for classroom libraries. Writing materials are generally not expensive, but a variety should be available. Paper for making books and a book-binding machine should be as accessible as copying paper and a copy machine. Every classroom should have a few computers, a good printer, and some writing/publishing software.

The schedule is another area that classroom teachers should try to affect. In some schools, special teachers set their own schedules or have them set by a supervisor. Children come and go at all hours, and classroom teachers seldom have an uninterrupted hour in which to teach anything to everyone. In other schools, a certain period of time—between 45 and 90 minutes—is designated for special subjects for each grade level. In addition to having only one time period each day when the children go somewhere and then come back again, scheduling special subjects by grade-level blocks provides the classroom teachers with some grade-level planning time each week. Other schools work in the reverse but still achieve a similar result. These schools have "safe" periods for each classroom every day—periods of 90–120 minutes when no child is to be pulled out for any special service.

It is important that teachers and children have large uninterrupted blocks of time to work together. We have found that when schools set a goal of providing these blocks, they can almost always be achieved. Two- or three-hour uninterrupted blocks are worth fighting for!

(See also Recommended Resources lists in Chapters 2–10.)

## Children's Books

*Alphabet Annie Announces an All-American Album,* Susan Purviance and Marcia O'Shell

*Anastasia at Your Service,* Lois Lowry

*Are You My Mother?* P. D. Eastman

*Aunt Flossie's Hats (and Crabcakes Later),* Elizabeth Fitzgerald Howard

*Beast in Ms. Rooney's Room, The,* Pat Reilly Giff

*Biggest Tongue Twister Book in the World, The,* Gyles Brandeth

*Brown Bear, Brown Bear, What Do You See?* Bill Martin

*Caps for Sale,* Esphyr Slobodkina

*Carrot Seed, The,* Ruth Krauss

*Cathedral,* David Macaulay

*Clever Little Tailor, The* (various authors)

*Clifford the Big Red Dog,* Normal Bridwell

*Get On Out of Here, Philip Hall,* B. Greene

*Go Dog Go,* P. D. Eastman

*Goodnight Moon,* Marcia Brown

*Hattie and the Fox,* Mem Fox

*Hop on Pop,* Theodor Geisel

*How Things Work,* Time-Life Books

*I Went Walking,* Sue Williams

*Inside, Outside, Upside Down,* Stan and Jan Berenstain

*Island of the Blue Dolphins,* Scott O'Dell

*Little Engine That Could, The*

*Little Red Hen, The* (various authors)

*Missing: One Stuffed Rabbit,* Maryann Cocca-Leffler

*Once Upon a Sidewalk,* Jean Craighead George

*One Fish, Two Fish, Red Fish, Blue Fish,* Theodor Geisel

*Our Friend, the Sun,* Janet Palazzo

*Philip Hall Likes Me, I Reckon Maybe,* B. Greene

*Pyramids,* David Macaulay

*Robert the Rose Horse,* Joan Heilbroner

*Rosie's Walk,* Pat Hutchins

*Spiders,* Gail Gibbons

*Sun Is On, The,* Linda Michelle Baron

*There's a Wocket in My Pocket,* Theodor Geisel

*Three Little Pigs, The* (various authors)

*Treasure Island,* Robert Louis Stephenson
*What Makes the Weather?* Janet Palazzo
*When the Relatives Came,* Cynthia Rylant

## Children's Magazines

*3-2-1 Contact,* Children's Television Workshop
*My Weekly Reader,* Scholastic
*National Geographic for Kids*
*Ranger Rick,* National Wildlife Federation
*Scholastic News*
*Sports Illustrated for Kids*
*Sprint,* Scholastic
*Time for Children*
*Weekly Reader*

## Computer Software

Co: Writer, Don Johnston
Draft Builder, Don Johnston
IntelliTalk II, Intellitools
Kidspiration, Inspiration
Write: Outloud, Don Johnston

## Other Resources

Primary Reader's Theatre series, Curriculum Associates
*Ripley's Believe It or Not,* Time-Life Books
*Take Part Plays, Grades 3–6,* Sundance
*Take Part Starters, Grades 2–3,* Sundance
*The Baseball Encyclopedia,* Time-Life
*Traditional Tales and Plays* collection, Rigby

# references

Achilles, C. M. (1999). *Let's put kids first, finally: Getting class size right.* Thousand Oaks, CA: Corwin Press.

Adams, M. J. (1990). *Beginning to read: Thinking and learning about print.* Cambridge, MA: MIT Press.

Allington, R. L. (1983). The reading instruction provided readers of differing reading ability. *Elementary School Journal, 83,* 549–559.

Allington, R. L. (2002). Research on reading/learning disability interventions. In A. Farstrup & S. J. Samuels (Eds.), *What research says about reading instruction* (3rd ed.). Newark, DE: International Reading Association.

Allington, R. L., & Cunningham, P. M. (2007). *Schools that work: Where all children read and write* (3rd ed.). New York: Longman.

Allington, R. L., & Johnston, P. (2001). Characteristics of exemplary fourth grade instruction. In C. Roller (Ed.), *Learning to teach reading: Setting the research agenda.* Newark, DE: International Reading Association.

Allington, R. L., & Johnston, P. H. (Eds.). (2002). *Reading to learn: Lessons from exemplary fourth-grade classrooms.* New York: Guilford.

Allington, R. L., & McGill-Franzen, A. M. (1995). Flunking: Throwing good money after bad. In R. L. Allington & S. A. Walmsley (Eds.), *No quick fix: Rethinking literacy programs in America's elementary schools* (pp. 45–60). New York: Teacher's College Press.

Arens, A. B., Loman, K. L., Cunningham, P. M., & Hall, D. P. (2005). *The teacher's guide to Big Blocks.* Greensboro, NC: Carson-Dellosa.

Artley, S. A. (1975). Good teachers of reading—Who are they? *The Reading Teacher, 29,* 26–31.

Baumann, J. F., Kame'enui, E. J., & Ash, G. E. (2003). Research on vocabulary instruction: Voltaire redux. In J. Flood, D. Lapp, J. R. Squire, & J. M. Jensen (Eds.), *Handbook of research on teaching the English language arts* (2nd ed., pp. 752–785). Mahwah, NJ: Erlbaum.

Beck, I. L., McKeown, M. G., & Gromoll, E. W. (1989). Learning from social studies texts. *Cognition and Instruction, 6,* 99–158.

Beck, I. L., McKeown, M. G., Hamilton, R. L., & Kucan, L. (1997). *Questioning the author: An approach for enhancing student engagement with text.* Newark, DE: International Reading Association.

Beck, I. L., McKeown, M. G., & Kucan, L. (2002). *Bringing words to life.* New York: Guilford.

Becker, W. C. (1977). Teaching reading and language to the disadvantaged—What we have learned from field research. *Harvard Educational Review, 47,* 518–543.

Biemiller, A. (2004). Teaching vocabulary in the primary grades. In J. F. Baumann & E. J. Kame'enui (Eds.), *Vocabulary instruction* (pp. 28–40). New York: Guilford.

Biemiller, A., & Slonim, M. (2001). Estimating root word vocabulary growth in normative and advantaged populations: Evidence for a common sequence of vocabulary acquisition. *Journal of Educational Psychology, 93,* 498–520.

Blachowicz, C. L. Z., & Fisher, P. (2000). Vocabulary instruction. In M. L. Kamil, P. B. Mosenthal, P. D. Pearson, & R. Barr (Eds.), *Handbook of reading research* (Vol. 3, pp. 503–523). Mahwah, NJ: Erlbaum.

Caldwell, J. (2002). *Reading assessment: A primer for teachers and tutors.* New York: Guilford.

Calkins, L. (1994). *The art of teaching writing.* Portsmouth, NH: Heinemann.

Campbell, J., Voelkl, K., & Donahue, P. (1997). *NAEP 1996 trends in academic progress.* Washington, DC: National Center for Educational Statistics.

Carr, E., & Ogle, D. (1987). KWL plus: A strategy for comprehension and summarization. *Journal of Reading, 30,* 626–631.

Cataldo, S., & Ellis, N. (1988). Interactions in the development of spelling, reading and phonological skills. *Journal of Research in Reading, 11*(2), 86–109.

Chomsky, C. (1971). Write first, read later. *Childhood Education, 46,* 296–299.

Clay, M. M. (1993). *An observation survey of early literacy achievement.* Portsmouth, NH: Heinemann.

Cudd, E. T. (1989). Research and report writing in the elementary grades. *The Reading Teacher, 43*(3), 268–269.

Cudd, E. T., & Roberts, L. (1989). Using writing to enhance content area learning in the primary grades. *The Reading Teacher, 42,* 392–404.

Cunningham, P. M. (2005). *Phonics they use: Words for reading and writing* (4th ed.). New York: HarperCollins.

Cunningham, P. M., Cunningham, J. W., Hall, D. P., & Moore, S. A. (2005). *Writing the Four Blocks way.* Greensboro, NC: Carson-Dellosa.

Cunningham, P. M., & Hall, D. P. (1997). *Month by month phonics for first grade.* Greensboro, NC: Carson-Dellosa.

Cunningham, P. M., & Hall, D. P. (1997). *Month by month phonics for upper grades.* Greensboro, NC: Carson-Dellosa.

Cunningham, P. M., & Hall, D. P. (1998). *Month by month phonics for third grade.* Greensboro, NC: Carson-Dellosa.

Cunningham, P. M., & Hall, D. P. (2001). *True stories from Four Blocks classrooms.* Greensboro, NC: Carson-Dellosa.

Cunningham, P. M., Hall, D. P., & Cunningham, J. W. (2000). *Guided reading the Four Blocks way.* Greensboro, NC: Carson-Dellosa.

Cunningham, P. M, Hall D. P. & Gambrell, L. M. (2002). *Self-selected reading the Four Blocks way.* Greensboro, NC: Carson-Dellosa.

Cunningham, P. M., Cunningham, J. W., Hall, D. P., & Moore, S. A. (2005). *Writing the Four Blocks way.* Greensboro, NC: Carson-Dellosa.

Cunningham, P. M., Hall, D. P., & Sigmon, C. M. (1999). *The teacher's guide to the Four Blocks.* Greensboro, NC: Carson-Dellosa.

Cunningham, A. E., & Stanovich, K. E. (1998). What reading does for the mind. *American Educator, 22*(1&2), 8–27.

Day, J. P., Spiegel, D. L., McLellan, J., & Brown, V. B. (2002). *Moving forward with literature circles.* New York: Scholastic.

Duke, N. K., & Pearson, P. D. (2002). Effective practices for developing reading comprehension. In A. E. Farstrup & S. J. Samuels (Eds.), *What research has to say about reading instruction* (3rd ed., pp. 205–242). Newark, DE: International Reading Association.

Durkin, D. (1979). What classroom observations reveal about reading comprehension instruction. *Reading Research Quarterly, 14,* 481–533.

Dyson, A. H., & Freedman, S. W. (2003). Writing. In J. Flood, D. Lapp, J. R. Squire, & J. M. Jensen (Eds.), *Handbook of research on teaching the English language arts* (2nd ed., pp. 967–992). Mahwah, NJ: Erlbaum.

Echevarria, J., Short, D., & Vogt, M. E. (2003). *Making content comprehensible for English learners: The SIOP model*. Boston: Allyn & Bacon.

Edwards, P. A. (1991). Fostering early literacy through parent coaching. In E. H. Hiebart (Ed.), *Literacy for a diverse society: Perspectives, practices, and policies* (pp. 199–212). New York: Teachers College Press.

Ehri, L. C., & Wilce, L. (1987). Does learning to spell help beginners learn to read words? *Reading Research Quarterly, 22,* 47–65.

Ellis, N., & Cataldo, S. (1990). The role of spelling in learning to read. *Language and Education, 4,* 47–76.

Fall, R., Webb, N. M., & Chudowsky, N. (2000). Group discussion and large-scale language arts assessment: Effects on students' comprehension. *American Educational Research Journal, 37*(4), 911–941.

Faltis, C. J. (1993). *Joinfostering: Adapting teaching strategies for the multilingual classroom*. New York: Merrill.

Farnan, N., & Dahl, K. (2003). Children's writing: Research and practice. In J. Flood, D. Lapp, J. R. Squire, & J. M. Jensen (Eds.), *Handbook of research on teaching the English language arts* (2nd ed., pp. 993–1007). Mahwah, NJ: Erlbaum.

Gardner, H. (1993). *Multiple intelligences: The theory in practice*. New York: Basic Books.

Gibbons, P. (2002). *Scaffolding language, scaffolding learning*. Portsmouth, NH: Heinemann.

Graves, D. H. (1995). *A fresh look at writing*. Portsmouth, NH: Heinemann.

Graves, M. F. (2004). Teaching prefixes: As good as it gets? In J. F. Baumann & E. J. Kame'enui (Eds.), *Vocabulary instruction* (pp. 81–99). New York: Guilford.

Graves, M. F., & Watts-Taffe, S. M. (2002). The place of word consciousness in a research-based vocabulary program. In A. E. Farstrup & S. J. Samuels (Eds.), *What research has to say about reading instruction* (3rd ed., pp. 140–165). Newark, DE: International Reading Association.

Hall, D. P., & Cunningham, P. M. (1997). *Month by month reading and writing for kindergarten*. Greensboro, NC: Carson-Dellosa.

Hall, D. P., & Cunningham, P. M. (1998). *Month by month phonics for second grade*. Greensboro, NC: Carson-Dellosa.

Hall, D. P., Cunningham, P. M., & Arens, A. B. (2003). *Writing minilessons for upper grades*. Greensboro, NC: Carson-Dellosa.

Hall, D. P, Cunningham, P. M. & Boger, D. B. (2002). *Writing minilessons for first grade*. Greensboro, NC: Carson-Dellosa.

Hall, D. P, Cunningham, P. M., & Smith, D. R. (2002) *Writing minilessons for second grade*. Greensboro, NC: Carson-Dellosa.

Hall, D. P., & Cunningham, P. M. (2003). *Month by month phonics for second grade*. Greensboro, NC: Carson-Dellosa.

Hall, D. P., & Williams, E. (2000). *The teacher's guide to Building Blocks*. Greensboro, NC: Carson-Dellosa.

Hall, D. P., & Williams, E. (2003). *Writing minilessons for kindergarten.* Greensboro, NC: Carson-Dellosa.

Harris, V. J. (Ed.). (1997). *Using multiethnic literature in the K–8 classroom.* Norwood, MA: Christopher Gordon.

Hart, B., & Risley, T. R. (1995). *Meaningful differences in the everyday experiences of young American children.* Baltimore: Paul H. Brookes.

Harvey, S., & Goudvis, A. (2000). *Strategies that work: Teaching comprehension to enhance understanding.* York, ME: Stenhouse.

Hillocks, G., Jr. (1986). *Research on written composition: New directions for teaching.* Urbana, IL: National Conference on Research in English/ERIC Clearinghouse on Reading and Communication Skills.

Hodges, R. E. (2003). The conventions of writing. In J. Flood, D. Lapp, J. R. Squire, & J. M. Jensen (Eds.), *Handbook of research on teaching the English language arts* (2nd ed., pp. 1052–1063). Mahwah, NJ: Erlbaum.

Invernizzi, M., Juel, C., & Rosemay, C. A. (1997). A community volunteer tutorial that works. *The Reading Teacher, 50,* 304–311.

Ivey, G., & Broaddus, K. (2001). "Just plain reading": A survey of what makes students want to read in middle school classrooms. *Reading Research Quarterly, 36,* 350–377.

Johns, J. J. (2001). *Basic reading inventory* (8th ed.). Dubuque, IA: Kendall/Hunt.

Johnston, P., & Allington, R. L. (1991). Remediation. In R. Barr, M. Kamil, P. Mosenthal, & P. D. Pearson (Eds.), *Handbook of reading research* (Vol. 2, pp. 418–452). New York: Longman.

Juel, C., Biancarosa, G., Coker, D., & Deffes, R. (2003). Walking with Rosie: A cautionary tale of early reading instruction. *Educational Leadership, 60,* 12–18.

Juel, C., & Minden-Cupp, C. (2000). Learning to read words: Linguistic units and instructional strategies. *Reading Research Quarterly, 35,* 458–492.

Keene, E. L., & Zimmerman, S. (1997). *Mosaic of thought: Teaching comprehension in a reader's workshop.* Portsmouth, NH: Heinemann.

Knapp, M. S. (1995). *Teaching for meaning in high-poverty classrooms.* New York: Teachers College Press.

Kozol, J. (1991). *Savage inequalities: Children in America's schools.* New York: Crown.

Langer, J., & Allington, R. L. (1992). Writing and reading curriculum. In P. Jackson (Ed.), *The handbook of curriculum research* (pp. 687–725). New York: Macmillan.

Leslie, L., & Caldwell, J. (2001). *Qualitative reading inventory—3.* New York: Longman.

Macon, J. M., Bewell, D., & Vogt, M. (1991). *Responses to literature.* Newark, DE: International Reading Association.

Manning, G. L., & Manning, M. (1984). What models of recreational reading make a difference? *Reading World, 23,* 375–380.

McGill-Franzen, A. M., & Allington, R. L. (1991). The gridlock of low achievement: Perspectives on policy and practice. *Remedial and Special Education, 12,* 20–30.

McQuillan, J. (1998). *The literacy crisis: False claims, real solutions.* Portsmouth, NH: Heinemann.

Nagy, W. E., & Anderson. R. C. (1984). How many words are there in printed school English? *Reading Research Quarterly, 19,* 304–330.

National Reading Panel. (2000). *Teaching children to read: An evidence-based assessment of the scientific research literature on reading and its implications for reading instruction: Reports of the subgroups* (National Institute of Health Pub. No. 00-4754). Washington, DC: National Institute of Child Health and Human Development.

Ogle, D. (1986). K-W-L: A teaching model that develops active reading of expository text. *The Reading Teacher, 39,* 564–570.

Palmer, B. M., Codling, R. M., & Gambrell, L. B. (1994). In their own words: What elementary children have to say about motivation to read. *The Reading Teacher, 48,* 176–179.

Pearson, P. D., & Fielding, L. (1991). Comprehension instruction. In R. Barr, M. Kamil, P. Mosenthal, & P. D. Pearson (Eds.), *Handbook of reading research* (Vol. 2, pp. 815–860). New York: Longman.

Peregoy, S., & Boyle, O. (2004). *Reading, writing, and learning in ESL* (4th ed.). Boston: Allyn & Bacon.

Pikulski, J. J. (1994). Preventing reading failure: A review of five effective programs. *The Reading Teacher, 48,* 30–39.

Pilla, M. L. (1990). *The best high/low books for reluctant readers.* Englewood, CO: Libraries Unlimited.

Pittleman, S. D., Heimlich, J. E., Berglund, R., & French, M. P. (1991). *Semantic feature analysis: Classroom applications.* Newark, DE: International Reading Association.

Pressley, M. (1998). *Reading instruction that works: The case for balanced teaching.* New York: Guilford.

Pressley, M., Allington, R. L., Wharton-McDonald, R., Block, C. C., & Morrow, L. (2001). *Learning to read: Lessons from exemplary first-grade classrooms.* New York: Guilford.

Pressley, M., & Wharton-McDonald, R. (1998). The development of literacy, Part 4: The need for increased comprehension in upper-elementary grades. In M. Pressley (Ed.), *Reading instruction that works: The case for balanced teaching* (pp. 192–227). New York: Guilford.

Raphael, T. E., Kirschner, B. W., & Englert, C. S. (1988). Expository writing program: Making connections between reading and writing. *The Reading Teacher, 41,* 790–795.

Read, C. (1975). *Children's categorization of speech sounds in English.* Urbana, IL: National Council of Teachers of English.

Shanahan, T. (1988). The reading–writing relationship: Seven instructional principles. *The Reading Teacher, 41,* 636–647.

Share, D. L. (1999). Phonological recoding and orthographic learning: A direct test of the self-teaching hypothesis. *Journal of Experimental Child Psychology, 72,* 95–129.

Shepard, L. A., & Smith, M. L. (Eds.). (1989). *Flunking grades: Research and policies on retention.* Philadelphia: Falmer.

Sigmon, C. M., & Ford, S. M. (2002) *Writing minilessons for third grade.* Greensboro, NC: Carson-Dellosa.

Slavin, R. E., Karweit, N. L., & Wasik, B. A. (1993). *Preventing early school failure: Research, policy, and practice.* Boston: Allyn & Bacon.

Snow, C. E., Barnes, W. S., Chandler, J., Goodman, I., & Hemphill, L. (1991). *Unfulfilled expectations: Home and school influences on literacy.* Cambridge, MA: Harvard University Press.

Spivey, N. (1997). *The constructivist metaphor: Reading, writing and the making of meaning.* New York: Academic Press.

Stahl, S. A., Duffy-Hester, A. M., & Stahl, K. A. D. (1998). Everything you wanted to know about phonics (but were afraid to ask). *Reading Research Quarterly, 33,* 338–355.

Stanovich, K. E. (1986). Matthew effects in reading: Some consequences of individual differences in the acquisition of literacy. *Reading Research Quarterly, 21,* 360–401.

Stanovich, K. E. (1991). Word recognition: Changing perspectives. In R. Barr, M. Kamil, P. Mosenthal, & P. D. Pearson (Eds.), *Handbook of reading research* (Vol. 2, pp. 418–452). New York: Longman.

Stanovich, K. E., & West, R. F. (1989). Exposure to print and orthographic processing. *Reading Research Quarterly, 24,* 402–433.

Sudduth, P. (1989). Introducing response logs to poor readers. *The Reading Teacher, 42,* 452–454.

Sulzby, E., & Teale, W. (1991). Emergent literacy. In R. Barr, M. Kamil, P. Mosenthal, & P. D. Pearson (Eds.), *Handbook of reading research* (Vol. 2, pp. 727–757). White Plains, NY: Longman.

Taylor, B. M., Hanson, B., Swanson, K., & Watts, S. (1998). Helping struggling readers in grades two and four: Linking small-group intervention with cross-age tutoring. *The Reading Teacher, 51,* 196–209.

Taylor, B. M., Pearson, P. D., Clark, K., & Walpole, S. (2000). Effective schools and accomplished teachers: Lessons about primary grade reading instruction in low-income schools. *Elementary School Journal, 101*(2), 121–166.

Topping, K., & Paul, T. (1999). Computer-assisted assessment of practice at reading: A large scale survey using Accelerated Reader data. *Reading and Writing Quarterly, 15,* 213–231.

Visser, C. (1991). Football and reading do mix. *The Reading Teacher, 44,* 710–711.

Wharton-McDonald, R., Pressley, M., & Hampston, J. M. (1998). Literacy instruction in nine first-grade classrooms: Teacher characteristics and student achievement. *The Elementary School Journal, 99,* 101–128.

Wheelock, A. (1992). *Crossing tracks: How untracking can save America's schools.* New York: New Press.

Wylie, R. E., & Durrell, D. D. (1970). Teaching vowels through phonograms. *Elementary English, 47,* 787–791.

Young, S. (1994). *The Scholastic rhyming dictionary.* New York: Scholastic.

# index

## Photo Credits

Michael Newman/Photo Edit: pp. i, 15, 52, 120, 139, 173, 184, 204, 225, 284, 292; Tony Freeman/Photo Edit: pp. 1, 10, 82, 228; T. Lindfors/Lindfors Photography: pp. 11, 14, 19, 24, 25, 26, 44, 51, 64, 73, 137, 144, 159, 179, 203, 216, 236, 249, 250, 264; Robin Sachs/Photo Edit: pp. 18, 174, 200; Patricia M. Cunningham: pp. 42, 49, 67, 69, 70, 71, 100, 102; Brian Smith: pp. 45, 86; Comstock Royalty Free Division: pp. 72, 149, 153, 201, 205, 214, 215, 235; Bob Daemmrich/Photo Edit: pp. 83, 111, 131, 138; Michelle D. Bridwell/Photo Edit: pp. 87, 110, 124, 176; Frank Siteman: pp. 125, 160; Rosalyn D. Morgan: p. 247; David Young-Wolff/Photo Edit: pp. 265, 283

## Text Credits

Extracts on pages 230 and 239 from *Brown Bear, Brown Bear, What Do You See?* by Bill Martin, Jr. Copyright © 1967, 1970 by Harcourt Brace & Company, renewed in 1995 by Bill Martin, Jr. Reprinted by permission of Henry Holt & Co., LLC.